The Myth of Prison Rape

The Myth of Prison Rape

Sexual Culture in American Prisons

Mark S. Fleisher and Jessie L. Krienert

With a Foreword by James B. Jacobs

ROWMAN & LITTLEFIELD PUBLISHERS, INC.
Lanham • Boulder • New York • Toronto • Plymouth, UK

ML—

ROWMAN & LITTLEFIELD PUBLISHERS, INC.

Published in the United States of America
by Rowman & Littlefield Publishers, Inc.
A wholly owned subsidiary of The Rowman & Littlefield Publishing Group, Inc.
4501 Forbes Boulevard, Suite 200, Lanham, Maryland 20706
www.rowmanlittlefield.com

Estover Road
Plymouth PL6 7PY
United Kingdom

British Library Cataloguing in Publication Information Available

Library of Congress Cataloging-in-Publication Data:

Fleisher, Mark S.
  The myth of prison rape : sexual culture in American prisons / Mark Fleisher and
Jessie Krienert.
      p. cm.
  Includes bibliographical references and index.
  ISBN-13: 978-0-7425-6165-6 (cloth : alk. paper)
  ISBN-10: 0-7425-6165-8 (cloth : alk. paper)
  ISBN-13: 978-0-7425-6166-3 (pbk. : alk. paper)
  ISBN-10: 0-7425-6166-6 (pbk. : alk. paper)
  eISBN-13: 978-0-7425-6599-9
  eISBN-10: 0-7425-6599-8
 1. Prisoners—Sexual behavior—United States. 2. Prison violence—United States. 3.
Male rape—United States. I. Krienert, Jessie L., 1974– II. Title.
  HV8836.F55 2009
  365'.6—dc22

                                                                    2008033983

Printed in the United States of America

⊚™ The paper used in this publication meets the minimum requirements of American
National Standard for Information Sciences—Permanence of Paper for Printed Library
Materials, ANSI/NISO Z39.48-1992.

Table of Contents

List of Figures and Tables

FIGURES

TABLES

Foreword

The Myth of Prison Rape fits comfortably in a long tradition of social problems publications that deconstruct social problems. Previously, social science researchers have shown how many social problems (e.g., marijuana, child abductions, hate crimes, campus sexual violence) have been defined and exaggerated by advocacy groups. Moral panics often ensue. Politicians respond by passing legislation that provides the advocacy groups a symbolic victory and satisfies the public for remedial action. Invariably the "problem's" salience recedes, at least for a time.

The promotion of every social problem has its own unique history. The politics of "stop prison rape" would itself warrant a book. The release of Human Rights Watch's report *No Escape: Male Rape in U.S. Prisons* (2001) would certainly deserve special mention. Suffice it to say that in the late 1990s and early 2000s, a one-issue advocacy group called Stop Prison Rape (www.spr.org), supported by a slew of religious, human rights, and prisoners' rights organizations, brought prison rape to the top of the social problems agenda.

Congress responded by unanimously passing the 2003 Prison Rape Elimination Act (PREA), which asserted that at least 13 percent of U.S. prisoners will be raped while serving their sentences and that one million inmates had been raped in the previous twenty years. These claims found a receptive audience in an American population prepared to believe the worst about U.S. jails and prisons, their "knowledge" having been drawn mostly from sensationalistic movies, TV dramas, and media exposés.

PREA provided a variety of remedial measures. It required that the U.S. Department of Justice create a review panel designed to conduct hearings on prison rape and make the prevention of prison rape a top priority in each prison system. It mandated that the Bureau of Justice Statistics produce an annual report on its activities concerning prison rape and directed the National

Institute of Corrections to provide training and technical assistance, establish a clearinghouse for information, and produce an annual report to Congress. It also authorized the Bureau of Justice Assistance and the National Institute of Justice to make research grants.

The Myth of Prison Rape was produced under the auspices of one of the first grants. It is based upon in-depth structured interviews with more than 500 randomly selected inmates in diverse prisons in different parts of the country. To say that it will disappoint the Act's proponents is an understatement. (Interestingly, the other PREA-sponsored research grants also have failed to confirm the rape epidemic on which the Act was predicated.) Fleisher and Krienert do not try to estimate the prevalence of prison rape. Rather, they try to illuminate how prisoners understand rape and sexual interactions more generally. They find that prisoners overwhelmingly see most sexual relations in prison as normal, predictable, and voluntary and that they have little fear of the kind of violent sexual attack that one who watches HBO's brutal prison drama *Oz* might think is an everyday occurrence. When Fleisher and Krienert released their initial report, they were excoriated by PREA proponents who "know" that violent sex is pervasive in American prisons. The chairman of the National Prison Rape Elimination Commission (established by PREA) called the study "unscientific." Stop Prison Rape issued an entire report attacking the study (www.spr.org/pdf/PREAUpdate0206.pdf).

Anthropologist Mark Fleisher and sociologist Jessie Krienert are not the first social scientists to study prison rape, but their study is by far the most comprehensive and sophisticated yet undertaken. Among its many important contributions are its exposure of the homophobic bias of most of the early twentieth-century researchers of prison sex, a devastating critique of the received wisdom about prison rape, the scientific execution of a qualitative field research study, and the compilation of a dictionary of prison sexual argot. Most importantly, they have illuminated the complexity of a subject that heretofore was marked by sensationalism and simplistic understanding. I believe that open-minded readers will be impressed by the scholarship that underlies *The Myth of Prison Rape*.

Fleisher and Krienert persuasively argue that prison rape cannot be understood without understanding prison sex and that prison sex is complicated. There is a lot of sex in prison. Like sex outside of prison it ranges along a number of continua, from wholly voluntary to wholly involuntary, from mutually fulfilling to asymmetrically manipulative and exploitive. Illuminating how prisoners understand these sexual interactions is a valuable contribution to our understanding of prisons, prisoners, and human sexuality.

James B. Jacobs

Preface

Well before we interviewed our first inmate we met with a high-ranking administrator in the National Institute of Justice. She said she wasn't interested in a study of prison rape prevalence statistics. Instead, she wanted to know the meaning of rape within prison inmate culture. "Meaning" is a powerful word. It is easier to count incidents of alleged prison rape than to dig around in the abstraction we call prison culture to cull out the contextual meaning of sexual violence from the enormous complexity of an American mega-prison housing thousands of inmates.

Simply asking inmates "what does homosexual sex mean?" gets us nowhere. Sigmund Freud, Carl Jung, Joseph Campbell, and other familiar twentieth-century philosophers of human thought taught us that inner forces motivate and interpret human behavior and that these inner forces are outside of cultural participants' conscious recognition. Practically speaking, if knowledge of how we behave, how we speak, and how we see ourselves and others were consciously available to us like arithmetic on a chalkboard we'd have little need for clinical psychologists and the pharmacopeia of psychoactive medications psychiatrists dispense to keep us sane in the modern world.

Accepting the premise that humans are driven by inner forces outside their conscious recognition, we had to devise a methodology that would allow us to gather data, which would provide an opening into the symbolic world of prison inmate culture. Cultural meaning isn't formed in a vacuum absent of human thought, emotions, and feelings. To study rape in men's and women's prison culture meant that we had to study the history of the interpretation of homosexual sex in America (and its European influences) over the twentieth century.

To study the culture and symbolism of prison homosexual sex and sexual violence we gained a thorough knowledge of 70 years of research literature on prison culture. We also had knowledge of the intellectual history of relevant multidisciplinary research, which strongly influenced early prison scholars' interpretation of homosexual sex in prison. Early scholars' nascent thoughts on homosexual sex and sexual violence formed the bedrock of today's theory of prison culture and homosexual sex. Finally, we had a tool kit of methodologies to collect and analyze data. In our study, data are the raw spoken words of inmates. Analysis means the derivation of meaning, or interpretation, of those spoken words within the specific cultural context of prison inmate culture, social life, and systems of thought.

The Myth of Prison Rape examines systems of cultural meaning embedded in the symbolism of inmates' collective, verbal expression of sexual violence in American prison culture. A cultural boundary distinguishes American prison culture from the culture of free communities. We can test the existence of that boundary quite simply. An inmate can walk away from prison and fall back into his life on the street, knowing what to do, what to say, what the world around him means. However, if you were walked into an American penitentiary and plopped down in the middle of the prison compound—a big yard— would you know what to say, what to do, and the meaning conveyed by social life on the yard? We will tell you the answer would be a resounding NO.

Why? You have crossed a cultural boundary. It would take months for you to become comfortable enough to walk the compound without envisioning a graphically violent end to your stroll. Inmate-to-inmate conversations would be largely impossible for you to understand. The appendix is a dictionary of prison sex terminology. Give yourself a vocabulary test. See how little you know about prison sexual dynamics. The point is this: prison inmates like those whose words you'll read in our book, look like us, sound like us, and seem "culturally familiar," but we'll assure you they don't think like us.

Our research is based entirely on inmates' raw speech. Since we couldn't spend months watching inmates in cell houses and dormitories, waiting to see or hear about sexual violence, our study explores prison sexual violence from an inside view, as prison inmates talk about it. In prison there are many reasons inmates engage in violent activity; there are also a myriad of reasons why inmates choose to engage in sexual contact.

The juncture of violence and sexuality finds its dominant form of expression through *conversation*, not through action, among prisoners and prison staff. We gathered an extensive body of narratives about sexual violence, its players, causes, conditions, circumstances, contexts, and outcomes. We quickly learned that prison rape cannot be explained by looking at sexual behavior or sexual dysfunction or nonsexual violence as it occurs outside prison. In a real sense, a study of the culture of prison rape is a study of the concepts of sexuality, personal identity, and institutional social roles forged to a study of actual or purported violence.

Prison sexual violence as we define it refers to forced nonconsensual sex under the threat of armed or unarmed violence. We learned from hundreds of interviews with men and women prisoners that prison sexual violence rarely occurs as a real-life behavior men and women inmates fear will happen to them.

We also learned that prisoners *say* they know a lot about prison sexual violence. A large percentage of the men and women we interviewed were serving their first prison sentence, facing the confused uncertainty of a life of confinement. Others who were veterans of the American prison system had foreknowledge of what faced them.

First-timers had to learn about prison life by watching and listening to inmates and staff. Not everything that is said about prison rape finds behavioral expression; talk is talk. Many of our inmate interviewees never saw an actual act of sexual violence, not even over decades of doing time in different prisons in different states. Nevertheless, they knew a lot about prison rape.

CULTURAL CONTRAST IN THE INTERPRETATION OF SEX

Prison culture is not a representative slice of free American culture. Sex acts inside and outside prison may appear similar, but the behaviors have radically different interpretations. Acts inmates see as sexual experimentation outsiders may interpret as sexual violence.

Our study found that inmates' tales of sexual violence in and of themselves are culturally significant artifacts, which obtain serious meaning in the absence of actual sexual violence. Simply put, inmates don't need to see real-life sexual violence or be sexually victimized to learn enough about the process of sexual violence to hold them in good stead inside prison. Tales of sexual violence like the boogeyman stories we tell children are sufficient in most cases to raise inmates' awareness of contextual dangers and bluntly remind them that a penitentiary is a serious place.

INTERPRETATION OF SEXUAL VIOLENCE

Prisons are places of ultimate self-interest. Quickly learning as much as possible about survival has great benefit to individuals. Prison rape tales regulate inmates' association with the larger community by teaching them about proper behavior within the context of the prison community. By learning more about their association to the larger inmate population, inmates are also sharpening their self-interest in survival. Always, however, personal self-interest regulates inmate behavior. "Mind your own business," "don't do somebody else's time," "there are no friends in prison" are common in the verbal script of prisoners and clearly express inmates' dominant self-interest. The inmate population never takes on more importance than a single inmate's role in it. There is a balance of inmates' self-interest and their role in institutional social dynamics. Prison rape tales facilitate that balance between what inmates need to know to keep themselves safe and what they must know to maintain their safety within the prison walls.

The Myth of Prison Rape analyzed what inmates need to know in their own lives and their lives within a broader institutional context. Rape tales are a perfect transmission vehicle of lessons that will get anyone's attention. Most inmates are illiterate, so folktales—tales about prison rape—are the best means of attracting and maintaining inmates' attention to mechanisms of cultural survival. We are not saying that American prisons are out of control and that prisoners are in imminent danger of sexual and physical assault. Prisons are not out of control. As our analysis shows, inmates who learn as much as possible about conditions and causes of sexual violence worry less and are far less fearful of sexual victimization.

Let's clarify a significant point before it causes confusion. Prison culture is embedded with tales of sexual violence and infamous folkloric characters whose sexual exploits are legendary across the United States. To be sure, however, the ubiquity of sexual violence tales has no necessary relationship to the prevalence of prison rape. A grievous error in thinking would occur by using the (il)logic "there are a lot of rape tales so therefore there must be a lot of rape" or "prisoners wouldn't talk about rape if it didn't happen."

Prison rape tales convey information through surface characters in those tales, but the meaning of those characters' behavior lies deep within the prison culture. To approach that issue we cross the line between the literal and the symbolic nature of human culture.

Prison rape tales are about sexual violence, but prison rape isn't the point of prison rape tales. Rape catches inmates' and our attention. However, rape tales have one system of meaning within prison culture and another meaning system within the culture of the community. Problems arise when citizens believe or insist they believe that they know the meaning of prison rape. What citizens know about the symbolic complexity of prison rape boils down to what citizens know about community rape as those tales are told by magazines, newspapers, television news shows, and exploitive shows that plead to citizens' most immoral side.

A CULTURAL UNDERSTANDING
OF PRISON SEXUAL VIOLENCE

The goal of our research was straightforward but analytically difficult to accomplish. When the research began we wanted to know (1) what inmates know about sex, sexual violence, sexual assault, and rape; (2) how inmates learned it; and (3) how inmates use their specialized knowledge of sexual behavior in the everyday social dynamic of prison.

Prisons are institutions different from any place citizens visit. Except for convicted felons, no one really knows what prison life holds in store. An understanding of sexual violence from an inmate cultural perspective provides correctional personnel the best basis to create sexual violence intervention and prevention initiatives. We cannot prevent something we don't really understand. Although the word *rape* is used to describe sexual violence inside and outside prison, the cultural reality of prison life provides its own unique twist on sexual violence. Why should we assume that lawful citizens share views of sexual life and interpretation of sexual behavior with addicts, murderers, robbers, thieves, and rapists who are our constituents in prison populations? If we assume criminals' and our worldview share symbolic interpretations of cultural symbols, our initial assumption grossly misunderstands both citizens and inmates.

There is uniqueness in the way inmates conceptually express their vision of homosexual sex and sexuality and interpret others' sex and sexuality. We describe in our book their unique symbolic vision. When you finish reading *The Myth of Prison Rape*, don't sit back and say, "Fleisher and Krienert didn't tell me anything about the prevalence of rape in prison." You may read our book dozens of times and examine each table and figure and you won't find estimates of the prevalence of prison rape. We left prevalence studies to others. Later in the book, we give you references to the most current studies of estimates of prison rape prevalence. Our job was to make cultural and symbolic sense of what inmates said, using their words. Based on the axiom that thought influences culture and culture influences thought, the only "true" expression of inmate culture comes through the words inmates use to talk about the world they live in.

Acknowledgments

Former prison inmates, correctional professionals, professional correctional organizations, directors and commissioners of correctional agencies, scholars in universities and private research organizations, Institution Review Boards of universities and prisons, prison wardens and their staff, the senior administration of the National Institute of Justice, and men and women doing time in America's prisons aided in the conceptualization and implementation of our research design and methodology. Of course, we are responsible for the analysis and interpretation of inmate interview data.

The research reported here was funded by National Institute of Justice, grant number 2003-RP-BX-1001. Opinions expressed in this document do not represent the official position or policies of the National Institute of Justice, Case Western Reserve University, Kent State University's Institute for the Study and Prevention of Violence, Illinois State University, or its trustees.

Chapter One

Introduction

Our book analyzes the complexities of the cultural idea of rape inside American prisons. We didn't study allegations of prison rape, confirmations of rape, rape court cases, or prison records. We didn't study the prevalence of rape. We only talked to inmates.

Our research purpose was to understand how inmates "think" about prison rape. "Think about" means that we wanted to know what *they* know. What do inmates know about rape? How did they learn what they know? And, how do they interpret what they know in the broad social context of prison life?

We studied the idea of prison rape as it exists in the minds of men and women inmates. We didn't ask inmates if they ever consented or refused sexual advances or how many times they refused or consented. Answers to those questions do not provide the type of data we need to understand sexuality and sexual behavior within the broad context of prison society. With the type of data we gathered we cannot tell you how many allegations of sexual abuse there were in any of the prisons we visited.

What did we find when we studied the idea of prison rape in 10 states and 30 prisons across the United States? We found inmates' ideas on prison rape and rapists[1] have little variation. All 564 inmates we interviewed gave us similar answers to interview questions. It seemed as if all inmates[2] had known the same rapist and rape victim and were familiar with the same sex acts and social interactions that led to rape. When all interviews were analyzed we corroborated Johnson's (1971) finding that there was no epidemic of prison rape. Inmate observations that rape was infrequent and not a major prison safety concern have been further corroborated in decades of published prison research (Lockwood, 1994; Smith and Batluk, 1989).

Prison researchers who studied the social life of inmates never asserted that rape was a major disruptive factor in prison life. However, from the 1930s to the

1950s researchers' sociopsychological perspective on prison homosexuality was steeped in psychoanalytic-oriented theoretical interpretations of homosexuality. Given American culture's strong bias against homosexuality and homosexual sex, it isn't a surprise that prison researchers' antihomosexual bias was supported by medical diagnosis. A few examples illustrate prison researchers' discovery of the pathology of homosexuality.

Homosexuality has strong footing in decades of diagnosis as a psychiatric pathology reinforced by destructive prison environments embedded in and reinforced by an antihomosexual American society. Prisons were pathological environments that transformed heterosexuals into sexual predators (Fishman, 1934). Homosexuals were deviants (Fishman, 1934; Sykes, 1958). Homosexuality was caused by inner psychic turbulence (Devereux and Moos, 1942). Homosexuals were psychopaths whose sexual perversion spread like an infection (Clemmer, 1940). With an intellectual history that framed homosexuality as a psychiatric disorder expressed in violent behavior, the ensuing inference was clear: prisons were packed with pathological homosexuals whose sexual violence seemed a byproduct of prison environment or mental disorder. Indeed, with such an intellectual history and civil bias against homosexuality little question exists about the origin of the idea of a prison rape epidemic.

Why do citizens believe that prison rape has reached epidemic levels? Let's advance three cultural assumptions. First, perhaps citizens share the belief in epidemic levels of prison rape, because rape occurs in the community, ipso facto citizens extend their concept of community rape into prison social life. Perhaps too, since community rapists are convicted and sent to prison, citizens believe those rapists keep on raping inside. Finally, perhaps citizens in the free community have been so steeped in their own conceptualizations of prison rape, including epidemic levels of prison rape, that their cognitive image of prison life has been confused with the reality of prison life.

We are hopeful that you will table your assumptions about prison rape before you read our book. Unless you've done time, you have no direct experience with prison life. Whatever you "know" about prison rape was learned from television shows and movies. Even listening to tales told by former inmates who allege they were raped in prison are second-, third- or fourth-hand observations. We, the outsiders, have no way to separate a former inmate's thoughts about stories of rape from actual occurrences of prison rape. After years of studying prison rape, including interviews with 564 inmates, we can share first-person tales about prison rape that would make the hair on your neck stand up.

Years of interviewing inmates reinforced our view that inmates love to talk, particularly to outsiders. We spoke with inmates who had not shared a conversation with an outsider in years. On the street, only speech conveys information. Inside, every service or commodity inmates receive depends on what they say and how they say it.

Inmates were not intimidated by questions like "why do inmates have sex in prison?" "How many inmates out of 100 picked at random would you say are gay?" "What does it mean for an inmate to be turned out?" In the twenty-first century in normal social life in the free community, are there citizens who don't know what it means to be turned out or to come out of the closet?

Everyone knows something about sex. Sex acts inside and sex acts outside prison may appear similar but observers—citizens and inmates—will "see" very different acts and interpret those sex acts in widely divergent ways. Why? Sex acts occur and are interpreted through the lens of a cultural construction of the sex acts' meaning. Prison culture and free community culture aren't the same. Why should sex acts in dissimilar places have the same interpretation? Prison sexual violence interpreted through the lens of a free culture's construction of rape perpetuates a major conceptual and analytic error.

Prison culture does not represent a slice of free American culture. Prisoners does not a representative sample of the free American population, and we should be thankful for that. Scattered among the tens of thousands of nonviolent drug users and drug dealers in our prisons are prisoners who committed murder, burglary, felonious assault, rape, home invasion, serial killings, slaughter of their own children, and drive-by shooting, among other heinous crimes. Why then should prison culture, molded and influenced by the minds of violent inmates, interpret any human behavior in the same way as a culture molded by the minds of free citizens?

Inside prison, sexual violence tales are not interpreted as oddities or unusual or particularly frightening. Prison staff and inmates interpret sexual violence stories as "normal," even ironic. On the one hand, prisoners learn and talk about sexual violence and accept the stories as normal. On the other hand, prisoners summarily and without ambiguity condemn the behavior of inmates who threaten to sexually attack fellow inmates. Prison culture views prison rapists as weak and cowardly. They are inmates whose behavior falls outside the pale of successful inmate life.

Despite the obvious dangers of prison life, inmates report little fear or worry about rape. With good reason; an inmate pressed for sex in prison is probably safer than a coed pressed for sex at a drunken fraternity party. At least in prison, inmates said, a man can fight and might even get help from other inmates, or he can run, or scream for help from staff. Despite what some outsiders believe, inmates consistently report that prison correctional staffers try to keep inmates safe. The coed secreted off to some dark, out-of-the-way bedroom with a 6-foot-tall, 190-pound fraternity brother doesn't share the same safety protection available to inmates across the country.

Our research was not designed to test the truth or falsity of inmates' statements to us. That we leave to criminal investigators. We are only concerned with common themes uncovered in interviews shared among our inmates. No doubt the most interesting interview data shared by our inmates was their explanation for and interpretation of sexual behavior prison outsiders would call nonconsensual sex. Inmate interpretation of nonviolent sexual behavior is refreshing in modern America: inmates don't judge homosexuals to be immoral or depraved. When it comes to sexual behavior, inmates have a live-and-let-live attitude, at least most of the time. As one female inmate explained, *"I had to come to prison to find sexual freedom."*

Our research purpose was a *cultural and social analysis* of the *idea* of prison rape as a system of knowledge, beliefs, norms, values, social processes, and symbols *shared by* inmates in men's and women's prisons. By idea we mean a "thought," a snippet of a broader system of cultural knowledge, characteristic of the way members of a population think. The idea of prison rape must be understood in the broad context of prison life as a social process, which involves numerous actors over different periods of time. Sexual violence shouldn't be conceptualized as a solitary act. Delving into prison rape means studying prison rape and the complex array of other ideas and behavior to which it links. What types of behavior precede and follow violent sex? What are aggressors' motivations for violent sex? What are the consequences of sexual victimization for an aggressor and inmate?

The idea of prison rape exerts a powerful influence on inmates' lives. We asked inmates when they first heard about prison rape. Not surprisingly, they first heard about prison rape on the street, well before they came to prison. Their first sources of information were family members and street companions who had done jail and prison time. Street-based notions of prison rape were later solidified in county jail, where they lingered for months or years awaiting trial or a transfer to a prison. In county jail they heard the infamous "don't-drop-the-soap" prison shower tales.

Language philosophers and social scientists who study sociolinguistics and psycholinguistics taught us that language influences thought and thought influences language. Every parent knows that when their children begin to speak, their conceptualization of the world expands in complexity with their language ability. A three-year-old and a six-year-old "see" and experience different worlds largely as an effect of the degree of sophistication of language differences that occur between ages three and six. Prison inmates learn more about prison life and hear more sexual violence tales as they do their time. Two things happen over time. First, inmates' general knowledge about the causes and conditions of prison rape increases; however, inmates, like youngsters, acquire their knowledge from listening to conversations and repeating what they hear. Eventually, once they acquire a storehouse of knowledge, they are able to create "original" rape tales. Second, inmates learn more about sexual violence as the months and years pass, but their fear of and worry about prison rape stays at a relatively low level. Herein lies the irony of the myth of prison rape: the more inmates know about sexual violence, the less they worry.

THE MYTH OF PRISON RAPE

Our cultural study uses the concept of *myth* as the basis of the analysis. Our definition of myth is "a collection of culturally rational narratives that have knowledge fundamental to the culture itself." A myth is not a lie or a denial of the significance of an act. A myth contains a culture's most significant symbolic elements.

The myth of prison rape isn't 1, 10, 25, 50, or 100 rape tales. The myth of prison rape has no specific geographic and temporal dimension. It's shared by men and women whose life course landed them in a penitentiary. There they learn the rape myth. East Coast and West Coast inmates share the myth of prison rape; they tell similar rape tales and explain them in similar ways. Men inmates in prisons thousands of miles apart, men who have never traveled beyond the confines of their home neighborhood, knew the tales of legendary prison rapists—by name. Old tales spawn new tales. The names of characters may change, the time frame may change, the characters' personality may change, but always rape tales share the core themes of the rape myth. The content of our book is an exploration of the rape myth's core themes, their interrelationships, and their meaning within inmate culture.

The rape myth generates tales that have a cultural function and a social function. A tale's cultural function carries beliefs, attitudes, values, and perceptions that are the warp and weft of inmate culture. The excerpt below illustrates the cultural function of rape tales.

> A rapist wouldn't be looked on nicely. He'd be totally disrespected. Say an individual come in here first time and he's weak. Someone will take him under their wing and educate him. If someone came along and just took the guy off, someone would take that guy off, because that's disrespectful. We all recognize that everybody was in the same boat, so we tried to keep peace. Us old guys stay with our old-fashion ways. We have inside policemen, we have our justice system too, except it's all [of us].

In this rape tale we learn that sexual violence is sordid and can lead to wholesale inmate unrest. The rejection of rapists endorses the shared desire to maintain peace and social order for the benefit of everyone living and working in prison. The complexity of the information conveys to new generations of inmates the hidden complexities of prison culture and prison society's shared ethos of common social order.

A tale's social function carries rules of prison behavior, the do's and the don'ts of staying alive. There is no manual that teaches children how to be productive members of society. Children learn by listening and watching others. So do inmates. Rape tales carry an overabundance of prison cultural knowledge. In their simplest form, rape tales provide basic socialization advice: don't talk to strangers; don't accept anything from anyone; mind your own business; don't gamble, or sell or use drugs; don't get involved in activities that might have violent repercussions. When inmates learn those rules from rape tales, they learn cultural information. They learn that a violation of any rule might have an unambiguous yet definitive outcome. The details of that outcome are immaterial. The critical cultural information denotes the process leading to the outcome.

So valuable are rape tales generated by the myth of prison rape that if we had no more information about American prison life than hundreds of rape tales, we could write an ethnography of inmate life. We'd know prison culture's core beliefs, values, attitudes, and perceptions that guide inmate and staff interpretations of their world. But the myth presents a philosophical dilemma. Myths trap us. We cannot think outside of our culture. We are compelled to see the world through the lens of myth. However, we can gather discourse on prison sexual violence and rape tales from a culture's native inhabitants (inmates) and analyze that discourse for the cultural content it provides.

Cultural knowledge is conveyed via speech. In our case, knowledge of sexual violence is conveyed via inmate speech. All sexual-violence speech is generated by the myth of prison rape or by knowledge embedded within prison inmate culture. We don't think inmates lied or told us purposefully distorted tales. Why? Our data provided the same or very similar information that prison researchers have heard over decades. Whether inmates lie or distort information about sexual violence is of no consequence. In an analysis of culture via language content everything inmates say has the same source. Truth and accuracy are generated by the same source that generates lies and distortions. But in the end, truth, accuracy, lies, and distortions are cultural constructs. Truth and accuracy are assessed in cultural context. We may see a twisted tale, but inmates see a cultural truth. Knowledge is relative to cultural context. In short, everything inmates say is necessarily conveyed via the myth of prison rape transmitted through and interpreted by inmate culture.

NOTES

1. In this book the word *rape* refers to rape inside prison; *rapist* always refers to inmate rapists inside prison.
2. The term *inmate* is generic and inclusive of men and women inmates. We specify men and women inmates when necessary.

Chapter Two

Intellectual History of Prison Sexual Culture

Karoly Maria Benkert, a late-nineteenth-century German psychologist, coined the term *homosexual* (Feray and Herzer, 1990). While homosexuality is a relatively recent concept, homosexual sex surely is not a recent behavior. In this chapter we offer an abridged history of research literature on prison culture, prison homosexual sex, and psychological and social theories of homosexuality (see Fleisher and Krienert [2006] for a thorough literature review). This chapter explores past research by decade. We use this arrangement to illustrate the growth of intellectual exploration in theories of prison sexual culture.

On the topic of women inmates' sexuality, studies commonly begin with "few studies address," or "there seems to be a void." In fact, there are even articles written about how little research has been done (Tewksbury and West, 2000). Women's prison research has a relatively short and narrow scholarly focus. There are no large-scale studies of culture and women inmates' sexual behavior and scant mention of sexual coercion or sexual assault. What little research exists historically focuses on consensual same-sex behaviors and pseudofamilies (Hensley, Tewksbury, and Koscheski, 2002). Only recently have researchers begun to examine female coercive sexual behavior. In fact, it is only within the past 20 years that researchers even recognized the possibility of sexual assault committed by a female inmate and not a staff member (Alarid, 2000; Calhoun and Coleman, 2002). When available, we infuse women's literature within the broad discussion of sexuality and rape.

EARLY DECADES OF PRISON SEX RESEARCH: 1930s TO 1940s

The 1930s through 1950s can arguably be recognized as the single-most influential period in the intellectual development of prison culture research.

7

Early prison research is significant in the history of prison culture studies for three reasons. First, the concept of culture as a legitimate topic of research was introduced to scholars. Second, Freudian psychoanalytic theory influenced the interpretation of prison homosexuality and homosexual sex. In latter decades, Freudian theory persisted, but not in a strict psychoanalytic form. Freudian concepts were "translated" into sociological theory of prison homosexuality and used to illustrate the influence of sexual "deprivation" on prison culture. Third, the discovery of World War II Nazi concentration camps had a pronounced effect on the study of homosexuality, sexual violence, and the interpretation of prison life and effects of confinement on inmates through the present day.

Fishman's *Sex in Prison* (1934)

Joseph F. Fishman's 1934 book, *Sex in Prison*, explored a theoretical premise that later became known as deprivation theory. It is the belief that incarcerated men, driven by the irrepressible need for sexual release, and deprived of "normal" heterosexual outlets, engage in same-sex relations. He distinguished between men who succumb to their need for sexual release and those men who are forced or coerced into same-sex relations.[1]

> Should you doubt that deprivation of liberty constitutes the real punishment to a prisoner, imagine yourself living a first class hotel, the only condition being that you do not leave the building. I am sure you would tire of it in a week. Then imagine yourself confined there for from five to twenty-five years, and you can get some idea perhaps of how monotonous and irksome incarceration becomes even under the best of conditions. . . but you are just one person. Assume now that there are about two thousand of the same sex in the hotel with you under exactly similar conditions, and that you see these same people, and no others, day in and day out, month after month, and year after year. (p. 165)

His work gave a broad outline of the culture of prison sex, and a limited lexicon of prison sociosexual terminology. This was an important first step at recognizing the interplay between verbal labels and social roles. He recognized openly homosexual men known as "fairies," "fags," "pansies," or "girls." They exhibited effeminate traits, and were common targets of sexual predation. There were "wolves" or "top men" who were predators who targeted fairies and younger inmates of slight build perceived to be effeminate. The ascription of sexual proclivities to physical characteristics became a dominant theme in prison sociocultural research, which continues to the present day (see Hensley, Tewksbury, and Castle, 2003). Fishman considered the majority of wolves to be formerly heterosexual men who were driven to homosexuality and sexual predation as a result of sexual deprivation.

Fishman captured the social dynamics of sexual pursuit. He noted that wolves may "court" other inmates, sometimes quite persistently and over a long period of time, and shower them with gifts and favors, hoping to make the target into a "girl."

> They usually begin with a friendly offer to protect the newcomer, and to see that his life in prison is made as easy as possible for him. This offer is often gratefully accepted by the new inmate because he is not yet accustomed to prison life. . . . The first advance is usually followed by the giving of small presents, such as a box of cigarettes purchased from the prison commissary. Unless the new prisoner has someone to 'put him wise,' assuming that he does not know the object of these advances, he gradually slips into a position of helpless dependency on his self-styled protector. When the final purpose of these attentions becomes known, and if the object of them resists, he is very often threatened with physical harm. (p. 84)

In addition to the physical violence often suffered by targets of sexual aggression, Fishman emphasizes the moral degradation of becoming a "pervert" and facing the physical harm he believed to be caused by long-term homosexual activity.[2]

Clemmer's *The Prison Community* (1940)

Clemmer's *The Prison Community* (1940) made a major conceptual contribution to prison research by identifying culture as a topic of formal study:

> [A] a more obvious principle is that the prison, like other social groups, has a culture. "Culture" may be defined as those artificial objects, institutions, modes of life or thought which are not peculiarly individual, but which characterize a group and have both special and temporal contiguity; or, in the oft quoted words of Tylor (1924 [orig. 1871]),[3] as "that complex whole which includes knowledge, belief, art, morals, law, custom, and any other capabilities and habits acquired by man as a member of society." Culture, therefore, is supra-individual. . . . To understand the culture of the prison, knowledge of certain fundamental processes of human interaction is necessary. To the sociologist culture is societal structure, and the social processes are functions. (p. 86–87)

The Prison Community exposed structures and functions of prison culture and described the process by which inmates become socialized to prison culture, a process Clemmer dubbed *prisonization*, a seeming analogy to anthropology's concept of enculturation. Clemmer saw prison culture as an amalgam of many influences, including the characteristics, norms, values, and knowledge brought into the prison from their previous lives by a diverse group of inmates; the characteristics of the prison as an isolating and segregating society; and the physical architecture and organization of the prison itself.

The unique interplay of social forces and physical context influenced inmates' prisonization experience. For example, an inmate who, by sheer luck, received a work assignment that allowed him to remain relatively isolated, and a cell mate who was not violent, predatory, or involved in drug trafficking, would be prisonized to a lesser extreme of prison life than another inmate whose cell and job assignments forced him into closer contact with hard-core inmates. Clemmer viewed these chance placements of cell mate, cell block, and work assignment as the strongest determining factors in the degree of inmate prisonization.

Clemmer viewed homosexuality of any kind as sexual perversion, and men who engaged in homosexuality as either not having followed a "normal" course of male sexual and emotional development, or else as relapsing due to the pressures unique to prison life. These pressures include deprivation of normal heterosexual outlets, but they also include the relative promiscuity of the average inmate prior to being incarcerated; ubiquitous sexual stimuli in the form of radio and magazine advertisements; the focus on sex in prison argot and humor; and the disquieting effect of the presence of inmates committed for sex offenses and inmates who are openly homosexual.

Deprivation theory remained unnamed in Clemmer's work. Nevertheless the premise of sociosexual deprivation was a core theme in Clemmer's analysis of prison sex. Unlike later uses of the deprivation concept, Clemmer did not consider deprivation a crucial factor in shaping the culture of prison sex. "Without further elaboration it may be stated categorically that sex yearning and lonesomeness for feminine companionship is for the great majority of prisoners the most painful phase of incarceration" (p. 256).

Clemmer's only mention of sex-related violence was in reference to fights that break out between jealous inmates competing for the attentions of the same man. In such cases formerly "straight" convicts initiated sexual advances toward openly homosexual convicts. Clemmer concluded:

> The all-male environment, the absence of strong social controls, the impersonalization of social relationships, and, most of all, the existence of centers of infection in the penal culture, stimulate abnormal sex conduct. The most important of the infectious foci are the definite homosexual psychopaths who spread perversion throughout the community. (p. 264)

Psychoanalytic Interpretations of Homosexual Sex in Prison

Early research on prison culture focused on psychiatric interpretation of homosexuality and homosexual sex, diffused with a medical interpretation of homosexuality, common in the nineteenth and twentieth centuries. Generally a medical interpretation posited that homosexual sex was a consequence of humans' inability to meet their biological demands for opposite-sex sex. Given that assumption, same-sex prisons inevitably cause psychiatric disease, manifested through sex-related violence. By that argument, prisons are the context but not the immediate cause of sexual violence.

Homosexuality was diagnosed as a psychiatric disorder in the early 1940s. Devereux and Moos (1942) suggested that homosexuality was not a condition of "human or criminal nature," but rather a medical problem. As a medical problem, homosexuality was caused by inner psychic turbulence. "The process [of becoming a homosexual] is facilitated by the fact that there is always a potential infantile homosexual lurking behind the 'manly' mask of the beast of prey, which rejoices in male society" (pp. 306–24). Perhaps prison researchers' current concept of the prison sexual predator finds its intellectual genesis in Devereux and Moos's beast of prey.

Soon after Devereux and Moos, Karpman (1948) continued the psychiatric interpretation of homosexual sex. He wrote that "[a]s the hope of gaining access to a person of the opposite sex recedes farther and farther, the transition from this type [of sex] to the more abnormal expressions takes place sooner or later." He continued: "phantasies gradually develop an abnormal character picturizing paraphiliac situations, the masturbatory practice assumes a definitely pathological aspect, and the nearest thing to a 'real' female is the feminine homosexual." Same-sex sex was considered an abnormality that only emerges as a deviant form of sexuality rather than a natural expression of human sexuality. Masturbation was also considered pathological behavior. Karpman asserted that the only intervention taken by prison staff to resolve sexual abnormalities was "violent suppression" and that abnormal influences of prison sexual life were carried by inmates back to the community. Those two 1940s assertions emerge again decades later in the federal Prison Rape Elimination Act of 2003.

Forced or coerced sexual activity was not mentioned in early women's prison literature. Any discussion of sexuality was relegated to the realm of unnatural relationships where racial and class differences were prominent topics (Otis, 1913). In discussions of homosexuality, black women were thought to be more aggressive and dominant; white women fell into relationships with them to gain safety (Freedman, 1996). Low-socioeconomic-status women were thought to be more susceptible to lesbianism than those from an upper-class upbringing. Prison and community homosexual relationships were thought to be a perversion. Early research for both genders reflects homosexual perversion as a predetermined conclusion of prison life. The prison environment became the focal point for the transformation of (normal) heterosexual inmates into homosexual deviants.

Early Decades: Summary of Key Findings

The early decades of prison culture research created groundwork for decades of later research. An enumeration below finds early research outcomes keyed to scholar and date of research. The conceptualization of prison sexual predators illustrated their manly qualities and manhood while their prey appears weak and defenseless. These psychological stereotypes of sexual aggressors and prey persist into modern research.

* Deprived of heterosexual relations, men inmates will develop irrepressible urges for sex and will engage in same-sex behavior. Sexual predators were heterosexuals driven to sexual violence by sexual deprivation (Fishman, 1934).
* Prison culture has the power to alter sexual propensities (Fishman, 1934) and transform heterosexuals into homosexuals (Clemmer, 1940).
* Homosexuality (Fishman, 1934) and masturbation (Karpman, 1948) are deviant, even pathological behaviors.
* Prison was a pathological environment and caused inner psychic turbulence and untold psychosexual harm (Deveureux and Moos, 1942; Fishman, 1934; Karpman, 1948).
* Homosexual psychopaths spread sexual perversion, like an infection, among inmates and adversely influence multiple domains of prison life (Clemmer, 1940).
* The infantile homosexual lurking within men inmates' psyches cause them to become beasts of prey (Deveureux and Moos, 1942).
* Prison authorities try to punish homosexuality "out of" inmates (Karpman, 1948).
* Deviant sexual behavior in prison extends to post-release community behavior (Karpman, 1948).

MIDDLE DECADES OF PRISON SEX RESEARCH: 1950s TO 1970s

A Freudian interpretation of homosexuality, homosexual sex, and homosexuality's strong influence on the evolution of prison culture persisted in the scholarship of Gresham Sykes. Sykes's (1958) study influenced prison research from the 1950s into the 2000s. Studies from this period saw a shift from cultural examinations of sexuality to prevalence, classification and rhetoric. During this period emerged the idea that homosexual sex was strongly influenced by gender. Prison research shifted emphasis from detailed descriptions of prison life to quantifiable expressions of inmate behavior.

Sykes's *The Society of Captives* (1958)

Arguably the single-most theoretically influential prison study was Gresham Sykes's 1958 *The Society of Captives*. Sykes was a Princeton University sociologist who studied inmate social life at the New Jersey State Maximum Security Prison. He collected data from approximately 20 inmates who served as a "panel" he could question whenever he needed (p. 135). Sykes wrote in the early post–World War II era. His writing compared prisons to Nazi concentration camps; at that time a natural comparison. Sykes infused prison life with multiple sociopsychological deprivations, including the deprivation of liberty; the deprivation of goods and services; the deprivation of heterosexual relationships; the deprivation of autonomy; and the deprivation of security. Taken together, these deprivations threatened inmates' ego structure and created a defiant survival adaptation. Defiance was also manifest in the prison argot with its emphasis on being a "real man," or someone who could do his time; take what the guards dished out to him; refuse to complain; and remain cool. A real man "confront[ed] his captors with neither subservience nor aggression" (p. 102).

A contextual theory of prison culture and inmate sexuality emerged in the sociology of Gresham Sykes. Sykes proposed that the deprivation of heterosexual relationships lies at the heart of the majority of prison sexual activity:

> There are, of course, some "habitual" homosexuals in the prison—men who were homosexuals before their arrival and who continue their particular form of deviant behavior within the all-male society of the custodial institution. For these inmates, perhaps, the deprivation of heterosexual intercourse cannot be counted as one of the pains of imprisonment. They are few in number, however, and are only too apt to be victimized or raped by aggressive prisoners who have turned to homosexuality as a temporary means of relieving their frustration. (p. 71)

Sykes's analysis of prison argot identified sexually aggressive prisoners—the wolves—as situational homosexuals[4] driven by deprivation of heterosexual outlets.

> And the inmates, too, attempt to distinguish the 'true' sexual pervert and the prisoner driven to homosexuality by his temporary deprivation. In the world of the prison, however, the extent to which homosexual behavior involves 'masculinity' and 'femininity' would appear to override all other considerations and it is this which provides the main basis for the classification of sexual perversion by the inmate population. (p. 95ff)

The outward structures of prison sex culture were seen as rooted in the deprivation of heterosexual relationships. However, in addition to these outward structures, Sykes pointed to the deep-running psychological effects of deprivation, which were the true mechanisms through which deprivation created the culture of inmate sex:

> Shut off from the world of women, the population of prisoners finds itself unable to employ that criterion of maleness which looms so importantly in society at large—namely, the act of heterosexual intercourse itself. Proof of maleness, both for the self and for others, has been shifted to other grounds and the display of 'toughness,' in the form of masculine mannerisms and the demonstration of inward stamina, now becomes a major route to manhood. But for homosexuals and non-homosexuals alike, the emphasis placed by the society of captives on the accompaniments of sexuality rather than sexuality itself does much to transform the problem of being a man in a world without women. (p. 97)

A crisis of self-image and self-understanding induced by the deprivation of heterosexual relationships creates the culture of prison sex. Such deprivation stands as the dynamic force in creating aggressive sociosexual characters— wolves—and their weak prey, punks.

Sykes's Influence on the Future of Prison Intellectual Thought

In the history of prison research, Sykes's significant conceptual contribution was the introduction of the prison-as-concentration-camp analogy. Positing that prisons and concentration camps share a core culture, Sykes proposed that prison culture was primarily the product of deprivations imposed on and endured by inmates.

Out of the prison qua concentration camp analogy evolved themes and concepts still accepted as axiomatic in prison culture research. Nazi brutality against homosexuals diffused into prison scholars' worldview. Inmates were necessarily defiant against "guards." Snitches were men who aided the enemy and were justifiably punished by other inmates. Wholly inadequate, even brutal prison conditions maintained a helpless and hapless prisoner population guarded by cruel keepers. The sociopsychological consequences of imprisonment caused permanent life-term damage.

Not until the 1960s did prison scholars seriously consider less harsh and judgmental ideas about the sociopsychological nature of prison homosexuality and reappraise the damage caused by homosexual conduct. What had been at minimum 30 years of negative judgment about prison's near-inevitable damage inflicted on inmates' sociosexual lives began to shift, with a few exceptions (Davis, 1968) in the 1960s. Macrosociological changes in American culture, such as civil rights legislation, likely opened prisons to considerations more enlightened than previously recognized. Several mid-1950s studies foreshadowed this change.

Smith (1956) examined homosexuals' quality of life at the Medical Center for Federal Prisoners, in Springfield, Missouri. He concluded that institutions need "a closely supervised program for homosexuals," (p. 43) more effective diagnostic criteria and methods, and a means to increase the validity of classifying homosexual inmates. He also concluded homosexual inmates were content with themselves and their sexual preference.

Ward's (1958) examination of institutionalized adolescents, while distinct from adult prisons in many ways, had findings similar to others' research in adult prisons. He found there are nonhomosexual aspects of homosexuality in institutions, and that "[b]ullying and aggressive homosexual behavior become confused with manliness." Ward proposed that a lack of rape investigations was linked to American culture's bias against homosexuality. "Because of the stigma which our society places on homosexuality, and because of society's demand that such behavior be eliminated, officials are reluctant to encourage investigation of homosexual practices in their institutions. The possibility of unfavorable publicity brings with it the real danger of dismissal from office by public demand (pp. 301–14)."

The Gendered Path of Prison Homosexuality

By the 1960s, male and female inmate homosexuality had distinctly different and gender-biased interpretations. While male inmate homosexuality was perverse and psychopathological, female inmate homosexuality was a supportive and situational activity exacerbated by women's customary need for social and emotional support. Ward and Kassebaum (1964):

> The process of turning out seems to represent socialization of the new inmates into practices which provide support, guidance and emotional satisfaction during a period when these are lacking. . . . Inmates believe that most homosexual involvement occurs early in imprisonment, that most affairs are situational with heterosexual relationships to be resumed upon release and that many are 'once-only' affairs. (p. 174)

Few changes occur in the description of women's prison homosexuality. Gagnon and Simon (1968) found women inmates did not have an overpowering sexual urge. In consensual relationships, the "femme" role and the "stud," or butch, role were usually defined. The femme was more likely to be a heterosexual outside prison and display traditionally feminine characteristics. The stud played the male sex role. "He" adopted male behaviors, dress, hairstyles, and language (Giallombardo, 1966). African Americans and street lesbians were more likely to play the stud role (Alarid, 2000) and were expected to pursue the femme (Ward and Kassebaum, 1964).

By the 1960s, researchers expanded their theoretical focus and looked at social and sexual roles and their influence on institution social control. Sykes and Messinger (1960b) noted inmates have a conscious appreciation of institution social control and make deliberate efforts to achieve and maintain it. Garabedian (1963) described a variety of inmate social roles and how they accommodated prison life. He argued that "pains of imprisonment" diminish over time, and when they do, inmates became more involved in positive prison life (Leger, 1973).

Gagnon and Simon (1968) identified patterns of sexual adjustment among men and women inmates by examining sexual deprivation and its effects on sociosexual relationships. They argued that positing inmate homosexuality as an effect of prison sexual deprivation was too strict and too simplistic an interpretation of prison homosexuality. They had two significant theoretical assumptions. First, a study of prison homosexual sex should include consideration of inmates' sexual and nonsexual lives prior to imprisonment. Second, the responses to sexual and nonsexual experiences outside prison influenced their adaption to a single-sex environment and loss of freedom.

Gagnon and Simon concluded that "women have fewer problems than men in managing sexual deprivation" (p. 27) and that "most prisoners do not seem to feel an overwhelming sexual need" (p. 25). Those conclusions support previous (but not necessarily valid) research findings that (1) women inmates' sexual behavior was supportive and reflected women's customary need to obtain social and emotional support; and (2) men's homosexual behavior was deviant. The idea that female homosexual sex was normal but men's was deviant was then firmly implanted in the intellectual history of prison inmate sexual research.[5]

Homosexual Adaptations

Johnson (1971) found homosexuality was not epidemic and devastating but rather an adaptation to prison life. He suggested that through constant contact among men, the inmate's "whole life is predicated on homosexualized group contact" (p. 85). The social organization of the prison environment caused inmates to create a "class of women substitutes" (p. 85) and to engage in inmate marriages, which "serve[d] to release sexual and emotional frustration" (p. 85). There was no protection for homosexuals who were raped. Staff, he said, had negative attitudes toward homosexuals. He described how a raped homosexual's lover would seek revenge on the predator. However, he had no empirical data to support the retaliation contention.

Kirkham (1971) identified five points about prison homosexuality. (1) There were only three possible adaptations open to members of the inmate community: sexual abstinence; masturbation; or participation in institutional homosexuality. (2) Situational homosexuality was fostered by a tendency on the part of sensational writers to grossly exaggerate the actual incidence of the phenomenon. The "number of inmates who participate in any form of homosexual behavior while imprisoned is relatively small when compared to the vast majority of prisoners who adapt to sexual frustration by masturbating" (p. 330). (3) Inmates who engaged in homosexual activity[6] presented a facade of toughness, "manliness," to escape being defined as a homosexual. (4) The marital relationship between a man inmate and his male wife was largely instrumental; a male wife would obtain goods for her man, and in turn he provided physical protection. Women, he said, moved among relationships; social shifting among relations caused jealousy and conflict. (5) Sex roles, he said, such as a wolf or jocker, were not considered "real" homosexuals.

Kassebaum (1972) identified sexual affairs as coercive, commercial, or romantic. Coercive relationships were those when a person gave in to the requests of others out of fear of actual or threatened violence. In commercial relationships, money or goods exchanged hands for sexual favors. Romantic relationships were characterized by affection and willingness of both parties to engage in sex. Kassebaum classified prison sexual orientation, ranging from inmates who were openly homosexual inside or out to inmates who avoided homosexual contact and used masturbation as an outlet. Finally, he found that approximately 50 percent of women inmates had had some form of in-prison sexual experience.

The Epidemic of Rape

The end of this era began with a handful of panic-inducing writings about prison rape. Davis (1968) found sexual assaults in the Philadelphia prison system were epidemic. Reviewing 3,304 administrative reports, 156 sexual assaults were documented in the 26-month study (seven in sheriff's vans, 149 in prisons): 82 were buggery; 19 fellatio; and 55 were attempted coercive solicitations involving 97 different victims and 176 different aggressors.

Davis studied only administrative reports and did not provide data on substantiated reports of sexual aggression. In the 30 years preceding, and 40 years after Davis's study, prison researchers did not report epidemic levels of sexual aggression and violence. In 70 years of prison studies, researchers' most common observation about sexual dynamics is that squabbles emerge in competition for sexual partners. Up to the present day, Davis's findings remain anomalous.

Soon after Davis's study, Linda Charlton, a journalist, published the article "The Terrifying Homosexual World of the Jail System" (1971). She alleged that new inmates were approached for sex very shortly after they came in; that homosexuality in jail alienated inmates and further separated them from the normal outside; and that a prison should create conditions that parallel the outside world, allowing inmates heterosexual behavior.[7] Creating an inside world that mirrored the outside, she wrote, would decrease the devastating effect of prison on inmates.

An unspecified number of conversations with former inmates and a self-selected literature review convinced Charlton that homosexual behavior and sexual aggression in jail were a significant problem. She brought to the popular media the stereotypic inmate homosexual, the stereotypic sexual predator, the stereotypic prison-as-concentration-camp image, and a reinforced notion that prison rape had reached epidemic levels.

Daniel Lockwood's *Prison Sexual Violence* (1980) used data collected in 1974–1975 in the New York state prison system. Lockwood defined "sexual aggression" as:

> behavior which leads a man to feel that he is the target of aggressive sexual intentions. . . . We see sexual aggression as a continuum marked by different levels of attempts to exploit, and different levels of reaction to exploitations. At the bottom of the continuum we might see a target imagining aggression from an aggressor's overture. At the top we might see the gang rape. Along this continuum, any incident of aggression is created as much by the interaction that unfolds as by the intentions of the aggressor. (p. 6)

Lockwood identified characteristics of targets and aggressors and salient features of different kinds of aggressive incidents important to understanding the culture of prison sex. He found targets were significantly more likely to be white, while aggressors were significantly more likely to be black. Targets were generally younger than aggressors and of relatively slighter build and lower weight than aggressors. They had effeminate characteristics; were fairly inexperienced in prison life; and were particularly vulnerable in the first few weeks of initial imprisonment or transfer to another institution. Aggressors sought newcomers; they were naive and easy prey and unaware of aggressors' hustles. Aggressors, Lockwood found, did not view themselves as homosexuals but did view victims as women.

Lockwood elaborated Fishman's descriptions of the context and dynamics of sexual aggression and offered a tentative typology of aggressor approaches.

(1) *The Propositioning approach*—no threats or use of force are present.
(2) *The Player approach*—combines force and threats with verbal tactics.
(3) *The Gorilla approach*—relies exclusively on force or threats. "Gorillas," also known as "booty bandits," "asshole bandits," or simply

"bandits," are prisoners who pounce on other men and attempt to sodomize them.

Prison culture recognizes several approaches to handle sexual threats. Lockwood documented the effects of sexual aggression on targets. Effects included chronic anxiety, depression, and suicidal ideation. A frequent outcome of sexual victimization was victims' aggressive withdrawal from prison social life via self-isolation or protective custody. A threatened inmate has the dilemma of whether to report the aggressor to the authorities. Reporting would incur the label of snitch and may make him vulnerable to reprisals. Such a situation, Lockwood wrote, may be worse than the sexual aggression a potential victim seeks to avoid. A snitch may opt for protective custody; however, protective custody severely restricts job access, exercise, and recreational opportunities. The only alternatives to snitching would be fighting or submitting to an aggressor. A target's preemptive public display of force may prevent an assault. A retaliatory post-assault strike may stave off future problems. Sexual pressure and responses to it are cultural blueprints. They are matters of thought and discussion, but neither may be acted out.

Lockwood reaffirmed deprivation theory as the motivating force propelling aggressors:

> The idea that violence is an end in itself, which is mentioned in the rape literature, has little supporting evidence in our study. Violence for its own sake is not explicitly present. . . . Aggressors who spoke openly about their behavior sometimes expressed guilt and remorse over having been driven to such lengths. On the other hand, they saw a peremptory sex drive behind their activities, and blamed the prison and other external forcers for creating the pressing problem which inevitably forced their actions: How can you cope with being sexually deprived for three years, for two, for even five years at a time? . . . Paradoxically as it may strike us, aggressors can thus not only justify their acts but can argue that they, ultimately, are the real victims. (p. 338ff)

Middle Decades: Summary of Key Findings

The middle decades of prison research amplified earlier findings and added to the literature new concepts, ideas, and interpretations. They are enumerated below.

- American prisons were analogous to Nazi concentration camps in their effects on inmates (Sykes, 1958).
- Deprivation of heterosexual sex caused prison sexual activity (Sykes, 1958).

- Sex deprivation was the dynamic force driving sex-related aggression (Sykes, 1958).
- The deprivation of imprisonment lessens over time (Garabedian, 1963).
- Male-inmate homosexuality was perverse but female inmate homosexuality was a supportive and situational activity and exacerbated by women's customary need for social and emotional support (Ward and Kassebaum, 1964).
- Homosexuality may not be epidemic and devastating, but an adaptation to prison life (Johnson, 1971).
- Inmates' preferred form of sexual expression was masturbation vs. homosexuality (Kirkham, 1971); and
- Sexual relationships can be coercive, commercial, or romantic (Kassebaum, 1972).
- Sexual targets suffer chronic anxiety, depression, and suicidal ideation that result from the stress of targeted sexual aggression; sexual targets are likely to become violent (Lockwood, 1980).

MODERN DECADES OF PRISON SEX RESEARCH:
1980s TO 2000s

The 1980s had a proliferation of prison sex and violence research. However, few new ideas were forthcoming. Scattered projects sought to identify the prevalence and scope of rape and other types of prison sexual behavior without the identification of a framework for common understanding. Cultural examinations of prison sexual behavior were virtually nonexistent.

Prevalence

Nacci and Kane (1982; see 1983; 1984) studied sexual aggression in federal prisons. Based on a survey methodology, they found that one in 330 male inmates had been a target of sexual aggression but that less than 0.3 percent had been raped. Sexual targets were homosexuals or bisexuals 70 percent of the time. The stereotypic image of the sexual-assault victim emerged. Victims were slender, effeminate, and had long hair. Sexual targets, Nacci and Kane found, discussed sex openly in public earshot.[8]

Tewksbury (1989a) examined 88 male inmates at the Lebanon Correctional Institution in Ohio. Group-administered survey questionnaires were distributed to college-program inmates in their classrooms. They found that inmates estimated rape in the general prison population at a much higher rate than self-reported incidence. Seven percent of the inmates reported attempts at coercion and no inmates reported being raped; however, they estimated that 14 percent of all inmates had been sexually assaulted or raped while in prison[9] (pp. 34–39).

Corroborating Tewksbury's finding, Lockwood (1994) reported that male homosexual rape was a rare event and that large numbers of offenders are propositioned for sexual favors. Researchers and inmates, Lockwood (p. 98) said, "have been perpetuating certain ideas about prison sexual violence that are not supported by systematic research on the topic."

It is only within the past 20 years that researchers recognized the possibility of female-inmate sexual assault committed by female inmates instead of a staff member (Alarid, 2000; Calhoun and Coleman, 2002). Much of the modern work focuses on a coercive system of economic exchange between female inmates. Decades of studies reported that inmates became "canteen punks," or "box whores," to avoid beatings and reap the economic benefits of homosexual behavior (Bowker, 1977). A clear distinction between consensual and coercive sex fades into ambiguity when a coerced inmate seems to consent in exchange for canteen goods or protection (Alarid, 2000).

Homosexual Behavior

Tewksbury (1989a) found that male inmates reported rates of homosexual activity at or below the general [free] population. Hensley, Tewksbury, and Wright (2001) in the men's maximum-security Southern Correctional Facility in Lucasville, Ohio, studied masturbation and consensual sex. Hensley et al. (2001) found that 79 percent of inmates said they were heterosexual prior to incarceration; 69 percent continued to be heterosexual after incarceration; 36 percent received oral sex from another male inmate; and 32 percent performed anal intercourse on another male inmate. Hensley and Tewksbury's (2002) literature review found a lack of clear definitions of sexual behavior and sexual terminology used in research studies. They noted further, a comment not in literature until their study, that 60 to 70 percent of America's inmates were illiterate (pp. 226–43).

In the past 30 years, few changes occurred in the description of women's prison homosexuality. In consensual relationships, the "femme" role and the "stud," or butch, role were usually defined. Women inmates who reported participation in homosexual prison activities involved younger inmates or those with longer sentences (Hensley et al., 2002). Younger inmates' prison homosexual behavior was explained by their sexual experiments outside prison (Koscheski and Hensley, 2001).

Pseudofamilies

Women inmates' pseudofamilies have stimulated research over many decades (see Selling, 1931). Modern pseudofamily research has reinforced the association between prison deprivation (boredom, forced associations with others, and lack of privacy) and participation in familial roles. Giallombardo (1966) and Propper (1981; 1982) noted that pseudofamilies provided asexual emotional ties. However, some research identified women's fear of closeness to inmates (Greer, 2000, pp. 461–62). Inmates' perceptions vary on the issue of the personal functions of a pseudofamily.

> Christian families call each other sister. One girl calls another inmate mommy. After you spent some time at the facility, the juveniles get into plays, activities; older inmates are reminded of their children on the outside. It is just a name, no actions are taken, nothing sexual. This is a form of friendship terminology.

Women inmates' sociosexual identity within a pseudofamily extends their outside sociosexual identity and allows them to maintain a sense of self (Culbertson and Fortune, 1986, p. 33). Hensley, Tewksbury, and Koscheski (2002) suggested that women who closely identified themselves with the roles of wife, or daughter, or mother prior to incarceration would most likely engage in pseudofamilies. Pseudofamilies help women cope with family deprivation by forming substitute relations (Pollock, 2002a). Most women did not participate in same-sex behavior prior to incarceration, and would not likely be committed to a postrelease homosexual lifestyle. Instead, homosexuality was a cultural adaptation to incarceration and a means of obtaining affection and attention.

Prison socialization: pseudofamily vs. the mix. Recent research suggests that women's prison culture has changed and become less stable and familial than in the past (Greer, 2000). Owen (1998) discusses "the mix," or female subculture at Central California Women's Facility. Although inmate personal interactions have emotional, practical, material, and sexual value, Owen identified the mix as an arena for sexual coercion and assault. Pseudofamilies were a social adaptation that worked to keep women out of the mix.

Alarid (2000) examined one woman inmate's prison life over five years via correspondence. Her work found that a woman's social relations play a role in coercive sexual behavior. She found examples of retaliatory sexual assault in cases where a sexual attack was a reprisal for a nonsexual wrong against a friend of the attacker. Greer (2000) examined 35 Midwestern inmates and found sexual relationships were based on economic manipulation, paralleling Owen (1998), who also discussed the sale or trade of sexual favors for commissary. Unfortunately information on this subject remains limited.

Greer (2000) suggested that changes in popular culture influenced change in women inmates' sexual behavior. She argued that since women are not as strongly tied to their once-traditional roles, women have social options in addition to mother or sister or daughter. Modern housing architecture structures in women's prisons, coupled with sociosexual changes, led to change in interpersonal role relationships. Researchers documented that family programs and furloughs strengthen outside biosocial family ties and decrease the significance of pseudofamilies (Pollock, 2002b). Owen (1998), however, found women still involved in play families and dyadic sexual relationships; the pervasiveness of these relationships are unknown.

Institutional Factors

Correctional institutions' architecture has been cited as a possible correlate to sexual behavior. Gaes and McGuire (1985) measure a range of factors contributing to prison assault rates in men's institutions. Flanagan (1983) assessed male inmate misconduct and found that inmate age at commitment, drug use, and race contributed to a high rate of infractions. Struckman-Johnson and Struckman-Johnson (2002) found that in three women's units housing 295, 113, and 60 inmates, women reported a range of coercive sex, mostly genital touching, from 19 percent in the highest-population unit to 6 to 8 percent in the lowest-population units. Similarly, Owen (1998) cites increases in prison population and an increase in drug offenders as characteristics likely to change the dynamics of sexual coercion.

Race, Ethnicity, and Aggression

History of prison rape research has no definitive analysis between rapists' and rape victims' race or ethnicity. There are, however, indirect references to a black rapist and white victim. Racial affiliation independent of physical size and strength and social affiliation, such as religious group membership, gives little to no definitive analysis of how race functions as a deciding factor in sexual assault. Researchers have yet to assert that inmates engage in behavior that in the community would be labeled racially motivated sexual assault.

Moss, Hosford, and Anderson (1979) conducted a pilot study of 24 federal inmates: 12 known rapists were compared to 12 randomly selected inmates from a federal prison population. Researchers posited that inmate age at the time of imprisonment correlated positively with lower involvement in homosexual rape. Study participants were divided into four groups: black-rapists, black-non-rapists, Chicano-rapists and Chicano-non-rapists. Statistical analyses determined variations on study variables between rapists and comparison inmates. Twelve rapists were members of a minority group (7 blacks, 5 Chicanos), 10 of 12 victims were white. All rapists selected targets of a different race.

Chonco (1989) conducted interviews with all male inmates passing through the prerelease center of a minimum-security Midwestern prison. Interviews were open ended, with the author seeking to gauge the role of race in the targeting of victims of sexual assault. Race was not mentioned by inmates as a victim-selection criterion, so the author concluded that race was not a factor in victim selection. However, this conclusion may have had as much to do with the nature of the questions asked as the actual role of race in victim targeting.

Fear of Sexual Assault

Several studies have suggested that the *fear* of rape and sexual assault shapes prison culture as much as actual incidents. Smith and Batiuk (1989) examined 66 inmates at a single institution and concluded that, even if the actual incidence rate of sexual victimization in prisons was relatively low, the pervasive fear of such victimization dictated inmate behavior and dominated a majority of inmate interactions.

> [O]ne type of performance comes to dominate all others. This performance is directly related to the fear which permeates the entire inmate population of being labeled a homosexual, or worse, being raped. . . . This pervasive fear of sexual victimization leads to a performance which emphasizes strength and masculinity and de-emphasizes characteristics which are considered weak or feminine [such as compassion, love, and the like]. (p. 32)

Jones and Schmid (1989) provide another view of how the new inmate conceptualizes prison life, and how that conception changes over time. Participant observation (one of the authors was an inmate) was used over a 10-month period at a Midwestern state maximum-security facility. Twenty inmate interviews revealed the fear of sexual assault inmates feel. Fear, they concluded, dominated new inmates' concept of prison life. Fear led to a rudimentary "isolationist" survival strategy. Inmates adjust in the first few days and weeks. Once they acquire a more realistic assessment, they release their fear of sexual assault until a rape or sexual assault occurs.

> [T]he critical incident need not and generally does not, involve the new inmate himself; the fact that he hears about the event is sufficient to destroy his feelings of relative security. . . . The effect of a reported sexual assault is so powerful to a new inmate that a temptation often exists—a few days after the event—to 'write off' the incident as an isolated occurrence, and to struggle to regain the sense of well-being that had gradually been developing. Although some inmates are successful in recapturing a feeling of security, it is again sabotaged by another dramatic event a few days or weeks later. (p. 56)

Over time, the authors contend, the inmate learns to make sense of these violent attacks. Thus, for example, he learns that a murder that occurred was payback for a bad drug deal, that a "rape" was the toll exacted for an inability to repay a debt. In essence, the authors argue that over time a new inmate comes to understand these events in their cultural context and comes to see them less and less as random and unpredictable acts of violence. He may even welcome them somewhat as "a dramatic disruption of an increasingly tedious prison routine" (p. 59).

Modern Decades: Summary of Key Findings

The past 25 years of research has contributed nuanced interpretations of prison sexual aggression.

- Sexual violence has metaphoric value functioning to filter inmates' interpretations of prison life (Smith and Batiuk, 1989).
- Inmates' estimates of sexual coercion are higher than self-reported incidents; there were no inmate-rape self-reports in Tewksbury's (1989a) study.
- Fear of sexual assault dominates new inmates' isolationist adaptation to prison life; over time inmates' adjustment becomes more realistic and their fear of sexual assault wanes until a rape or sexual assault occurs (Jones and Schmid, 1989).
- The actual incidence rate of sexual victimization appears relatively low; however, the pervasive fear of victimization dictates inmate behavior and dominates a majority of inmate interactions (Smith and Batiuk, 1989).
- Prison rape rarely occurs (Lockwood, 1994).

FINAL COMMENTS

Deprivation had its conceptual origin in the early twentieth century as a psychological theory of homosexuality (Gay, 2002, p. 66). Deprivation diffused into prison research on homosexuality in the 1930s (see notes 1 and 2). Since the 1930s, prison researchers removed inmates' conscious motivations for their choices of sexual behavior and replaced individual, conscious deliberation with unconscious forces compelled by sexual deprivation. Researchers continue to account for variation in inmates' sexual behavior with the concept of sexual deprivation. If deprivation were removed from an explanation of prison homosexuality, the absence of deprivation would leave a gaping hole in the theoretical landscape.

There are no studies in the vast literature on prison culture that acknowledge humans' sexual flexibility. In all-male and all-female prisons the absence of heterosexual partners may establish cultural conditions that allow the expression of homosexual sex, but the proximal causal factor is cultural sexual malleability.

The history of homosexuality over thousands of years demonstrates the normalcy of a hetero- to homosexual continuum. Prison variations on a sociosexual continuum range from abstinence, to homosexual sex where one or both parties are not culturally seen as homosexuals, to female surrogates ("queens") who can provide "symbolic" heterosexual sex.

NOTES

1. Fishman's concept of deprivation seems to derive from Freud's 1905 exposition of sexuality in *Three Essays on the Theory of Sexuality*. Freud made the distinction noted here. He wrote that people deprived of sexual expression will resort to (his word) "intercourse" with members of their sex. Freud wrote: "under certain external conditions—of which inaccessibility of any normal sexual object [exists] . . . they are capable of taking as their sexual object someone of their own sex and of deriving satisfaction from sexual intercourse with him" (Freud, 1905/1962, p. 3). Fishman may have misinterpreted Freud's connotation of "normal." Freud's intent was not abnormal or deviant as interpreted today. Freud's technical use of *normal* would be synonymous with "baseline," as a baseline form of sexual expression.

2. Fishman refers to homosexuality as moral degradation. Freud did too, but Freud did not judge homosexuality. Freud did not use degradation to imply moral degeneration. In the Genteel time of the day, Freud called homosexuals inverts and homosexuality inversion. Inverts, wrote Freud, "do not have a compelling need for sex. Inversion and sex do not coincide. . . . outpourings of emotion . . . are commoner among [inverts] than among heterosexual lovers" (Freud, 1962, pp. 11–12). The association of prison homosexuals with publicly displayed emotions (vs. the stoic image of the nonemotional heterosexual male) appears often in the literature. Additionally, Freud wrote: "Several facts go to show that in this legitimate sense of the word inverts cannot be regarded as degenerate: (1) Inversion is found in people who exhibit no other serious deviations from the normal" (Freud, 1962, p. 4).

3. Edward B. Tylor, 1924 [orig. 1871] *Primitive Culture*. 2 vols. 7th ed. New York: Brentano's. Tylor proposed that cultural regularities were determined by general laws of culture rather than biological determinism.

4. Eigenberg's (1992) article discusses "normal" heterosexuals who, as an effect of deprivation, engage in prison homosexuality. She described a typology ambiguity in the distinction between homosexuality and heterosexuality and how the ambiguity influenced the interpretation of prison rape. This argument raises a significant theoretical issue. It poses a (1) dichotomous classification of homo- vs. heterosexuality or (2) condition of variable states of "normal" sexuality. Variable states of homosexuality argue for a type of baseline sexuality with conditional variation induced by situational conditions; this position seems consistent with a Freudian theoretical perspective on sexuality.

5. There are no theoretical or research-based challenges to this gender-based interpretation about men's and women's sexual behavior in the history of prison sexual research. Today's research still uses women's need for comfort and emotional support as the basis for explaining women inmates' pseudofamilies.

6. Note the cultural distinction between inmates who engaged in homosexual behavior and inmate homosexuals.

7. The 1970s saw a period of reform in the philosophy of correctional management. On the assumptions Charlton noted, correctional administrators experimented with an inmate-inclusive style of prison management. Prisons permitted inmate advisory boards to meet with senior administrators to offer opinions that reflected the collective voice of the prisoner population. The movement toward "normalizing" prison society didn't persist. Inmate disorder and violence dramatically increased, which led to a tightening of prison management (see Fleisher, 1983).

8. Inmates reported that incidents of sex play, "grab ass," as they called them, get out of control and can lead someone to feel as if he'd been grabbed too hard or mocked.

9. Since the inmate sample was not representative of the general population's education level, this finding may be partially an outcome of differential prisonization.

Chapter Three

Research Design and Methodology

Our study followed the canons of social scientific research. We made explicit the smallest details of our research design and methodology. Our sampling design, interview instrument and interview data, and analytic procedures are available to other researchers. Ours was the largest randomly selected inmate sample ever used in cultural research on American prisons. In this chapter we discuss key elements of our research design and methodology.[1]

RESEARCH PROCEDURE

Research requires a number of steps. First, we read every published study on prison culture since 1940. Second, we designed a theoretically grounded interview instrument sufficient to gather cultural data. Third, we designed a sampling strategy. In our study, sampling included both selecting prisons for doing interviews and once in a prison, a sampling strategy to select inmate interviewees. Fourth, we conducted interviews and prepared interview data for analysis. Fifth, we analyzed our data using a systematic coding scheme. Codes were derived from cultural data; thus, our analysis was grounded in the interviews of inmates. Sixth, we interpreted the results of the analysis within the chosen theoretical context. We now provide a brief summary of each research step.

Development of Interview Instrument

Specific types of interview questions gather culturally specific, or ethnographic, data. There are ethnographic and nonethnographic queries. Examples of nonethnographic questions include "have you been forced to touch someone's genitals?" and if yes, "how many times have you been forced to do it?"

The responses may be "yes" and "five." These responses are affirmations and a frequency of an act. A cultural study focuses on what it "means" to be forced to touch genitals. What does it mean to be "forced"? What distinguishes a "forced" from a consensual context? How many types of forced and consensual contexts are there? How are they similar? How are they different?

In the field: asking former inmates about prison sex. Our research goal was a cultural and symbolic study of sexual violence. The only way to approach such a study, short of going to prison ourselves, was to go to the "experts." Those experts were former inmates. The research team[2] spent five days in a high-crime community in a Midwestern city where Fleisher had conducted research over many years. There, he knew dozens of adult men and women whose ages ranged from late teens to sixties. These former inmates had been to prison at least once. Some had been imprisoned six to eight times, including adolescent males and females who had been jailed in juvenile detention. Older former inmates knew Fleisher well and felt comfortable discussing with the research team the dynamics of their own sociosexual life in prison.

The topic of prison sex and prison rape didn't frighten them away. Rather, they were eager to talk about what they saw and heard in jails, juvenile institutions, and adult prisons. Unstructured interviews were conducted with one or several former inmates on the street or in front porches or living rooms.

To capture inmates' meaning of sexual aggression, former inmates were given a chance to create research questions. In this way, cultural information they thought was important would emerge. Former inmates were prompted with a set of ethnographic questions: if you were studying prison rape, what questions would you ask? What questions should we ask? What are the most important ideas to cover? How can we be sure we don't get bogus answers? Then exploratory queries shifted to more specific topics: "tell me about prison sex"; "tell me about prison rape." Old-timers gave a life-history account discussing their memories of life in penitentiaries 20 to 30 years ago vs. prison life 10 to 15 years ago vs. today.

Each day provided a series of interview topics (themes), such as bartering for sex; behavior of bootie bandits; rapists today vs. rapists decades ago; debt repayment and sex; gangs, sex, and rape; religion, sex, and rape; and institutional control of sex and sexual violence. Additionally, we took careful notes on sex-related vocabulary and anecdotes about sexual aggression and aggressors.

Interview data were organized into categories including: rape, rape and debts, rape and retaliation, rape and gangs, rape and religious groups, and prison control of sex and rape. Interview questions were constructed using this general structural framework of categories. For example, the question "what's the reputation of a rapist in the general population?" was based on comments made by middle-age former inmates who said that back in the day, bootie bandits were seen as comedians and were well-liked by the general population. Younger respondents, however, reported that bootie bandits had lost their humorous connotation and were considered rapists.

Office interviews with former inmates. After conducting field-based focus groups, we selected former inmates for preparatory interviews. Four men, each with 10 to 15 years of prison experience, volunteered for a group discussion on prison sex and prison rape. We asked them to draft questions, share opinions about whether they thought inmates who didn't know us would answer questions with a high degree of truthfulness, and used the questions to generate an unstructured interview about prison sex and prison rape.

Finally we asked each former inmate to give us a typical answer to each question; that is, what would an inmate likely say in response to the question. We wanted to know if questions would elicit prison sex vocabulary in a natural way, if responses were long or short, if responses required a few or many follow-up questions, and if categories of questions had to be asked in a particular order. For example, should management questions about prison rape appear before or after inmate-culture questions about rape? In the end, former inmates agreed that if we ask culturally sound questions inmates would be less likely to "game" us than if we sounded like university professors. In short, the more inmates thought we knew, the better their responses would be.

Testing the instrument in prison. By the time we field-tested a draft instrument we were well steeped in inmates' perceptions and vocabulary of prison culture and prison rape. In the field we found that our first draft version, which tried to include all topics the former inmates said were important, was too wordy and unwieldy, too complex, and took hours to complete a single interview. An example of a single question on version one follows below.

∞ Have you ever known an inmate who was killed behind sex? Explain.
   o Follow-up question to inmate: Are there terms for this type of killing?
   o Follow-up question to interviewer: Elicit term and mutually exclusive definitions. Identify synonyms and near synonyms. Ask inmate to give the correct use of each term.

A second draft version attempted to hone in on culturally important variables, such as inmates' attitudes toward rape inside and outside prison. Inmates said this version was redundant, and asked for the same information in too many ways. An example follows below.

∞ What do inmates think of a free man/woman who rapes a free man/woman outside?

∞ What do inmates think of a man/woman inmate who rapes a [man/woman inmate] inside?

∞ What do dudes think of a man/woman who rapes a [man/woman] inside?

∞ Are there terms for free men/women who rape free men/women outside?
  o Follow-up question to inmate: Are there terms for this type of rape?
  o Follow-up question to interviewer: Elicit term and mutually exclusive definitions. Identify synonyms and near synonyms. Ask inmate to give the correct use of each term.

The third version narrowed the questioning by shortening questions to make them less complex and tiresome. We also decided to move vocabulary to a separate section. This grouped similar questions together in one location to maintain a single train of thought. Additionally, answers to some vocabulary questions stimulated thinking about other vocabulary, making it easier to elicit natural responses. In the end, however, the most effective way to elicit vocabulary was found in long responses wherein inmates used vocabulary in a natural way.

Questions from the second and third drafts were field-tested at a men's and a women's prison. At first, some questions were ambiguous to some inmates in the sense that they weren't sure how to respond, or didn't understand what the question was asking. Some questions were too terse and needed additional explanation, or too wordy and caused a loss of inmate concentration. Standard English vocabulary was sometimes too complex. Some questions exceeded inmates' education level, impeding their ability to give answers. In such a case, "I'm not sure how to say it," or something similar was their response.

We field-tested our interview instrument. Interestingly, we found that the term *rape* seemed somewhat baffling to inmates. We thought that perhaps the term *rape* did not mesh well with inmates' worldview, or the way they think and categorize knowledge. Nevertheless, inmates answered our questions about rape, but their answers didn't flow naturally, giving us the impression that they were searching for any answer that made some sense.

Skipping to the outcome of our dilemma in cultural semantics, we learned through open-ended questions that the word *rape* "made cultural sense" if it was inserted within the social context of domestic violence. Men and women inmates associate rape with broken love affairs (see Fleisher and Krienert [2006] for the final interview instrument).

Sampling Strategy

Correctional institution site selection. Clemmer's (1940) theory of culture, re-
lying on differential experiences in a prison, led to the selection of high-security
prisons instead of lower-security institutions.[3] High-security inmates were
chosen based on the following assumptions: (1) high- vs. low-security inmates would have longer criminal histories; (2) they would have more involvement in violence; (3) they would have a greater likelihood of physical,
emotional, or sexual victimization at some time in their lives; (4) they would
have a greater likelihood of drug use outside and/or inside prison; (5) they
would be more likely to have served multiple terms at different prisons; (6)
they would have more years of imprisonment; and (7) the likelihood was
greater that they witnessed or engaged in sexual assault, sexual coercion,
and/or prison rape.

The only prison-selection variable was high security. Once satisfied, we
then visited institutions made available by directors of correctional agencies.
Research confidentiality requirements prevent us from disclosing the identity
of correctional institutions.

Prison-site selection was consistent with a research assumption predicated
on Clemmer's (1940) theory of culture. To refresh, his theory of culture assumes that prison culture has universal dimensions. Prison culture, all things
being equal, would show greater cultural homogeneity than heterogeneity. In
other words, prison culture in institutions anywhere would be more alike than
different. Cultural variance would come from prison culture history, inmates'
street experiences, and their community socialization.

A sample of 400 male and 200 female inmates was set for the project's
interview objective. Also agreed upon was the number of prisons where interviews would occur. Thirty correctional institutions—23 male and 7 female, in 10 states, was the target. With National Institute of Justice approval, the sample focused on regionally based geographic representation.
This focus resulted in the division of the country into four regions with vis-
its to several states within each geographic region of the United States.

The 23 men's institutions were the highest-security-level men's prison
available in each state. When women's institutions were multi-security level
and housed minimum-, medium-, and high-security women inmates, we selected inmates from the highest-security-level housing units within the institution. Therefore, all 30 institutions contained high-security-level, general-
population inmates.

Inmate sampling. The research goal was an objective analysis of inmates'
subjective perspectives on sexuality and sexual violence. Given our goal,
sampling did not require targeting interviews with alleged rapists and rape

victims. Rather, this study sought to gather a broad cross-section of general cultural knowledge.

Sample procedures were based on classical population probability sampling. We used a systematic sample, selecting a random start and a fixed selection-interval number thereafter. At each institution we had a single contact person. Each contact person provided us with an inmate general-population roster.[4] The number of general-population inmates on an institution's sample roster was divided by the number of subjects required for the projected number of interviews conducted in a week. Forty male inmates and 30 female inmates were the minimum number of weekly interviews. The general-population count was divided by 40 or 30 to create an interval number. A staff member was asked to pick a number from one to the interval number. This number was applied to the roster to find the first interviewee. To select the second inmate, the interval number was added to the number of the first inmate selected. This pattern continued until the minimum number of inmates was selected.[5] Then, 15 to 20 inmates per institution were added to the interview roster using the same procedure. Additional inmates were needed to cover refusals, transfers, hospitalizations, and other unexpected circumstances.

A precise, replicable sampling design was critically important in two ways. First, our sampling procedure was easily replicated in each of the 30 prisons, and could be replicated by future researchers. Second, a random sampling design assured a prison executive staff that we were not "stacking the deck," as some institution staffers referred to it, by preselecting a cohort of inmates who, in some way, carried a grudge against prison staff. Institution personnel were told that sampled inmates would be asked exactly the same questions; that personal information about anyone—inmate or staffer—cited in an interview would not be collected; and that specific incidents of and participants in alleged prison rape or other types of sexual assault would not be discussed with staffers or sought for interviews. Once inmates gave us their written consent to interview, they were explicitly warned to withhold information about previous and future institution rule violations and warned that prior or future incidents of violence of any type mentioned in the interview would be reported to the warden's office.

Interviews[6]

Doing interviews in a penitentiary may seem like a risky venture; however, no prison researcher, to our knowledge, has been hurt by an inmate interviewee. Similarly, after an interview, despite movie and television writers' exaggerated imaginations, inmates are not assaulted, maimed, or killed for talking to

"The Man." Fact is, men and women inmates thoroughly enjoy talking to outsiders, if the outsiders know how to talk to them.

The worst thing an interviewer can do is look terrified when an inmate—a killer, a bank robber, a gang leader, a street rapist, a child molester, a multiple murderer, serial killer, or drug dealer, walks through the interview room door. Unless you're interviewing in a super-maximum-security penitentiary, inmates walk in on their own accord. In a super-max inmates are chained, hand and foot. Those chains make these inmates look even more frightening. Although general society may believe inmates without chains will jump over the interview desk and assault, kill, or rape the researcher, in reality, inmates prefer a few hours of conversation with a woman interviewer, or a man interviewer who jokes and tells tales.

Successful inmate interviews must be done in a natural style, in the same way you'd talk to your friends in a neighborhood coffee shop or tavern. Interviewers must be loose, friendly, and attentive. Good interviewers will laugh (when appropriate), and smile when an inmate tries to shock them with deliberately obscene talk. Additionally, if you are a woman interviewer you should always expect that a male inmate may try to masturbate while looking at you, or even expose himself to you during an interview. If you can't handle those things with ease and calm, don't interview penitentiary inmates.

Even with a structured interview in hand, inmate interviews are difficult. Inmates love to talk, and they can talk for hours nonstop. It's your job to guide an interview where you want it to go, which means you cannot be timid. You can actually tell an inmate to "*STOP*, let's get back to what we're doing."

Here is an intellectual piece of advice. If you know everything you need to know about theory and methodology, but nothing about criminal justice and prison, stay away from prison research with inmates. If you cannot talk fluently about prison operations and programs, prison security, prison-staff management hierarchy, the criminal justice system, court proceedings, unfair sentencing, police procedure, inmate talk (see the appendix), inmate sociopolitical and economic dynamics, inmate life history, and the effects of affective disorders on patterns of perception and speech, find a different research location. Otherwise, although you'll take copious notes, you won't be able to construct on-site follow-up questions that make cultural sense to inmates. Even a brilliant statistical analysis will be absent of cultural validity if the researcher can't transfer that analysis into a narrative about prison life.

We want to give you some idea of what it's really like to conduct prison interviews with violent men. Carefully read the tales of Max. In prison jargon, Max had no "discernible mental illness."

Max

From the moment we were buzzed in through the gate, this super-max prison had the appearance of the set of a futuristic science fiction movie. Armed officers were in plain view, doors were equipped with iris scan technology, and attention to security was clearly of utmost concern. We passed through three separate sets of locked doors before reaching our final interview destination. Upon arrival we were led into a large, sterile room that contained a mesh holding cell, a strip cell, a centralized officer control unit, and a small glass cubicle isolated in the center. We were asked to wait on a mesh bench, where our graduate assistant nervously mentioned that her dog run at home was bigger than the cage they were currently using to hold an inmate.

Our respondent was brought to the area in handcuffs and shackles, escorted by two correctional officers. He was then stripped, issued new clothing, and resecured to walk the 20 feet into a glass chamber located inside the glass cubicle in the center of the room. Once in the chamber he was cuffed behind his back to a solitary stool. Our research team was then escorted into the glass cubicle, where we struggled to get close enough to the intercom to talk to our subject. Our first obstacle became obtaining informed consent, as inmates in this facility were not normally allowed to use pens or be passed anything from the outside.

When we were able to begin, we introduced ourselves and spent the next three hours talking to our subject, Max,[7] about the subtleties of prison sexuality. We took turns asking questions and were rewarded with a very forthcoming, to-the-point discussion about sex behind bars.

> People come to reception you have nothing and it's quite a while until you can get anything, no boxes, no mail, no money cause it takes a while to follow you from where you were, old time bootie bandits would lend things to guys to a point where they can't pay it back and would then collect in other ways. Or straight out beat someone down and physically traumatize them until they consent, that's less now, staff seem to be more aware of it, or if not aware more concerned. The word *rape* I've never heard, it's always *bootie bandits* or *taking his ass*.

Max held a master's degree and was a very eloquent, articulate subject. We soon forgot our location and were able to drift in and out of the interview with the cadence of old friends. Max shed light on the intricacies of sexuality inside prison culture.

> You have drug culture, sex culture, violent culture, and gang culture, some play games in all fields, the different sects stick together because that's the thing that they're into, sometimes they are even arranged in housing units

that way. One corner for drug users, one corner for gangs, one corner for crazy sex offenders, birds of a feather flock together. Cliques form on the basis of common interest. Consensual sex is very common. I've seen four guys in a cell one time, looked like a Roman orgy. I've seen an officer come out [of a cell] with a store-bought dildo in a shakedown.

We asked about inmates who have sex with men in prison but did not have sex with men in the outside world, and he provided a different take on the seemingly fluid dynamic of prison sexuality.

I can't imagine that, that's like an alcoholic working in a brewery. If they have sex in here they had sex out there. You don't wake up some morning out of the blue and say gee I'll suck a dick today, it doesn't happen, it's a continuing activity even if you were hiding it.

Nearly an hour into the interview we asked Max a question about the likelihood of retaliation if a rape were to occur inside. He sat back, crossed his legs, and replied in an even conversational tone:

The only type of rapes gangs would be ordering would be for retaliatory purposes, it's not a sexual act, it's same reason on the outside, you'd cut a guy's dog up and put it on the porch, or put a fish in their mailbox.

Max was mentally healthy, more or less, even though he was nonplussed by the idea of cutting up a dog and throwing its pieces on someone's porch. Before we move on to methods of analyzing such interviews, we want to introduce you to Joe. Unlike Max, Joe's mind was a home to serious mental illness, which had a direct effect on what he told us.

Joe

Mental illness runs rampant through American prisons. At midyear 2005, more than half of all prison and jail inmates had a mental health problem, including 705,600 inmates in state prisons, 78,800 in federal prisons, and 479,900 in local jails. These estimates represented 56 percent of state prisoners, 45 percent of federal prisoners, and 64 percent of jail inmates (James & Glaze, 2006).

One respondent truly exemplified the myriad of problems surrounding a mentally ill yet fully functional general-population inmate. Joe was very cheerful when he was escorted into the case manager's office for an interview. After he introduced himself and shook my hand, it took him several minutes to decide where to sit. While conducting a very fast-paced

(Continued)

conversation he vacillated between the two available chair choices at least five times before finally choosing a resting place. Joe was more than happy to participate in an interview. Demographic questions were easily answered without incident. As shown in the following interview excerpts, when he encountered a question that required thought, however, his answers became a hyperspeed journey through the mind of an unmedicated bipolar inmate.

> Researcher: Have you ever voluntarily requested mental health treatment in prison?
>
> Joe: I'm bipolar, but I don't take medication. I'm the reason Coke came up with new flavors, I wrote them and told them to make eggnog Coke in Christmas tree bottles and have it in an igloo thing, you know the coolers where you press the button where the soda comes out. It would have a star that lights up on the top and turns and stuff. They never wrote me back, but eight months later they came out with the commercial for Vanilla Coke, that was just showing me that they got my letter, they did it. They didn't do eggnog flavored though, that made me upset.
>
> Researcher: What are the reasons inmates get raped?
>
> Joe: I've written all the NFL teams you know, I can make them win. I have a guarantee for them that they'll win two back-to-back Super Bowls. I left them all 1-hour voice mails that really told them how to do that. The New England Patriots, they used my plan and they won, I'm not sure why they didn't win back to back, but they did come back and win. I don't know why they didn't contact me or thank me for it, that makes me mad, but I told them how to do it. I told them if it didn't work I'd be willing to come out there and blow my brains out on the field right in front of them. Maybe I'll try contacting the Cowboys, I could make them win, I haven't decided, maybe this year.

Although Joe was very forthcoming and upbeat throughout the interview, his responses hinted at an underlying inner turbulence. The following examples were seamlessly woven into his narrative responses:

> If I could, if I had a nuclear warhead I'd drop it on this unit. . . . I want to tell my mom I'm sorry I'll never see you again but I went on a rampage and told the news reporter why I did it and that's it.
>
> I tell her [female officer] you know that I get out soon, I better never see you in [CITY NAME] if I see you there I'll put a double barrel and blow your fucking head off, and she's like yeah whatever.

Joe's problems did not begin during his incarceration. Common to so many inmates, Joe highlights the systemic problem within general society. Prison becomes a last resort when all other resources have failed, and for some it becomes the only place they can truly coexist without a problem. Joe describes his childhood:

Lonely, didn't have too many friends, I thought about running away when I was 6 or 7, was really lonely. I stay with my mom every now or then, when I was in [STATE NAME] I was a beach bum, they got homeless shelters and stuff. I tried to be a walk-on with [NAME OF UNIVERSITY] for their football team you know, but they said I had to be enrolled, that don't make sense.

When it became clear that Joe would be unable to provide coherent answers to the interview questions, I attempted to thank him for his time and end the interview. Joe, however, could not be dissuaded; his response was that in the informed consent we said the average interview lasted 60 minutes, and by his count we still had 34 more minutes to go. Joe continued to engage in nonstop disjointed conversation until his 60 minutes had ended. On the outside, Joe represents an average citizen; he looks no different than anyone else. He was in good physical shape and had no physical signs of an illness. His condition was tolerated and even humored by officers and fellow inmates alike; it is unlikely that upon release he will face a similarly tolerant crowd.

We conducted 564 interviews, ranging in length from 90 minutes to 6 or 7 hours, depending on inmate knowledge. Interview length resulted in tens of hundreds of hours of interviews, providing thousands of pages of narrative text. Interviewing was the best part of our research; the fun part; next we had to "make sense" of what inmates like Joe and Max told us.

We did not use a recording device during our interviews; if we had, we'd probably still be transcribing interviews to this day. Instead, we used laptop computers to type inmate response word for word. Even if, hypothetically, our Institution Review Board,[8] inmate interviewees, senior prison officials, and other government stakeholders close to our work, would have granted us permission to usc a digital recorder, we would have chosen not to use one.

First, the police use recorders. Inmates are skeptical enough without making ourselves look like crime investigators. Second, we learned after years of interviewing inmates that recorders make you lazy. You believe that since the recorder captured the conversation, your interview is done; that belief would be a massive error in data collection. Third, the best interviews engage inmates, which is difficult to accomplish while taping.

Interviewers must convey with body language, facial gestures, smiles, puzzled looks, excitement, and laser-like stares into an inmate's eyes that he is the only person on the planet you care about at that moment. Body language must be relaxed, as if you are watching football after Thanksgiving dinner. Finally, and vitally important, you must learn to type quickly and accurately, think quickly enough to ask intelligent follow-up questions and follow-up questions to those, all the while maintaining your laser-like stare into the inmate's eyes and following our instructions above.

At the end of each day we removed all interview data from the institution. A day's interview data were never brought back into an institution. We cleaned interviews in the privacy of our local residence. We corrected spelling and reread responses to ensure we understood precisely what inmates told us. All responses in an interview made up a narrative text. When we finished interviewing 564 inmates we had thousands of pages of narrative text. Now our job was to analyze the narrative.

Techniques of Thematic Analysis: Codes and Coding

Information that repeats across dozens or hundreds of interviews points to cultural information we call themes. A theme refers to a redundant pattern. The inductive process of thematic analysis finds cultural themes and then links them into cultural systems of thought. Themes possess the experience of inmates whether such experience refers to actual behavior or the act of listening to someone else talk (Ryan & Bernard, 2003, p. 87).

Codes and coding. Codes are shorthand versions of significant content in interview narratives. Applying a set of codes to interview narratives for the purpose of identifying code frequency, code-use patterns, code co-occurrences, and tracking ideas, attitudes, social processes, and interviewees' interpretations has been called *text analysis*. Text analysis "discovers" and then applies codes. Codes provide word labels for acts, events, processes, and their combinations, enabling researchers to identify and track acts, such as "Coco ripped off T-Man's shoes"; social processes, such as debt: "T-Bone owed Jimmy John $200 and got beat up behind it"; attitudes, such as "rapists are psychos"; beliefs, such as "rapists are weak"; and, interpretations, such as "Tim didn't get raped, he likes hard sex."

Themes and Subthemes

Below you'll see two sections of our thematic code book (figure 3.1). A thematic code book is a summary of the semantic logic of cultural themes. Semantic logic includes cultural content and cultural logic. Cultural content is "what we think." Cultural logic is "how we think." Content and logic together represent a culture's unique worldview.

In the thematic code book, themes are marked (a.) and (b.). Subthemes are marked with (i. ii. iii.). Themes and subthemes represent cultural content derived from inmate interview data; we didn't create these themes beforehand and apply them to the data. Themes are defined by their subthemes. The placement of particular subthemes under their culturally appropriate themes represents the structural arrangement of cultural knowledge in prison inmate culture. The meaning conveyed by the hierarchical unit (theme + subthemes) represents semantic logic embedded in prison inmate culture. The single-most significant goal in a cultural analysis is accurately representing the logic of cultural thought unique to a society. An illustration helps to understand this abstract idea.

Clemmer (1940) postulated that inmates experience prison life differently depending on their living conditions, social interactions, work environment, and so on. The knowledge that cohorts of inmates acquire in different contexts makes cohorts somewhat different from one another. By virtue of living in prison all cohorts share a body of knowledge about prison life. Shared knowledge creates cohesion among a population of inmates. Cohesion means inmates know how to live together. What makes inmate culture different from free community culture is how inmates and how free citizens think about what they know.

In figure 3.1, themes are marked as [a. Inmate Relations] and [b. Inmate Social Roles]. These two themes occupy the same "level" in the hierarchy of codes. Occupying the same level means that [a. Inmate Relations] and

a. Inmate Relationships
   i. Individual relationships (generic code for dyads, sexual relationships, including marriage and wedding ceremonies) *T_Inmate_Relations*
   ii. Stables/Slavery (any discussion of sexual slavery, pimping, stables, etc) *T_Inmate_Stable*
   iii. Being on the down low, undercover, or hiding their sexual relationship *T_Inmate_DL*
b. Inmate Social Roles (use relevant anytime these roles are discussed, or if someone defines or possesses that trait)
   i. Predators: Any *T_Inmate_SR_Predator*
   ii. Victims: *T_Inmate_SR_Victim*
   iii. Queens *T_Inmate_SR_Queen*
   iv. Punks/Boys/Kids/Fags (passive male sex role) *T_Inmate_SR_Punk*
   v. Man/Daddy (dominant male sexual role) *T_Inmate_SR_Man*
   vi. Stud (dominant female sex role) *T_Inmate_SR_Stud*
   vii. Femme (passive female sex role) *T_Inmate_SR_Femme*
   viii. Weak *T_Inmate_SR_Weak*
   ix. Strong *T_Inmate_SR_Strong*
   x. New (new to prison, or young): *T_Inmate_SR_New*
   xi. Old (oldtimer, lifer): *T_Inmate_SR_New*
   xii. Child Molester: *T_Inmate_SR_Molester*
   xiii. Homosexual: *T_Inmate_SR_Homosexual*

Figure 3.1.   Thematic Codebook

[b. Inmate Social Roles] are mutually exclusive themes, which are composed of mutually exclusive subthemes. Sublevels are listed below themes.

Application of Themes and Subthemes

Our interview data were entered into Atlas/ti, 1997, which facilitates the application of thematic codes to narrative text. In our case Atlas/ti held our data set of 564 complete interviews and our scheme of themes and subthemes. Each subtheme was assigned a specific code, which contrasted with definitions of all other codes as shown in figure 3.1. As we read each interview we selected appropriate subthemes to apply to portions of the narrative, which met the subthemes' definition. Since words in combination carry more than one meaning, more than one subtheme can be applied to the same portion of narrative. Portions of narrative, or terms, that are marked by multiple subthemes are semantically complex ideas. We'll illustrate the nature of semantic complexity using two common prison terms.

Prison inmate culture has an entire lexicon devoted to inmate sexual culture. The appendix to this book is a comprehensive dictionary of terms and expressions inmates used in our interviews. The lexicon includes vocabulary and expressions that label inmates and social processes in a prison's sex scene. Punk, queen, killer (an inmate who masturbates in public), and hundreds of other sex-related terms are linguistic entry points into culture. Specialized terms have two meanings. Denotative meaning points to actions and people; connotative meanings are the concepts and ideas formed when there's a link among themes and groups of themes. The following is an illustration of complex connotations.

The prison expression "he's a punk" carries an overabundance of cultural information. Experienced speakers of inmate talk can use *punk* appropriately and can explain, if we ask the right questions, the meanings of the term *punk* and expression *he's a punk*. Speakers of prison talk and skilled listeners can fill in the cultural and semantic blanks if they are culturally skilled in prison speech genre. In other words, the term *punk* has a learned cultural meaning. *Punk* denotes specific types of inmates. *Punk* connotes abstract traits of those inmates.

The term *punk* frequently occurs with the term *weak*. A punk is a weak person, but connotations of being weak, or showing weakness, are culturally complex and have significant behavioral implications for inmates. An inmate who can bench press 300 pounds is physically strong but may show weakness if he can't control his urge to engage in same-sex relations.

Consider the term *prison rape*. Rape denotes actions of one person toward another, but the connotations of prison rape are a spoken shorthand for complex patterns of cultural ideas and concepts (themes and subthemes). When inmates (and we) hear the term *prison rape* its denotations may be (at least hypothetically) similar, but the term's connotations differ. Different connotations have multiple cultural meanings. In a cultural analysis, denotations that represent different acts are assigned themes. Subthemes and combinations of subthemes form cultural interpretations.

Prison rape is culturally unique, because it's based on learned themes and patterns of themes, which symbolically represent acts and their meaning that are off-limits to community folks. However, inmates and community folks share an important source of information about prison life and prison rape. That source is prison rape myth. Given the cultural difference between the free community and prison, we'd expect free community culture to interpret prison rape myth in a manner quite different from prison inmates. Next we'll illustrate abstract meanings conveyed in a sentence that conveys multiple meanings and how those meanings are coded.

The sentence below is an example of a single code: [T_Sex_Theory_Time]. The elements in the code are theme [T]; inmate theory of sexual behavior [Sex_Theory]; and, sexual behavior changes over time [Time]. This code refers to inmates' "theories on how doing time influences inmate sexual behavior."

> There really is no straight person, just someone who has never been touched yet, especially here, they might start off that way, but if they got 90 years it's just a matter of time, so they're just not touched yet.

That narrative represents a segment of inmate culture's theory of homosexuality. The theory is that a straight inmate who serves a lengthy sentence will eventually engage in homosexual sex as the effect of a long sentence, such as Life + 120 years.

Text coding requires an intensive familiarity with thematic codes and their distinctive features. Coding text requires the ability to spot narratives that correspond to thematic codes and to spot narratives that express important concepts for which there are no thematic codes.

The analysis of the interview narrative text was designed within the study's theoretical framework. Speech carries "pieces" of knowledge. Pieces of knowledge aggregate to form comprehensive categories of cultural information. Our analysis was targeted to identify pieces of knowledge (themes) embedded within cultural information.

Barring mental illness or organic damage, inmates should say similar things about similar topics. This would be analogous to free citizens on the East and West Coast, people who've never spoken to one another, sharing, for instance, knowledge of breakfast food or kinship terms.

Clemmer's theory of culture and language predicts that by virtue of prisonization, inmates on the whole will share a specialized body of knowledge.

Although inmates in different housing units or jobs will acquire different in-formation, we expected that prison culture, as expressed in the aggregate data of 564 interviews in 30 correctional institutions, would be more similar than different.

Significance of Cultural Knowledge

A snippet of knowledge includes such statements as *rapists are cowards, rape occurs infrequently*, and *debts may lead to forced and consensual sex*. Simi-lar snippets of knowledge might recur in 20 or 50 or 100 interviews. Although frequency of occurrence may indicate degree of shared knowledge, it does not necessarily impute cultural significance. That a majority of inmates know the recreation yard opens at eight in the morning and closes at dusk doesn't mean recreation yard information carries cultural significance. Knowing recreation yard hours is instrumental information, and is likely less significant than knowledge about "personal ways to prevent sexual assault."

How then does a cultural analysis assess significance of information with-out using statistical measures of significance? Cultural significance is attrib-uted to concepts, acts, attitudes, or perceptions of prison quality of life, which have a central role in inmates' prison life. Prison knowledge with the highest level of cultural significance generates rules of social behavior assessed as critical to prison survival by inmates themselves. Such knowledge would very likely be shared by a high percentage of inmates, creating a shared con-sensus of knowledge.[9] We identify significant cultural knowledge by deter-mining how inmates' knowledge about a topic (rape prevention strategies) in-fluences their behavior within a broader scheme of inmate social life.

Clemmer's theory of culture does not provide a mechanism to determine the significance or value of cultural information. In the context of Clem-mer's theory, inmates may know relatively little information about prison rape by virtue of where they are housed (a cell or dorm), their place of em-ployment (kitchen or grounds crew), or the criminal behavior of friends of their friends (gang members or inmate religious leaders). On the other hand, inmates' strong opinions, beliefs, and attitudes about prison rape are cultur-ally significant but have no necessary relationship to inmates' firsthand per-sonal experiences with rape. Inmates don't need to be sexually victimized before they learn the dangerousness of sexual violence on the social fabric of inmate life.

Our book's focus is the culture of homosexual sex, sexual violence, and in-mate social life in men's and women's prisons. Our cultural interpretation for homosexuality, sexual violence, and homosexual sex was based on inmates' explanations of the causes, conditions, and consequences of those behaviors.

To accomplish a cultural study of sexual violence we contextualized homosexuality and sexual violence within the context of prison life, and explained and interpreted homosexuality and sexual violence as inmates do. We also needed inmates' voice. Voice means word choice, semantic content, topic emphasis, attitude conveyed, mispronunciation, misuse of terms, use of prison terms, and so on. Our inmate transcriptions are, within limits imposed by simultaneously typing, thinking, and talking, true to inmates' voice.

The precision of our research design and methodology will allow prison researchers to replicate our data collection methods and arrive at a coding scheme similar to ours. A coding scheme is the first step in assessing cultural validity. Cultural validity means that we can explain homosexual sex and sexual violence within the cultural constructs of prison inmate culture. A culturally valid account for homosexual sex and sexual violence must be able to explain and interpret those behaviors by applying only information obtained from and firmly grounded in inmates' interview data.

NOTES

1. Fleisher and Krienert's (2006) final report to the National Institute of Justice includes a comprehensive discussion of research design and methodology.

2. The project's program officer accompanied the research team and sat in on unstructured interviews and on semistructured interviews, done at the end of the week, to test possible questions asked of men and women former inmates.

3. Various names were substituted for the term *high-security*. Some institutions had multiple custody levels within a high-security prison, where, for instance, high-custody and lesser-custody inmates made up a single general population. In this case, we sampled across custody levels. In other places, high- and lower-custody-level inmates were divided physically into distinctly separate general populations. In this case, we sampled only in higher-custody institutions. Often, however, medium-custody inmates had once been high-custody inmates and had their custody level reduced over time. We based our sampling design on a single method; sampling high-security or high-custody general populations. Efforts always confined sampled inmates to medium- or higher-security level.

4. Special inmate populations including inmates in administrative detention; disciplinary segregation; hospitalized inmates; inmates in residential substance abuse units; inmates in mental health residential units; protective custody; nonsentenced inmates; inmates in transit units; and INS detainees or deportees were not included.

5. If an institution has 1,000 research-eligible inmates provided on a general-population roster, researchers divided 1,000 by 40, to get the interval number 25. If in the range of 1 to 25, a staff member selected the number 5, the fifth inmate on the roster would be the first inmate subject. The second subject would be the thirtieth inmate (5 + 25), followed by the fifty-fifth, eightieth, and so on.

6. Inmate interviewees chose or denied to be interviewed. Interviewers read an informed consent statement, which specified the goals and purpose, risks and benefits, and research procedures to each potential interviewee. Potential interviewees were expressly told that their participation was voluntary and that they could choose not to participate without sanction. Inmates' intensive familiarity with the criminal justice system enabled them to make a decision that was best for them.

7. All names have been changed to protect the confidentiality of the respondents.

8. Case Western Reserve University's Institution Review Board's research restrictions and the sensitivity of the topic precluded tape recording. Anticipating the potential use of tape recordings in lawsuits filed by an interviewed inmate against an institution or agency, coupled with the fear that inmates' voices could be identified in court, even if regions, states, and institutions were anonymous, entered into this decision.

9. We can determine level of consensus with a consensus analysis. Our research did not propose a consensus analysis; however, we could nevertheless derive a research design from the results of this research.

Chapter Four

Learning the Rules of Prison Culture

"You have to realize the mentality of the inmates you're dealing with; it's one that is so unrealistic. They have their own logic and reality." [an inmate]

Prison culture has transmitted similar interpretations of sociosexual life over generations of inmates. Those same interpretations have been documented by prison researchers since the 1930s. Prison research literature reports consistency in an interpretation of sociosexual roles, perceptions of "weakness" vs. "strength," perceptions of vulnerability to physical and sexual victimization, strategies to protect oneself from victimization, and so on, in different prisons in different states across the country. The consistency in interpretation argues for a national culture, which socializes inmates to a similar body of prison knowledge no matter the prison's location. The consistency of prison knowledge traverses the boundary of male *and* female prisons.

VERBAL SOCIALIZATION INTO PRISON CULTURE

Clemmer's *The Prison Community* (1940) made a major conceptual contribution to prison research by identifying culture as a topic of formal study. Clemmer conceptualized prison culture as an amalgam of influences with at least three components. First, prison culture includes the characteristics, norms, values, and knowledge brought into the prison from their previous lives by a diverse group of inmates. Second, prison culture takes on the characteristics of the prison as an isolated and segregated society. Third, prison culture includes the architecture, policies, and practices of the prison itself.

Culture is a cognitive system of ideological and social constructs ("rules"). Rules guide behavior and ideology interprets it. Culture's rules, ideology, values, attitudes, and beliefs can be "heard" in verbal expression. Prison culture is transmitted verbally. Inmates don't learn to behave in prison or "think like inmates" by reading inmate handbooks. A high percentage of inmates are illiterate. Hensley, Tewksbury, and Wright (2001) estimate inmate illiteracy at 60 to 70 percent; thus verbal communication is critical to sustain prison culture. Knowledge of prison culture comes to inmates through conversations, gossip, rumors, and exposure to the general verbal barrage of social life.

Culture passes among individuals and between generations. That culture transcends individuals is captured by the expression *supraindividual* culture. The transcendent nature of prison culture becomes apparent in the comparison of prison research findings over the past seven decades. Clemmer's (1940) findings about male inmate sexual life in Illinois are fundamentally similar to Sykes's (1958) research in New Jersey and to Lockwood's (1980) research in New York state.

Clemmer's supraindividual theory of prison culture has implications for the nature of prison culture on a national (or perhaps international) scale. Prison culture isn't unique to a single prison, a group of prisons in a state, or a collectivity of prisons over a geographic area. We argue that prison rape mythology in its various expressions in rape tales are inherent in the culture of prison and shared by inmates nationally.

Of course, prison architecture, policies, and practices, have changed over the past fifty years. However, the characteristics, values, beliefs, and attitudes inmates expressed in early research on inmate homosexuality and sexual violence are shared with inmates today. Over the decades, prison researchers reported that sexual violence was not a regular quality of prison culture and society. If sexual violence occurs, it represents an exception to the behavioral regularities specified by prison culture. Past research showed that rape was a rare event (Lockwood, 1994), sexual violence incidents were relatively low in frequency (Smith and Batiuk, 1989), and more generally, homosexuality was not an epidemic and did not have devastating cultural consequences (Johnson, 1971).

The Prison Community exposed the structures and functions of prison culture. It also described the process by which inmates become socialized to prison culture, a process Clemmer dubbed *prisonization*. Inmates were automatically exposed to the forces of prisonization and had no choice in whether they would be affected. Once inside prison, prisonization affected all inmates and socialized them into prison culture.

Prisonization and community socialization operate in similar ways. Americans everywhere share cultural characteristics that make them similar to one another in many ways but different in others. Americans aren't identical; the privileged share a vision of the world different from the poor; some Americans think like Democrats, some think like Republicans; native New Yorkers are more similar to one another than to native Iowans. The differential exposure to more- and less-extreme experiences of prison life creates inmates who acquire attitudes, beliefs, and knowledge, which reflect the extremes of their experience. For example, if by sheer luck an inmate received a prime work assignment, allowing him to remain relatively isolated from others and including assignment to a passive cell mate, the prisonization effect of sharing a cell with a nonviolent, nonpredatory, or non-drug-involved cell mate would be positive. Both inmates would acquire a less-extreme vision of prison life than inmates whose cell and job assignments forced them into closer contact with hard-core inmates.

Prisonization draws prison cultural information from verbal messages about sexual behavior and sexual violence. Cultural information conveys simple but critical lessons about prison sex and social life. Learn how to behave, but learn quickly. Don't get too comfortable with people; they could be deceptive and cunning and want to exploit you. Avoid debt and theft; they won't be tolerated. Protect yourself physically and mentally. Stay strong. Handle your own battles. Be confident and decisive. Finally, sexual temptation increases with time; if you try it, you might enjoy it.

Verbal Exposure to Sexual Victimization

Clemmer's theory posits that inmates are influenced by what they hear in different contexts of prison life. Exposure to multiple types of personal experiences in prison would give inmates similar experiences on some issues but different experiences on others. Interview data would show variance on what, and how much, inmates know. They would also have different exposure to, and interpretations of, verbal messages. As a speech community, prisons are widely diverse in speech topics and ways of speaking. What's more, information brought into prison about sexual violence may influence inmates' initial perceptions of the dangerousness of prison life. Even before inmates enter prison they may possess knowledge, beliefs, and attitudes about prison sex and sexual violence. These may be opposite from or an exaggerated form of prison reality (Lockwood, 1980).

Past prison research suggested four data-collection dimensions. First, inmates' direct exposure to prison sexual violence as a perpetrator, victim, or on-the-scene observer gives inmates firsthand (direct) knowledge of sexual violence; firsthand knowledge should be distinguished from (indirect) knowledge conveyed in gossip and rumors. Second, inmates' perceptions of their environment are influenced by information they acquire via direct verbal messages. Third, if prison sexual violence were a serious problem it would threaten inmates' personal safety or at the very least cause them to worry. Fourth, messages of sexual violence conveyed in gossip and rumors are likely inflated, exaggerated, and twisted verbal accounts, which transforms the accounts into tales analogous to urban myths. Such exposure may influence how inmates perceive the prison environment and their perception of safety.

To measure these dimensions, we asked four basic questions: 1) Do you know for sure of a rape in this institution or any other prison you've been in? (2) If you haven't seen a rape firsthand, have you heard about an inmate being raped? (3) Are people worried about rape? Is it a big threat? (4) Is there rape folklore, like stories about notorious rapists of long ago?

The responses to these questions are cultural themes that appear regularly in interview data and are corroborated by previous modern and historical research. First, the percentage of inmates who report a "for-sure" knowledge of rape falls below inmates' reports of hearing about prison rape (Tewksbury, 1989b). Second, relatively high levels of hearing about rape do not necessarily influence inmates' perceptions of prison safety. Third, verbal messages of prison rape are not reinforced by visual experiences witnessing egregious prison rape. Fourth, despite verbal exposure to prison rape incidents and rapists, inmates express little fear of or worry about prison rape. Fifth, inmates recognize exaggerated tales of prison rape and rapists, distinguishing them from more realistic verbal messages; the exaggerated tales have no direct influence on inmates' perceptions of prison safety.

EMPIRICAL MEASURES OF PRISON RAPE MYTHOLOGY

We asked inmates four questions about prison sexual violence: did they worry about or fear being raped? did they know for sure of a prison rape? had they heard rape stories? had they heard about a rape? Figure 4.1 illustrates the relationship between male inmates' exposure to three types of rape knowledge and their level of worry about, or fear of, rape. Among men who have served less than five years, 55 percent heard rape stories, 37 percent heard of a rape, 10 percent knew of a "for-sure" rape, and 19 percent expressed some worry about or fear of rape.

> I'm not aware that any [rape] of it's going on. I hear stories that they caught so-and-so spooning in a bed or in the showers. I've never witnessed this going on. The worst I've ever had was a guy in the bunk above me masturbating in the middle of the night. I've heard about yada yada, being caught bent over a table while somebody else is butt-fucking them. I've only got my two eyes and ears to do all this. Narrow range in who you come into contact with. See black guys who wear their hair in curls, Kool-Aid lipstick, we chide them. . . . Every once

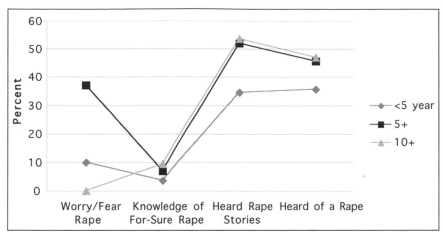

Figure 4.1.   Women Inmates' Exposure to Verbal Messages about Prison Rape

in a while I joke, "I wish I was gay; I'm in a men's prison, what better place to be gay," but no thank you.

Among men who served five or more years, 68 percent heard rape stories, 70 percent heard of a rape, 29 percent heard of a for-sure rape, and 23 percent reported some fear of and worry about rape. For men serving 10 years or more, 72 percent heard rape stories, 74 percent had heard of a rape, 35 percent knew for sure a rape had occurred, and 24 percent expressed some fear or worry about rape.

It was like three Mexicans, it was in a unit, they ran in on some young White kid, and that's just what I heard. It happened seven years ago. They ran into the cell. It was like two years later that I heard about it through another individual.

Percent increase or decrease of exposure to rape tales has little influence on worry about or fear of rape. As time served increased from less than 5 years to 10 or more, there was a 31 percent increase in exposure to rape tales, a 99 percent increase in exposure to hearing about a rape, and a 248 percent increase in self-reported knowledge of a for-sure rape. However, there was only a 3 percent increase in worry about or fear of rape.

Figure 4.2 illustrates the relationship between female inmates' exposure to the same rape tales. Data show that among women who have served less than five years, 35 percent reported hearing rape stories, 36 percent reported hearing of a rape, 4 percent reported knowing of a for-sure rape, and 10 percent had some worry about or fear of rape. Among women who served five years

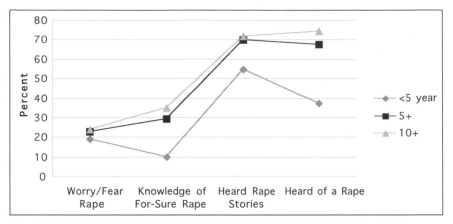

Figure 4.2. Men Inmates' Exposure to Verbal Messages about Prison Rape

or more, their reported level of hearing rape stories and hearing of a rape increased; 52 percent heard rape tales, 46 percent heard of a rape, and 7 percent heard of a for-sure rape, but there was a decline to 7 percent who reported worry about or fear of rape. Those serving 10 or more years continued the trend. Increases were reported in hearing rape tales (54 percent), hearing about a rape (47 percent), and knowing for sure about a rape (9 percent); however, **no** inmates serving 10 or more years reported a worry about or fear of rape.

Here, as with men's data, percent increase or decrease of exposure to rape tales has little influence on worry about or fear of rape. Comparing those who had served less than five years to those who had served 10 or more years, there was a 54 percent increase in exposure to hearing about a rape, a 31 percent increase in exposure to tales about a rape, and a 154 percent increase in self-reported knowledge of a for-sure rape. Higher exposure to rape knowledge produced a 100 percent decrease in worry about or fear of rape.

For-sure knowledge of rape and hearing about rape, controlling for gender and time served, show that inmates are exposed to a high level of verbal vs. visual messages about prison rape. Such a high level of verbal exposure in the context of a low level of visual exposure seems consistent with Clemmer's theory of supraindividual culture and cultural transmission of prison rape knowledge, independent of firsthand exposure to prison rape.

A Cultural Analysis of Increased Rape Knowledge

A careful analysis of inmate narratives provides a glimpse into patterns of increased knowledge exposure relating to rape. Four main themes were identified as important transmitters of cultural knowledge about rape in a prison setting: media portrayals, other facilities, definitional issues, and the time dimension.

Media portrayals. The media is a pervasive source of rape mythology. Prior to incarceration, inmates, as the general public, were hit with a barrage of movies, television shows, news reports, and multiple media sources that portray prison as a haven for rape and sexual violence. As one male inmate simply stated, *"I know about it [rape]. I read the paper and watch the news."* Many inmates claimed to "know for sure" of a rape through outside media portrayals; as one inmate described, *"That [rape] was a while back under the old administration. It was in the newspaper a while back in the '70s or '80s."*

Other facilities. Inmates often reported knowledge of "for-sure" rape in other institutions, where they were not currently incarcerated. While working on this project, the authors used to joke that they were chasing rape across the country. Upon arrival at each institution inmates would tell us that although rape was not happening at this institution we should talk to inmates at the prison down the road or in the next state because that was where rape occurred. Older institutions, especially institutions that had recently closed, were commonly cited as hotbeds for sexual violence. As one male inmate recounted, *"not in this one but heard of a couple of incidents in annex and old pen in [City Name] it was supposed to be common occurrence."* Some inmates maintained "for-sure" knowledge about rape at institutions they never occupied. As a single-term male inmate who had only been in one institution described:

> Go to [OTHER STATE PRISON] you'd hear a lot of that stuff [rape], because it's a violent unit. [OTHER STATE PRISON] or [OTHER STATE PRISON] you'll see a lot of sex and [hear a lot of sex] terms and [it's] known in [the] unit [that] you'll get punked. Bosses let it happen because they know they can't stop it.

Definitional issues. Inmates also report difficulty coming to consensus about what would constitute a "for-sure" rape. As discussed further in chapter 5, inmates have a complex cultural judgment system that takes many pre- and postassault activities into consideration when labeling an event as a rape. As one female inmate described, *"Yes; just a girl another girl was trying to talk to the other girl and the girl just gave in. The one had forced herself on her and she went ahead and gave in."* The line between consensual sex, coercive sex, and rape is not always clear cut in inmate culture.

> You hear about them but whether or not they were really rape is always a question, you never really know. They get in a situation and wish they hadn't been there and claim they didn't want to be there in the first place. They cry rape, you get that more than anything and that's not even really that common.

The time dimension. A final theme focuses on "for-sure" rape knowledge that involves incidents that occurred "back in the day," or many years in the past. In the following excerpt, an 18-year-old male inmate provides a detailed graphic description of a "for-sure" rape that occurred before he was born.

> A while back, two dudes raped a dude in the cell block, the doors was open at that time and they ran in there on the dude. Officers didn't find out, the dude was scared and was a real young dude. Dude was young, nice looking and they fig-ured, come in and seen he was scared you know so they went in on him. It was years ago, back in the early 1980s.

Some tales that are passed to inmates become "for-sure" rape knowledge for segments of inmate culture. The longer the time frame of occurrence, the more violent the story becomes.

> I saw this guy get raped here, he was a child molester, it was right on the tier by the toilet, he went over to take a leak and two guys came from either side and one dude hit him in his ear, the other guy kicked him he ended up on his knees in front of the toilet, everyone was laughing, 30 people were watching, officers were watching in the bubble, they came in after it was done, after the guys walked away, they didn't write nobody up or nothing. That's been years.

A Cultural Analysis of Inmate Worry about Prison Rape

Inmates unequivocally stated that they did not worry about rape in prison. Nearly 80 percent of men and over 90 percent of women reported they did not worry about rape or the threat of rape in the institution. Several cultural di-mensions demonstrate the reasons inmates share for their low reports of rape fear in prison.

Prison safety. Prison safety means that inmates don't have to worry about physical assaults and sexual victimization. Inmates we talked to resoundingly reported that prison was a safe place. Verbalizations of safety included de-scriptions of prison as "Prisneyworld" and "Camp Snoopy"; as one inmate explained, *"This prison is safe. If I don't search for drama it won't find me."* Inmates reported little reason to worry about or fear a physical or sexual at-tack inside the walls.

> I don't even give it a second thought. The first time I came in I was worried, you're tying the soap around your neck so you don't drop it. I was surprised when I got here, other inmates laugh and say "this is a prison? we don't believe that." If you're going to do time, this isn't bad. I don't have to worry that some-one is going to do something.

[are you worried about rape?] Not anymore; the wider areas, better lighting, better supervision with the guards, the way the pickets are set up, it's hard to get away with it. It's possible in the older units, but in the new units it just won't happen.

Sex is readily available. A common answer as to why rape was not a frequent occurrence in prison was the easy access to voluntary sexual activity inside. As one female inmate stated, *"No, it [rape] don't happen because so many are willing."* A male inmate echoed a similar sentiment, *"no, there's a lot of gays in [CURRENT STATE] who are willing, there's no need to get raped."* Inmates reported a lack of "need" for rape, as the sexual needs of fellow prisoners were easily met through consensual encounters.

Rape doesn't happen. Inmates said they don't fear or worry about rape because it is unlikely to occur inside prison. One male inmate told us that *"inmates don't think rape is a possibility, it doesn't really happen."* A female inmate was unambiguous in her opinion that *"it's [rape] not even a possibility."* Fear and worry lessens over time when their initial knowledge is verified through experience.

No, when you first come to prison you come in with all the TV stuff. At the yard you have open showers, it [rape] just doesn't happen. I've been down for 7 years and never thought about looking over my shoulder.

Inmates listed a variety of changes in prison over time as a reason to ease current fear of rape. As one female inmate explains, *"I've heard of it happening in the way past, not in a long time, it's been years, I don't hear about that at all."* Many changes were not "inside" changes, and instead reflect cultural changes that then affect the inmate's worldview.

In the early '70s, I'd say yes [worry about rape]. Nowadays it's not as it used to be. When I first got locked up I was worried, carried my shank. It [rape] kind of mellowed out, especially when AIDS came out—people worried about that.

Inmate narratives provide strong verbal support for the low levels of reported worry or fear about rape inside prison. In strong opposition to popular culture and media-infused beliefs about violent prison sexual assault, inmates perceive prison as a place relatively free of worry. The theory of cultural learning argues that inmates' knowledge depends on their exposure to different contexts within which they learn attitudes, beliefs, and opinions about prison social life. Exposure to different contexts means that some inmates may worry about rape while others don't, depending on their personal experiences. Personal experiences are not necessarily watching firsthand scenes of rape; rather personal experiences are exposure to gossip, rumors, innuendo, conversations in the chow hall, and general snippets of conversations here and there around a prison. Inmates' comments about a lack of worry and fear of rape because rape isn't a possibility cannot be interpreted as a proxy measure for rape's prevalence.

Why They Worry

Although most inmates report that they do not worry about or fear rape, what about those that do? A careful analysis of interview data reveals that many of the inmates who answered yes to our question about rape fear or worry did so for reasons far removed from prison sexual victimization. Inmates report that media, prior victimization, and just being new and naïve to the prison scene may produce a fear or worry about physical and/or sexual victimization.

TV/media. Knowledge of victimization begins long before inmates enter the prison walls. Before becoming inmates, they are exposed to the same barrage of pop media visualizations of violent prison rapes as you or I. Graphic rape imaging from *Oz, The Shawshank Redemption*, or *American Me* can easily cause fear for one who is new to the system. As one woman explains, *"the first-timers and women who hear rumors on the street and see rape in prison movies worry but when they get here they see it ain't like the movies."* Or similarly, a male inmate reports:

> Until you've done maybe 2 or 3 months maybe. The younger generation is worried, with all the rap and gangsta movies they watch; all they see are criminology and gangsta movies on TV, they're dumb-asses, they get here and for the first 6 months, you come through [UNIT NAME] and you're in an enclosed atmosphere, there's a guard on your ass the whole time, it is impossible for something to happen.

Past victimization. Inmates weren't always prisoners. When inmates were on the street, their worry about victimization kept them alert to danger. As would be expected, inmates with prior street victimization reported a greater fear of inside victimization.

> I am scared that people are going to come up behind you; when you come to prison after being raped out there, you are still going to be scared. My friend says he isn't scared; but I think he's making it up.

New to prison. New inmates, not yet savvy to the way of prison culture, report a greater fear of the unknown than inmates who have gone through the prisonization experience. As one female inmate reported, *"Yes, I am worried,*

I am new and I don't know about this place, do you?" For some, prison is an unknown quantity; they come with prior knowledge from the media and enter a foreign world they do not understand. Inmates report that fear or worry fades once they become assimilated into the culture. As one male inmate describes, *"Yeah, when you come through the door because you hear so much on the street, but then once you get settled and observe what's going around, but anything is possible."*

URBAN MYTHOLOGY

Urban myths are a type of modern folklore. These myths may be grounded in distant reality or truly fictional. They are distorted, twisted, and exaggerated, and told as if they were true. Fleisher's (1989) study of maximum-security penitentiary life discussed the social functions of inmate and staff urban myths. Topics were behaviors of penitentiary life, including homicide and severe physical assault. The tales themselves were judged by staff and inmates as fantastical but fun stories to share.

Narratives illustrate a thematically rich men inmate's verbal history about prison rape. Men's folklore has a broad geographic focus and seems more culturally significant than in women's prisons. In men's prisons cultural figures such as Boxing Betty, Purple Passion, Lick'em Lenny, and Brutus are identified either by name or activity across the country. These are not reported or interpreted as scary, foreboding characters; rather they are tales men laugh about. Women's prison culture has no sexually violent stereotypical, named characters analogous to men's characters. Unlike men's humorous reports of the antics of folkloric characters, women don't laugh and joke about sexual violence.

Male Folklore

Six main themes can be identified in male folklore. Stories focus on *retaliation*—inmates who were raped and then retaliated afterward in a violent display; *deserving it*—child molesters who are served penitentiary justice; and *errors in judgment*—inmates who don't fit homosexual stereotypes. Also common are stories about inmates who were raped in prison and enjoyed the experience—*raped but-liked-it stories*. We label the next category *lessons to learn*. These tales include stories that warn inmates what to expect or watch out for upon prison entry. Folkloric tales aid in the enculturation of inmates. These tales illustrate "proper" and troublesome prison behavior. For example, don't get too comfortable with people—they could surprise you (*errors in judgment*); or certain behaviors won't be tolerated in prison—watch yourself (*deserving it*). You should always take care of your own battles (*retaliate*), or, if you give into prison sex, you might just like it (*raped but liked it*). Finally, there are just some plain old *good old boy stories* that commonly serve as scare stories to encourage a riding/protective relationship with the person telling the story.

Errors in judgment. Inmates told us tales about the antics of Boxing Betty. Boxing Betty is, according to most versions of the tale, a former professional boxer, and on-the-yard bodybuilder. He does not look like a novice inmate's image of a prison homosexual, but Boxing Betty is an aggressive homosexual prone to extreme violence if he doesn't get his way. Boxing Betty, the tales goes, enjoys giving other men blow jobs. His request can be refused at some unsuspecting inmate's peril. Tales of his antics were repeated across the United States in prisons separated by hundreds and thousands of miles.

> Boxing Betty was a regular old dude, four dudes raped him in the shower at old [OTHER STATE PRISON] before they tore it down so he worked out and started lifting weights and came back five years later and raped and beat them up every single one of them, he got his get back, I was nine when this happened. He's gay now, but he made them suck his dick; he's considered a legend, he's a cool person you would never know.

> We used to have this one legend that this guy called Boxing Betty, a homo well-known. He used to box when they had the boxing program. He liked taking it both ways, and if he seen someone he liked that he wanted sex with, he'd beat them up and force them to fuck him in the ass.

The majority of inmates laughed at Boxing Betty's antics. Those inmates knew he was a folkloric character of prison culture. A few inmates, however, swore they personally knew Boxing Betty or knew where he was imprisoned.

> Boxing Betty, I met him, he is not to be fucked with, met him in [UNIT NAME] a year and a half ago; he lived up to his name; he targeted young guys when he was out of prison; he would beat you up until you would let him suck your dick or have anal sex with him. He learned from his ways. He went to [OTHER STATE PRISON] or [OTHER STATE PRISON].

Boxing Betty tales tell us that if you prejudge a man's sexual orientation by his physique then you can find yourself in serious trouble; if you prejudge any man by a sexual label then you can be quite mistaken and get into trouble; if you are approached and sexually propositioned, then fighting or arguing or giving in are probably not good strategies. Other versions of rape lore combine physical strength, fighting ability, and homosexuality. Folklore figures exemplify this combination of traits and illustrate the strength of homosexuals.

Got a big old dude down there who was called Fort Knox, got real old been on state 28 or 29 years, real big dude, was a professional weightlifter or something; the thing is, he the girl, he'll beat somebody up that he might like and while you laying there knocked out he going to get what he want. He's pressing 300 pounds but he like to suck your dick. If you don't let him, he knock you out and suck you. You wake up and your pants on down around your knees and you got a big old knot on your head.

There's this guy named Brutus; he's a really big guy supposed to be gay. He walked around with a weight belt on and told people "hey, you let me suck you off or I'm going to knock you out," and then he'd do it. I met Brutus in 1990. He was a big guy.

There's this guy they call Lick 'em Lenny; he's what they call a goop gobbler. He'll knock them out and then take them [have sex with them]. I don't know the guy's name, that's his nickname, but apparently he's a known homosexual who likes young boys and will suck dick on these young guys. He's some weirdo; he pays for cups of semen and will drink them.

Deserved it. The most graphically violent stories involve inmates who function outside of, or on the fringe of, prison culture. Child molesters and snitches are common characters in folkloric revenge stories. The stories serve to set boundaries for appropriate behavior and warn of violent repercussions for those who choose to operate outside the acceptable limits. Often these stories involve correctional officer approval, perhaps bolstering the claim that the inmate in question truly did *deserve it*.

Yes, they called him Trashcan, he raped a really, really good White boy, very young and still in his teens, and he raped him not knowing him that he was the big AB's boy, child. Trashcan raped him and they (you'll hear about this in [OTHER STATE PRISON]) they cut that dude's head off. They have hallways that are really long, [PERSONAL NAME] kicked that dude's head all the way to the searcher's desk. He got there and told the officer at the searchers desk, if you want the rest of this piece of shit he's back there at the back.

Retaliation. In prison, the actions that occur after a sexual assault determine whether the incident will be labeled as rape by inmate culture (see chapter 6 for a detailed discussion). Many stories describe violent reprisal for a rape or violent assault, as a way to maintain manhood.

Yes, I've heard stories of it; heard that 5 men had jumped on 1 man when he was a young man. He had a life sentence and he spent the rest of his sentence going from camp to camp killing them. It was added to his sentence but he didn't care. He was in here for life without parole.

Rape/sex and liked it. Some lore serves as a reminder that sexuality is an active part of prison culture. Many inmates willingly engage in prison sexual behavior. Stories of forced sex that brought enjoyment or sexual acceptance (see chapter 5) relay important cultural norms of sexuality.

> A drag queen come in the shower with two knives in his hand and said, it's my birthday and I'm not leaving until I suck everyone's dick. They called him Lisa and they let him. That was in [CURRENT STATE] Penitentiary. One of the guys that was in the shower I knew personally. They could have taken those knives away. I think they wanted it.

Lessons to be learned. Folkloric tales serve as warnings to inmates about things that are likely to happen upon incarceration. A common tale involved a character named "Big Dick Bob." In some places the name Bob was re-placed by Bill or some other name. Always however, his personal name was preceded by his title—Big Dick. Bob "took care of their old lady" while they were inside prison, said inmates jokingly. As one inmate described, *"'Where's your girl Saturday night?' With Big Dick Bob."* Is there a real Big Dick Bob? Doubtful, isn't it? But the lessons to be learned about doing time are expressed in Big Dick Bob tales. Experienced inmates know, and novice inmates will soon learn, that when they go to prison their wife or girlfriend will leave them soon afterward.

There are other types of sex tales that don't appear to be sex tales. When you are new in prison, if a friendly inmate offers you candy bars, what should you do? Sex tales have answers to these fundamental daily decisions. *"When I first went to prison the big scare tactic was when you first get to your cell and there are candy bars on your bed, don't eat them."* If candy bars are of-fered, then the wise decision is to be polite but refuse them. Accepting candy from "strangers" always leads to trouble. In prison it may lead an unsuspect-ing new inmate into a candy-for-sex trade. In the logic of prison culture, ac-cepting the candy comes with a firm obligation to offer some type of repay-ment. If a new inmate cannot repay with stamps or cash or commissary goods, then sex is the culturally defined exchange commodity. The next step, that is, being forced to give the candy-giver a blow job or hand job will not be considered coerced sex even if the candy-receiver feels threatened and trapped by the situation. Prison logic says if you accept candy then you must know the consequences.

Good old boy stories. Some stories serve to create fear in inmates for an in-strumental gain. These stories were often reported as the type of story that would be told to a new inmate to encourage that inmate to pay for the pro-tective services of the inmate telling the story. As one inmate described, *"They'll tell you these guys used to come in and we'd stand them up on the tables and auction them off to sexual predators."* Even if a new inmate doesn't really believe the stories, a "better safe than sorry" attitude may dictate their behavioral choices.

Female Folklore

Women's sexual abuse experience may in part account for women's prisons' paucity of sexually violent folkloric characters. However, there are recurrent tales of sexual assault. A rapist who assaulted victims with a hot curling iron was commonly cited; however, women who told the tale could not identify either the rape victim or rapist or where and when it occurred. The assault may have been grounded in reality but was reported, as urban myths are, as a "did you hear about" or a "friend of a friend" tale.

Female stories are wild stories that are much more violent than male stories. They usually have to do with women who were weak or had socially unacceptable crimes on the outside (molesting, killing their children) or women who stole money or in some other way acted outside the realm of culturally acceptable in-prison behavior. Women are much less likely to actually believe the lore, whereas men will not only swear they are true, but also swear they've met the cast of characters.

Socially unacceptable crimes. Women's folklore provides boundaries for acceptable behaviors. A common theme involves the abuse of other women or children. As one woman describes, *"The rape story you always hear is 5 women in the shower with a broomstick, they talk about it 'cause when people come in who do something to babies, that's what we do to them."* The stories serve as a warning that some behavior will not be tolerated in prison culture. As another woman explains, *"If you're a pedophile no one really does want to hang out with them. Some are hurt. Particularly people who attack child case convicts. [It's] like a police force in here because most of us were abused."*

In-prison rule violation. Culturally unacceptable behavior is not limited to preimprisonment actions. Female folklore defines the limits of prison culture through descriptions of violent reprisal for inmates unwilling to follow the informal rules.

That was a situation, where a girl had stolen an address off of another girl and was writing to her husband. That's a really big thing in here. The girl got really, really mad and I guess talked a couple of other girls into taking the girl in. They got duct tape and taped her up and raped in with a broomstick and cut her with razor blades. This happened on the compound in the minimum unit. Most of the really bad stuff happens in minimum. You only get cat fights in [UNIT NAME], more violence in [UNIT NAME] and the compound, way more. From my understanding there are buildings that are used for school, vo-tech, I guess they were in one of those rooms. That happened about 3 years after I got here. I remember seeing the girl, she was beat good. They butterflied all her cuts and she had stitches. One of the women was charged, sent downtown with that one. They were sent, they stood trial for that.

Yeah, they said they got a girl down on the bed and stuck stuff in her. They thought she had their money and they were going up in her to see if she had the money inside her, it was a loan-shark thing.

PRISONIZATION: VERBAL LESSONS OF SOCIALIZATION

Rape reports that may or may not have actually happened and stories about characters most inmates know are fictitious create subjective imagery inmates express via gossip, conversations, jokes, lore, secrets, and so on. Clemmer's (1940) theory of culture argues that verbal messages are the dominant form of socialization to prison life. These verbal messages carry information about practical issues and complex social dynamics. Verbal messages pass between generations. As they do, culture's supraindividual quality passes cultural information between generations. Messages about prison rape that actually occurred and stories like those described above pass between generations of inmates. Eventually, acts of rape and urban myths about rape are not easily distinguished as speakers twist and exaggerate tales with each telling, similar to a childhood game of telephone.

Inmates have heard stories about rape and rapists. However, few have baseline, firsthand knowledge of rape as a witness or victim or rapist or companion of a rape victim. Given inmates' wide range of experiences inside prison, some stories are more realistic than others. Without certain knowledge of an actual rape, a safe strategy would be to believe these stories until proven otherwise.

No matter if rape messages are believed or are descriptions of actual events, verbal accounts of prison violence and prison rape convey lessons about prison culture and social life. Lessons are conveyed via prisonization. Verbal messages are the single-most important dynamic in the transmission of cultural knowledge inside and outside prison. Prison rape messages impart motivations for violence and nuances in the meaning of prison behavior. From a broader social science perspective, actual inmate behavior and sexual behavior options captured by verbal messages indicate adaptive strategies available to men and women in a restricted environment.

Chapter Five

Prison Sexual Culture

Prison culture has evolved through an elaborate constellation of cultural sex symbols and cultural sexual dynamics. Clemmer's (1940) theory of culture and prisonization posited that through prisonization, inmates learn the rules of prison life. Prisonization would by definition include socialization into sexual subcultures inside the prison. Our term *sexualization* refers to the process of inmates acquiring cultural knowledge and rules of behavior that enable them to participate in the sexual subculture of prison. Participation does not necessarily mean inmates' personal involvement in sexual activity. Rather, participation refers to awareness of sexual culture sufficient to choose participation in, or avoidance of, a prison's sexual scene. In either case, inmates must know cultural rules of behavior to engage in sexual activity or remain outside the sexual scene.

Clemmer postulated that inmates bring with them into prison personal traits and behavior that influence the nature of prison culture. The history of prison culture research, as far back as Fishman (1934), described aggressive responses of an inmate population to homosexuals. Sykes's (1958) deprivation argument strongly suggested that prison life was devoid of sexual and social pleasures and that prison culture itself forced inmates into homosexual behavior. The importation of inmates by definition includes their sexual preferences. Clemmer's theory of culture argues that (1) sexual importation would affect sexual preferences of new inmates and (2) the dynamics between homo- and heterosexuals would influence future generations of prison culture. Theory of prison sex and sexual violence must abide by the concept that prison general populations are not asexual. Any theory of sexual violence must, by virtue of the composition of the general population, account for inmate sexual behavior.

Figure 5.1 reports data on preimprisonment sexual preference and experience. Our data indicate that women's prison culture may accept homosexual behavior with less resistance than men's prison culture. Thirty-eight percent of women reported a preimprisonment gay or bisexual preference, and 41 percent of women inmates reported same-sex experiences on the street. A culture of homosexuality may serve as a culturally acceptable mode of institutional adaptation for incarcerated women. By contrast, 16 percent of men reported a gay or bisexual preference, and 20 percent had same-sex experiences on the street. Men's prison culture may not as easily accept a homosexual adaptation, except on the fringes of prison society.

Figure 5.2 shows female sexual preference and preimprisonment sexual experience by time served. Women's data reveal less than 5 percent variation in reports of gay or bisexual orientation for those serving less than five years, five years or more, or 10 years or more in prison. Reports of same-sex street encounters decrease as length of time served increases, with 46 percent of women incarcerated less than five years, 35 percent of women incarcerated five or more years, and 32 percent of women incarcerated 10 or more years reporting same-sex street experiences.

Male inmates report different patterns of orientation and experience over time. Figure 5.3 indicates that 13 percent of men inmates with less than five years of incarceration, 18 percent of men inmates with five or more years of incarceration, and 20 percent of men inmates with 10 or more years of incarceration self-reported gay and bisexual preferences. Similar increases were found with respect to same-sex street encounters. Thirteen percent of men inmates with less than five years behind bars, 24 percent of inmates with five

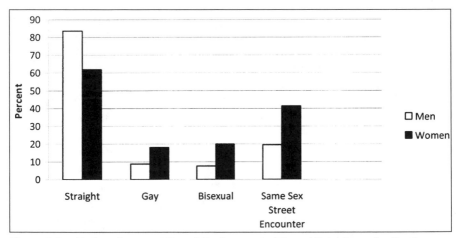

Figure 5.1. Preimprisonment Sexual Preference and Sexual Experience by Gender

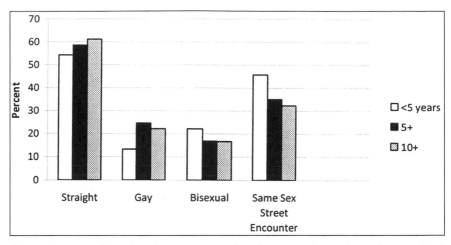

Figure 5.2. Female Preimprisonment Sexual Preference and Experience by Length of Time Served

or more years in prison, and 28 percent of inmates with 10 or more years in prison self-reported same-sex street experiences.

These data show that men and women inmates have experiences in a homosexual lifestyle prior to imprisonment. To be sure, new and experienced inmates are not naïve consumers of prison homosexual culture, albeit their involvement differs by personal preference. Upon entry into prison, men and

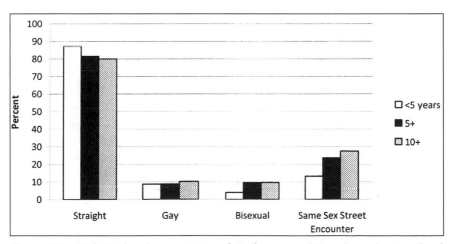

Figure 5.3. Male Preimprisonment Sexual Preference and Experience by Length of Time Served

women inmates bring sexual identity and experience. A cultural theory of prison rape and sexual coercion must abide by the fact that inmates (new or old) are experienced in homosexual culture. This fact suggests women and men inmates possess a level of cultural awareness high enough to cope with and respond to sexual pressure.

PRISON SEXUAL ROLES

The prison sexual hierarchy[1] does not exist on a simple continuum from homosexual to straight. In prison, the labels "gay" and "straight" are not necessarily mutually exclusive categories. Prison sexuality represents a complex socio-cultural network with increasingly fluid sexual roles. Each role can be identified through the public persona projected by the inmate. Two basic sexual tracks can be forged. The first involves openly homosexual behavior; actors in these categories define themselves as homosexuals and are considered homosexuals by the prison culture. The second track contains men who define themselves as straight, but may or may not participate in sexual acts with other men. Regardless of their behavior, they are seen as heterosexual by members of the prison culture. A separate hierarchy exists for each sexual track. Figure 5.4 displays narrative descriptions for the basic categories of prison sexuality.

Track 1: The Homosexual Persona

Punks, queens, and "true" homosexuals make up the sexual roles available for openly homosexual men. Inmates state that although it may be possible to move into different categories, for the most part, once identified they are static roles. Irrespective of their inner identity or preference, once labeled in the homosexual tract, they are viewed as open homosexuals within prison culture.

The "true" homosexual vs. the punk. "True" or "street" homosexuals occupy an elevated level of respect in the prison hierarchy. In an age of political correctness, men who were gay on the streets and do not hide their sexual preference find open acceptance from the different social groups in the prison. Street homosexuals are much more respected than inmates who were heterosexual on the street and turned to homosexuality by either choice or coercion after coming into the penitentiary. A clear distinction is made between a man who has led a homosexual lifestyle prior to incarceration and a person who chooses to participate in the gay lifestyle only in prison. The latter is known as a "punk."

Prison Socio-Sexual Roles

'True' Straight	Active	Down Low
"We still like females and that's all we interested in They are respected and strong if they don't have sex" *"Strong mother fucker; strongest man on the planet, almost impossible; impossible not to think, I know guys who try to do masturbation, you become a really freaky dude with books and TV screens [example: Oprah Winfrey fetish]"*	*"That's my man, husband, pimp; homosexuals prefer a straight man to be their man. There's a difference between a gay male and a heterosexual who messes with a homosexual, a heterosexual likes the female aspect, no flip flopping. Homosexuals want the strength and security of a heterosexual, not a gay man"*	*"You can keep it quiet for only so long, eventually guys will know, I know a couple guys who's undercover I just don't say nothing, I respect their privacy, it's not my business."*
Queen	**Homosexual**	**Punk**
"The girls [queens], we have more of the power. We're the chosen ones, whether you like it or not or want it or not. You all think I'm the bad person, I'm not; no men run me or tell me what to do. I control these guys. Officers know that I'm not a trouble maker."	*"If a guy comes to the joint and he's a homosexual on the street I'm more inclined to accept and respect what he is. If a man comes to the penitentiary and he's turned out I'll treat him differently. Just the level of respect or acceptance he has or will get."*	*"He'd be treated as a pressure punk, everyone would know he's been turned out, wouldn't be treated with the same acceptance as someone who came to the penitentiary as a homosexual. We wouldn't piss on him if he was on fire. It's respect to a degree, but it's more of an acceptance, not a respect. Guys would treat them a little different, I wouldn't have that animosity towards them if they were a homosexual on the street"*

Figure 5.4.   Inmates' Distinctions among Six Socio-Sexual Roles

If a guy comes to the joint and he's a homosexual on the street I'm more inclined to accept and respect what he is. If a man comes to the penitentiary and he's turned out I'll treat him differently. Just the level of respect or acceptance he has or will get.

Punks receive little respect in prison culture. They are viewed as having a lack of respect for themselves, due to their "choice" of sexual submission. In prison, personal protection is a key element of survival. Punks are considered weak, as they have not protected their own property. As one inmate states, *"ripping off a man's ass is like ripping off his radio. It's up to him to protect it."* The responsibility of protecting one's property and reputation depends on the weakness or strength of the individual.

He'd be treated as a pressure punk, everyone would know he's been turned out, wouldn't be treated with the same acceptance as someone who came to the penitentiary as a homosexual. We wouldn't piss on him if he was on fire. It's respect to a degree, but it's more of an acceptance, not a respect. Guys would treat them a little different. I wouldn't have that animosity towards them if they were a homosexual on the street.

A key difference between a punk and a "true" homosexual is knowledge. If an inmate enters prison as a known homosexual, he already knows the lifestyle. As one inmate indicated, *"some come in sexually oriented into the gay lifestyle and play the game without being abused in the process."* Inmates who enter prison as gay men will be better able to avoid sexual predation. Predators are less likely to press them or try to turn them out. As they already participate in the homosexual lifestyle, no power would be gained through sexual coercion.

The "true" homosexual vs. the queen. Moving up the hierarchy from punk to true homosexual, the top category is held by the "queen." Homosexuals are known by their sexual preference, but they do not need to play the female persona to be considered a homosexual. Queens, however, look, dress, and act like women. More importantly, they are treated as women by both inmates and staff. Queens play an important function in prison culture. They play an integral role in the dissemination of information between the "strong" men in the culture and the administration. They also control much of the sexual behavior that takes place in any given institution.

Need to learn to set down standards, they can't just get to the game and mess with an all-out queen, you can't con and trick an all-out queen. You can give game to a boy that you pick up, not to a queen, they ain't trying to hear that. An older person will be more likely to be in a relationship with a queen, young guys who try will end up being turned out by a queen. But they don't become someone's boy, there's no title for that. The queen knows who's more dominant and running the show, a man can still be in the relationship, just like on the street where the wife knows and is running things.

Track 2: The Straight Persona

Men who outwardly project themselves as heterosexual make up the second prison sexual track. Although they may be openly involved in sexual activities with other inmates, they are culturally identified as straight men.

The "straight" man. Sometimes viewed as mythical figures in prison culture, inmates recognize men who never delve into the sexual fray as "strong." Reportedly able to withstand the pressures of curiosity, time, and peer pressure, straight inmates are respected for their adherence to "masturbation only" as an outlet for sexual release. Status in the hierarchy grows with time served. Inmates who remain in the straight-man category for the duration of a lengthy or life sentence are accorded the top levels of cultural position.

> You'll talk to someone who's gay after 20 years, but not after 18 months. Time wears off on an individual. They are respected and strong if they don't have sex. But respect isn't taken away if they've been here a long time and have sex. The chances of doing 50 years and abstaining from sex are nonexistent; but not after 18 months.

When asked about inmates who choose to remain celibate, respondents indicate that their accorded strength is related to their ability to withstand the need for sexual contact. As one inmate notes, *"they say I am lying; some say [I am] abnormal because I been here 20 years [without indulging in sexual activities with male inmates]. I get credit because I am strong."*

Openly sexually active vs. the down low. Heterosexual men who receive sexual favors from others make up the middle level of the straight persona. Known for sexual relationships with women outside of prison, "active" heterosexual men do not hide their relationships with prison homosexuals. Often involved in short- or long-term relationships with "boys" or "wives," their masculinity is not determined through their sexual actions. As one male inmate describes, *"in here they don't look at it like that, the dominant is the man and the other person is gay, not a man; a man is not seen as gay."* Or from a different point of view, *"homosexuals prefer a straight man to be their man."*

Men who are not open about their sexual activity reside in the lowest rung of the straight hierarchy. While presenting a heterosexual identity, they are allowed fringe involvement in the sexual fray through hidden encounters. Inmates report a multitude of reasons for involvement in a down-low relationship, from worries about social group acceptance to fear of inside sexual activities becoming known to outside friends and family.

> They act like they're not into that and try to hide it from anybody, but it don't work out. They fear their mom or wife would find out, that's much more of a fear than another inmate finding out.

> Like say for instance you doing it but you don't want your players to know about it. You have, have a homo meet you somewhere or you shoot them a kite and say you want to hook up but you have to keep it on the down low so your people don't know about it. You be with a homo that won't say nothing.

Inmates report a cultural understanding of down low as a way to explore sexuality, by providing shared concealment of a down-low inmate's "hidden" status. As one inmate states, *"you can keep it quiet for only so long, eventually guys will know. I know a couple guys who's undercover I just don't say nothing, I respect their privacy, it's not my business."*

IN-PRISON SEXUAL ROLE TRANSFORMATION

Tomeka

Cross-cutting the dynamic social environment of the prison are a myriad of personal and group-based safe zones. These are social arrangements that afford inmates a sense of physical and emotional security. The underlying structure of sexual behavior in prison places many effeminate homosexuals (queens) in an overall power position. The social role of the queen revolves around a complex mix of sexual and nonsexual knowledge that afford her, and those associated with her, safety within the prison walls.

Gaining respect doesn't happen overnight; it takes time and ability. A queen's public image belies "her" inner identity as a woman. She dresses, talks, walks, looks, and acts like a woman. The continuous refinement of femininity is a lifelong goal of a true queen. Queens aren't just men in drag; in prison culture, they *are* female. They strive to become emotionally and socially attached to their emerging or existing feminine identity. Addressing a queen with her female name and referring to her as "she" is a sign of "her" public transformation into a woman.

We were able to speak with several queens throughout the duration of our project. Tomeka was a 34-year-old African-American self-identified queen who spoke of the difficulties of living in an all-male prison environment. When we spoke with Tomeka, she was a year and a half into a

10-year drug sentence. Combined, she had nearly 13 solid years of past incarceration and had been cycling in and out of DOC custody since she was 17. Tomeka was able to provide a frank and intriguing look into the culture of a prison queen.

She described the social role of a queen as an all-encompassing master status: *"from morning to night and to your soul, it's you completely, queen,"* and expressed her frustration with some of the men on her block—*"the guys that won't acknowledge my queendom and won't call me Tomeka. It's all the lady that I am, it's a queendom in me."* Self and cultural recognition of one's inner feminine identity, the ideal " woman" inside a queen, is her queendom. With a queendom comes acceptance from inmate and officer: *"Me, I'm openly gay, they have to accept me because I'm here."*

Much of a queen's role revolves around sexuality; however, even sexual behavior is governed by prison mores. True queens have their own social order when it comes to sexually appropriate actions.

> There's one queen here that's into S&M, she's really rare. She only wants to be penetrated and he puts his finger in his ass and eats feces and it's really gross; he wants guys to urinate on him and stuff like that. I'm like "you are not a queen," we don't do that. We have morals, we are self-respecting and a little bit more sensible. Big issue is the removal of the clothing. To be caught in a sexual position is embarrassing and degrading. As a queen I would never confess to having sex with another guy. As long as they don't have to imagine me having sex, it's OK, if they saw us the staff would be like "ugh."

Tomeka also spoke of the dangers of prison sexuality. Similar to date or marital rape, she described the difficulties of ending sexual involvement once in a relationship.

> When he made his advances instead of telling or causing a problem, I allowed him to have me but I told him I didn't want to more than once. I didn't have the [mental] strength to fight him off. I'm very terrified to this day, he has a reputation for putting his dick into every hole he finds and the last thing I wanted to do was have him do me knowing the risk of getting diseases. I let him have me, lay there and did his thing and it happens a lot on a mental aspect. These guys befriend other guys and they learn your weakness. Do you call it rape? Or talk about rape? No, you'd hear "Oh, I fucking had to do it with him again."

The fluidity of sexual roles is a defining element of inmate culture. Interview data show that inmates aren't ascribed to a sexual role because of physical size, hair length, and race or ethnicity; nor are they forced to accept a sociosexual role. Interview data show that sex roles shift from outside to inside as indicated by the expression "gay for the stay," heard across the country in women's prisons:

> I think over half this prison would try to say they're with so and so. People come in who are straight and the next day they are with someone. The next day a person is a wife. It's real childish. They do it to get attention. Couples hook up quickly, out of instability, to create a unit for protection immediately on entry to the prison. You get the feeling when you know someone's looking at you. They play that and it goes further. Sex is feeling good.

Male inmates also report the common occurrence of sexual exploration.

> I think there's just the normal level of curiosity, we have a lot of young people, who've never really seen it and there's a lot of old-timers too. The new kids see the old-timers who have been doing it [having sex] forever. They're kind of like turning out the younger kids, it's a whole new level of curiosity.

Inmate self-reports provide baseline data on sex-role shift in American prisons. Role shifts were measured over time served on current sentence. Inmates estimated the number of straight, down-low, and all-out gay inmates in a representative cross-section of 100 inmates on their yard. Men inmates estimated more men were straight and not down low than women inmates. Figure 5.5 shows the mean estimate of women on the down low was more than 60 percent lower than the men's estimates. Men inmates estimate that 15 percent of 100 men are openly gay, quite similar to men inmates' self-reported preimprisonment gay and bisexual orientation of 16 percent. Women inmates, however, estimate that 60 percent are openly gay inside but as noted in Figure 5.1,

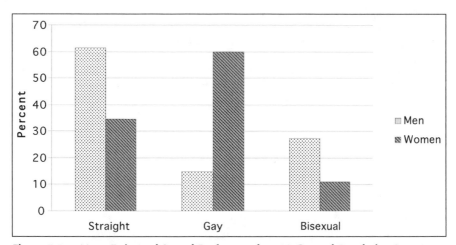

Figure 5.5.   Mean Estimated Sexual Preference for 100 General Population Inmates

only 38 percent self-reported preimprisonment gay and bisexual roles. This distinction fits the self-reported narrative pattern that self-identified straight women participate in homosexual relationships inside.

Table 5.1 shows estimated sexual preference by time incarcerated. The percentage of straight and down-low women remains relatively constant over time. The majority of women are not straight, and an overwhelming percentage of women are not on the down low. The percentage of straight women decreases, and numbers of down-low women increase, however slightly. Male inmate data supports a similar pattern. With an increase in time served, estimates of straight inmates drop and estimates of down-low inmates increase. This fact supports the narrative theme that "time will get you," meaning the longer a man remains inside the more likely he'll engage in same-sex relations. As one male inmate stated, *"I think that it's the time that causes the thoughts. If you was a straight person coming from the world to here, being here will change you up a bit, time takes its toll on everybody."* Interestingly, however, the mean number of open homosexuals doesn't show a significant increase. This suggests that if men become open with their sexuality, they do so early in their imprisonment; if not, they have the option of going down low.

INMATES' SUBJECTIVE PERCEPTION OF PRISON SEXUALITY

Prison worldview has a culturally unique rationale to account for same-sex behavior and inmate interpretation of sexual assault. Men and women inmates reported the cultural acceptability of living a celibate lifestyle; however, as time served lengthened to more than five and approaching ten years, inmates become more likely to slowly enmesh in the homosexual scene. To grasp a prison worldview of homosexuality requires stepping outside of a conventional, free society mode of interpretation of homosexual behavior and inside a culturally relativistic form of explanation.

Table 5.1.   Estimates of Sexual Orientation by Time Served

	<5 Years	5+ Years	10+ Years
Female Estimates (%)			
Straight	35.54	27.54	29.21
Gay	55.19	66.63	64.76
Down low	12.98	7.95	9.33
Male Estimates (%)			
Straight	65.34	58.52	57.09
Gay	14.41	15.11	16.62
Down low	23.48	30.03	28.80

Inner Homosexual

> It's [homosexuality] something in that individual. I don't take the credit for that.
> They are probably not facing whatever's inside of them. I believe there is some-
> thing over time that wears away that already exists. You have something in you.
> Eventually, if you never got locked up, you would have experimented.

Men and women inmates' narratives repeatedly refer to an "inner homosexual" or to one's "true homosexual nature." In inmate culture the inner homosexual bears on a wide scope of homosexual behavior. This concept emerged
from inmate narratives in different guises. Commonly, the inner homosexual
concept functioned to differentiate (what social scientists label) consensual
sex, coercive sex, and rape. For example, *"Every man is a homosexual. Every
man has sexual fantasies about a man."* Or *"Everyone is willing to do something; it's whether he's willing to hold it deep inside him."*

Cultural interpretation of sexual identity. Prison culture explains sexual behavior with a belief in an inherent homosexual nature. This homosexual nature may emerge on its own in specific cultural contexts. Context refers to
particular settings where the inner homosexual emerges. Prison provides such
a context. Inmates' expression "time will get you" refers to inmates' eventual
incapability to stave off the inner homosexual. Long prison terms—10 or
more years—weaken one's resistance to the inner homosexual.

> I believe the guys who are most open anti-gay . . . the more I'm convinced [they]
> got something in [them] that's gay. If you never got locked you'd have done it
> out there, maybe it would take alcohol or drugs but you'd do it. There is a sex-
> ual being in you that you didn't explore until you came to prison.

Looking from the outside in, the inner homosexual concept seems to help
neutralize and rationalize, and make more personally acceptable, inmates' homosexual behavior. Perhaps for straight inmates the concept of inner homosexual enables reconciliation between sexual behavior and self-concepts. On
the premise of an inner homosexual, straight inmates are homosexuals who
have not yet come out.

The inner homosexual helps explain women inmates' attitudes toward sexual assault victims. Victims, inmates said, have not accepted their inner homosexual. One woman explained, *"turning them out they are wanting it. I
think they have it in them, they are curious. You have to bring it out."* They are
more vulnerable to ridicule and social attack than women who joined the sex
scene and have friends and lovers "watching their back." In the logic of the
culture, rejection of the inner homosexual means weakness. By virtue of their
own physical or mental weakness, weak inmates can be victimized in a culturally justifiable act of sexual assault. It is important to note, however, that

sexual assault would be unlikely; women want to fit in with the in-crowd (Alarid, 2000), so they participate in social life and make friends.

Men and women inmates who enter prison and admit they were homosexual outside are better regarded by fellow inmates than those who are turned out. Open acceptance of homosexuality means, in inmate culture, that these inmates were "true to themselves," and did not hide or deny their inner homosexual. Inmate worldview declares that prison does not force homosexuality on anyone. Rather, narratives said, a prison's sexual scene offers opportunities to "become who you are as a sexual being" in relative safety, if sexual emergence proceeds along culturally acceptable pathways.

> Here homosexuality is accepted. I like to know who is around me, snitch, gay, straight. If you are an undercover fag you may have AIDS. Out and out is more accepted because you know your surroundings with them. There's more respect if you are out and out. You're less of a man if you are in denial.

Accepting one's sexual identity inside prison may be an arduous, perhaps violent, process. "Becoming who you are" as a sexual being requires accepting one's inner homosexuality. A homosexual or gay who doesn't conceal his or her identity upon admission to prison openly admits to the general population his or her acceptance of their own inner, homosexual nature. Prison sex worldview accepts inmates who recognize their inner sexual identity but balks when inmates try to hide it. *"I respect someone who is who they are. If they were homosexual on the street I respect that more, stay consistent with who you are."*

Cultural symbolism of the inner homosexual. Inmates' subjective perceptions of homosexuality focus on the inner homosexual concept. This concept has a powerful symbolic impact in inmate culture. Often, inmates' perceptions of homosexuality include strong, often brutal interpretations of inmate encounters with their own sexual identity. To disregard one's own nature signifies one's weak-mindedness. Physical weakness, the inability to physically protect oneself, or mental weakness, the inability to withstand external forces to engage in sex or resist threats, represent cultural anathema. Weakness can be met only with contempt.

Inmate sexual culture integrates three cultural assumptions: no one comes to prison naive; inmates are by nature homosexual; and resistance to accepting one's nature symbolizes weak-mindedness. The integration of these assumptions creates a sexual cultural continuum of social respect. At the extreme positive end are all-out queens; at the extreme negative end are men who must be forced by their own weakness to face and accept their own sexual nature. In this situation, a literalist interpretation of rape gives way to a merger of prison sexual culture's principle metaphors—the inner homosexual and rape. In this metaphoric merger of symbolic images the rapist disappears and the focus turns to an inmate with a clearer recognition of sexual identity.

Prison sex worldview interprets an unwillingness to accept one's own sexual nature as a cause of potential harm. In the logic of prison rape worldview, an inmate cannot be cajoled into oral sex but may "need" to be "pushed" into the process of sexual awakening. Inmate sexual worldview does not interpret such a push as coercion. Rather a push represents an act of a person enabling someone to accept the inner homosexual. The sooner an inmate comes to terms with the inner homosexual, the sooner personal tumult and social anxiety diminish.

This study provides an objective analysis of inmates' subjective perception of social and sexual life. Subjective perceptions are part and parcel of inmate interview narratives. An analysis of sex-related narratives led to abstract and often intuitively peculiar findings. The concept of an inner homosexual articulates the single-most significant conceptual process in inmate culture's worldview of consensual and coercive sex and prison rape. The inner homosexual concept does not mean that inmates believe everyone has a homosexual nature or that sexual coercion or rape does the victim a favor by raising his or her sexual consciousness. Inmates do not believe they have to be raped in order to accept their sexual identity. The inner homosexual exists only as an abstract symbolic expression[2] of inmates' dual sexual nature expressed in prison sexual culture.

CULTURAL CONSTRUCTION OF SEXUAL ASSAILANTS

The cultural dialogue of prison sexual aggression across the country included a variety of players on the sex scene. Some were vulnerable (punks), some violent (rapists and bootie bandits), others con men (turn-out artists). Rapists, bootie bandits, and turn-out artists are discernible social categories. Their ubiquitous cultural nature does not necessarily denote their actual existence on prison compounds nor does it imply that sexual assault occurs on compounds where inmates recognize these figures.

Rapists

Inmate culture conceives of rapists as weaklings and cowards. Their weakness expresses itself even in their inability to have sexual affairs absent of a surprise violent attack. Rapists are repellent; they cannot find willing sexual partners.[3] Alone, without companions, they fall to the margin of inmate society. In inmate parlance, rapists "*work outside the program.*"

Social marginality, if for no other reason, casts suspicion on rapists and makes them potentially dangerous. First, no one knows them, and this in itself makes mainstream inmates suspicious. Second, if they are unknown, mainstream inmates don't know what they do, who they may plot against, or who they may snitch on. Marginality also diminishes their protective affiliations with individual inmates and inmate groups. Rapists have few if any affiliations. As a male inmate described, *"It is like a circle, get him [rapist] out of the circle. Nobody wants them [rapists] in the group. They are pushed away."*

If they have social ties, prison rapists are linked to other socially marginal inmates. As a consequence, narratives noted, rapists do not have allies who will help protect them. Well-connected, mainstream inmates won't risk their reputation and their affiliations with their allies to support marginal inmates. Without allies, rapists are open to violent retaliation by victims and their affiliates. By sociocultural definition rapists are weak and cannot retaliate if they are assaulted.

Inmates abhor rape and rapists. Rapists are negatively stigmatized and may be targets of violent or nonviolent aggression within prison walls. Figure 5.6 examines the cultural feasibility of killing a rapist who refuses to abide by inmates' informal social rules.

Results indicate that women inmates rarely report knowledge of a rapist killed as the result of sexual assault. The lack of knowledge doesn't change with length of time served, staying under 5 percent for all three time points. Men inmates reported higher levels of knowledge of rapists who were killed with 7 percent of men who served less than 5 years. Although there were few narrative examples of a rapist being killed as a result of committing rape,

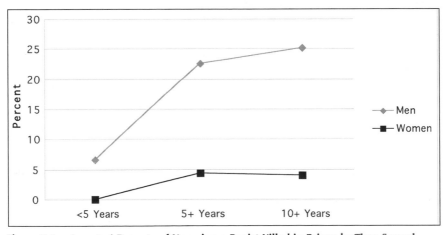

Figure 5.6.   Inmates' Reports of Knowing a Rapist Killed in Prison by Time Served

knowledge for male inmates increased to 23 percent for those serving 5 years
or more and 25 percent for those serving 10 years or more.

> An inmate who raped this one inmate turned around and waited until the dude
> was on the weight pile lifting and picked up a pillowcase with a weight and took
> part of his head off. Blood shot everywhere, he was dead after the first blow. He
> [the offender] was crying and shit and then told everybody. That was OK, he
> was wrong [the victim], he shouldn't have did what he did.

A rapist may try to create a strong social image. Weaker inmates may hang
out with a known rapist in an attempt to curry his favor out of fear. Hangers-
on "run a game." They stay close to a dangerous man, hoping he doesn't rape
them. However, social proximity won't prevent rape or physical assault for a
hanger-on. Rapists cannot be trusted.

Rapists on the compound are well known. They don't have safe zones. They
can't ask other inmates for protection; no one will come forward to protect
them. And they can be victims of a violent retaliation. Rapists don't retaliate
if they were assaulted. Victims are expected to *"do to them what they did to
you and more if you can."* A rapist's smartest move would be to "check" into
protective custody. As one inmate described, *"Cowards, he gots to get up
outta here, person gets caught, it gets around the yard, he gots to go or he's
going to get killed."*

Inmate culture allows a wide berth of sexual freedom; however, rape seems
on the margin of what otherwise would be culturally permissible sexual behavior, even of extreme types. As one male inmate stated, *"Street rapists and
chomos are pieces of shit, in everybody eyes. Rapist [inside] is no better than
a rapo outside."*[4] Prison culture sees rape as a pointless act of violence and irrational given the opportunities male inmates have to engage in sex with men
or women staff, and women inmates have to engage in sex with women and
male staff. A rapist has no power, no respect, and no influence. In the end,
rapists lose respect and companionship—no one wants to be associated with
a weak-minded coward.

Turn-Out Artists

A turn-out artist has smooth social skills and coaxes, often in a matter of days,
his prey into a sexually compromising situation. A new inmate who accepts a
chocolate bar or stamps, or loses a friendly card game, has enjoined a debt that
must be repaid. Rough turn-out artists whose harsh coercion and threats are on
public display are distinguished from rapists. A rough turn-out artist escapes a
rapist label if he's well liked, doesn't bully or stalk his victims, and doesn't show
physical or mental signs of weakness. A turn-out artist moves freely about the

general population; he has companions and doesn't avoid social interactions. Although he is known as a turn-out artist, his behavior carries no negative stigma.

> Turning out is a process of convincing a person that "you never tried it? How do you know what you like and what you don't like?" "There could be desires stored away that you know nothing about"; It's a process of making a person feel comfortable and convincing them they might like it and you never know.

Prison worldview finds that all turn-outs aren't rape. However, someone raped can later become a turn-out. Skilled turn-out artists are not rapists, inmates said. A rapist "steals" sex, whereas a turn-out artist initiates a relationship of exchange. Inmates commonly said "fair exchange is no robbery" or "commissary is necessary." These comments convey the meaning that an exchange of sex for property or protection can be a fair transaction.

Bootie Bandits

A socially determined distinction between a rapist and a turn-out artist becomes clearer in the comparison of a rapist and a bootie bandit. Old-school inmates, those who have served decades inside prison, distinguish bootie bandits from rapists. They said rapists stalk their prey and do not fight for sex if a victim resists. This point supports prison rape worldview's assertion that a man cannot be raped unless he wants to be (see Nacci and Kane, 1982, p. 16) and that a man doesn't have sex unless he wants to. Confronting force, inmates said rapists merely move on until they find a less resistant target. By contrast, a bootie bandit thrives on resistance to his sexual advances and does not back off if victims fight back. However, a bootie bandit sees the interaction as a game. He has polished skills in "talking people out of it." A bootie bandit doesn't fear apprehension or exposure to the general population.

> Just like a normal individual, you just whisper that he is, he be raping he be taking, but they don't call it rape, they call it trick. "He tricked Shorty out of his ass man." You might have an asshole bandit, he ain't going to take it but he keep pursuing it until he get it. It's like a form of brainwashing, and he befriend you first and give you what you want you move in his cell with him and once you get in the cell that's when he make his move.

Old-school inmates distinguish a rapist from a bootie bandit, but younger inmates may use the terms synonymously. Old-school inmates characterize rapists as dark, foreboding, and violent characters; however, a bootie bandit, by contrast, displays a cavalier attitude. Even though a rapist and a bootie bandit may have committed similarly violent sexual assaults, the behavior of a bootie bandit was interpreted by old-schools as comedic, a sexual clown figure of prison culture. Old-schools said bootie bandits "hop" from one boy to another, finding sexual pleasure often. Although narrative data are ambiguous on this point, a bootie bandit seems to have traits of both an aggressive turn-out artist and a rapist. This combination of traits makes a bootie bandit a significant cultural figure.

Stories about bootie bandits do not necessarily mean they existed as real-life characters. They are, however, embodiments of cultural traits. They are figures in the dark shadows of prison culture. While old-school inmates distinguish rapists from bootie bandits, the bootie bandit seems to better fit a colloquial vision of the prison rapist. Inmates reported that rapists avoid confrontation and find easy targets. Stripping away a bootie bandit's preference toward sexual violence leaves the bandit with personal traits desired by street hustlers: verbally adept; socially clever; friendly; manipulative; and always on the prowl for profitable hustle.[5]

Prison Sex Entrepreneurs: Country

Everyone has seen a *Law and Order* episode where a known child molester is beaten to death in a vicious prison attack. In fact, if you ask most inmates how they view pedophiles you'll be greeted with an onslaught of derogatory descriptions. Country's tales unite numerous threads in the myth of prison rape. The reality, however, is that money is the true equalizer in the cell block. It erases who you are by minimizing what you may have done in the past and ignoring what you're likely still doing inside.

Country was a middle-aged man with thinning hair and a very fair-skinned complexion. His looks, attitude, and even the tone of his voice composed an aura of creepiness that only sex offenders seem to be able to confidently display. He carried a superior attitude and from the start of our interview spoke to us as if he were a king holding court. We asked Country whether sex offenders were treated differently inside and his response spoke to the differences in perception of a prison insider.

> Seventy-five percent of the prisoners have some kind of sexual case. Seventy-five percent are sexual offenders from the streets, kidnappers, rape, child molesting, it doesn't matter for them.

Country was a self-described sex entrepreneur. As an old-timer who was openly involved in prison sex, he was seen by many as a go-to person for procuring sexual partners. We discussed the cost of a "Country-brokered" sex act.

> $1.50 for some sex, a bag of coffee, it just depends, each case is different. I might find a child molester who wants a real young cute 18-year-old boy and he might send me $100 cause he doesn't want anyone to know he's involved.

Later the conversation turned to Country's many sexual exploits, and in a chilling example of prison mirroring outside life, Country described a system of sexual grooming that he maintains inside the prison walls.

> All kids would be about the same age, 18 or so. If they're a little older, they can be spotters, and can go out and bring me new people. I'll tell them "Hey, keep an eye out and get me new people" they'd get rewarded with extra tobacco or marijuana.

We spent several hours talking to Country. During our conversation he tried to manipulate us into sending him money in at least four unique ways. Each time we would decline he would slowly shake his head, provide a charming smile, and state, "Hey, I gotta ask." When we talked with Country about victims of prison rape, he explained the difficulty of placing a person into a category based on the act alone. To Country and many other individuals who call prison their home, a rape victim is defined only by their actions after the attack, not through the actual event.

> If you come in here and I hold a knife to your throat and I tell you that I want you to fuck, and you do it, you're not weak. But if you don't come after me the next day with a knife or a club the next day, then you will be considered weak. The actual assault was not a weakness. It was smart thinking that you didn't get killed.

Within the context of these beliefs and social dynamics, inmates assess the distinctions among consensual and coercive sex and rape using culturally determined criteria. These are criteria mutually exclusive from those in a free-society worldview. Inmate culture does not have a standardized set of criteria to distinguish among types of sex acts. There are cultural issues to be resolved: Who consented to sex and why; who needed coaxing and why; who needed coaxing but later slid into a new sexual role; and who resisted coaxing but consented anyway as a means to find protection or commissary products, are questions needing resolution in the calculus of a prison sex worldview. Interview data show that rape vs. coercion vs. consensual sex are culturally defined but are not mutually exclusive categories. These are cultural classifications whose defining criteria shift as context shifts.

NOTES

1. The term *hierarchy* does not imply the operation of a formal system of ranked social statuses defined by rights and duties as we find in the military, corporations, or university professors. We use the term to denote prison culture's conceptualization of inmate sociosexual dynamics. As we use the term *hierarchy*, it means that prison culture creates mutually exclusive sexual roles by ascribing to each role a set of differentiating criteria. Sex roles and distinguishing criteria are universal features of American prison culture. These same role labels were identified by prison culture researchers as far back as Clemmer's (1940) study. Prison culture does not use the term *hierarchy*.

2. A late-nineteenth-century theory of homosexuality posited a third sex, with a man inside a woman's body, and a woman inside a man's. Thus homosexual behavior derived from an inner cross-sex identity (Gay, 2002, p. 66).

3. While inmates' narratives characterize rapists as socially marginal and therefore "weak," there are no studies on the social network structure of inmate society that demonstrate rapists are socially marginal, have few companions, and have no or few social ties to mainstream inmates.

4. *Chomo* and *rapo* refer to a child molester and rapist, respectively.

5. One of the former inmates who assisted in the conceptualization of this project called himself a bootie bandit but didn't refer to himself as a rapist. Now in his sixties, he had been imprisoned six times since his adolescence. Released from prison the final time in 1993, he claimed bootie bandits didn't exist in today's prisons.

Chapter Six

The Culture of Sexual Victimization

"It's like [victims] wear a sign on their head that says 'we're a victim.' There's something about them that's different. Every pedophile will say they look for children who are vulnerable. Rapists too. They just know who to get. It's like victims wear a mask rapists see." [woman inmate]

Prison culture's sexual worldview conceptualizes homosexuality, sexual affairs, and sexual violence as a symbolically complex interplay of unconscious forces emerging in a social reality. Prison worldview uses symbols of sexual violence contrary to and radically different from concepts of sexual violence in free society. Assumptions are predicated on physical and mental weakness, a "blame the victim" sexual victimization philosophy, and antipathy toward victims' pain and suffering. Paradoxically, however, prison culture worldview also abhors prison rapists and prison rape.

This section summarizes cultural themes embedded in inmate narratives on the causes and conditions of sexual violence. Cultural themes are not inmates' justifications and rationalizations for sexual violence. Thus far, analyzed data as well as the history of prison culture and sex research have shown sexual violence to be an infrequent occurrence.

CULTURAL PERCEPTIONS OF RAPE: WAS IT RAPE? IT DEPENDS

In here if you were raped, they'll think it could have been your fault.

Prison culture interprets sexual violence by its context. An act of sexual violence in one context may be interpreted as rape, but in another context, the same act may be interpreted as a turn-out, and in still another it may be an act of coming out of the closet. Inmates see sexually violent actions; however, their subjective perception of sexual violence dominates their interpretation of the violent act. When inmates identified contexts of sexual violence, some said an act was rape; others said the same act was not rape.[1]

Johnson (1971) wrote that there was no protection for a rape victim. Indeed, today's inmates, especially women, can be merciless on the condemnation of and disgust for a rape victim.

> Really they just get made fun of because they're so naive. I understand it could happen, but a lot of people say "how you gonna get raped by a bitch?" We have inmates who cheat on girlfriends and when they find out say they were forced. You not raped, you just got caught. They asked for it, or they did something wrong.

Prison worldview judged by free-society standards rests on a blame-the-victim form of explanation. Upon closer examination, prison cultural logic begins with a blame-the-victim philosophy and infuses it with complex forms of cultural explanations of homosexuality, homosexual violence, and sexual identity. Violent men and women inmates are not strangers to prisons. Their presence influences how social dynamics occur and are interpreted. Violence inside prison doesn't raise eyebrows or cause panic, but it does usually require some type of explanation. An explanation comes from the core premises that have emerged in American prison culture. While these premises are radically different from free-society standards, and while inmates do indeed blame victims for their sexual assault, inmates recognize sexual violence as abhorrent, unjustifiable acts.

A theoretical point must be reiterated. The complex differentiation among acts of sexual violence, sexual consent, and sexual coercion occur as a function of inmate culture's symbolic reinterpretation of sociosexual behavior. The cultural meaning of a sexual act finds its derivation in social context. In the way inmates use their culture, if an act of sexual violence remains constant in intensity and physical expression, inmates' subjective perception—the meaning of the act—varies by context. Thus, the primary mechanism used to determine an act's meaning focuses on contextualization. Since prison social contexts are open to others in addition to an aggressor and victim, others have a voice in the determination of the cultural meaning of sexual violence. In prison culture, the cultural decision—rape or not rape—about an act of sexual violence includes onlookers. Thus, when inmates were asked if a sex act was rape or not, their common response was "it depends."

> You hear rape like that [movie-like rape]. I don't know, I'm not saying it happens so frequently. I can't remember, but I can't put a number on it. I don't think

it happens every day. Within here it's like with anything else, there's a culture of inmates that participate in that type of stuff. You have people who can do 10 or 12 years and the thought of being with a man never come about but you have those who give in to those desires and do whatever it takes to get pleasure, they're wolves or bandits. You have people that guys go to who are able to talk others into doing sexual acts and those who forcibly can, it depends on the strength and fortitude of the individual. If four guys rape you it doesn't make you a punk. You could have just been overpowered. It's what you do after it happens, if it happens to you.

Witnessed or not, prison rape communicates a "public" message to the prison community. No matter how an institution assesses a sexual assault, inmate culture has its own cultural criteria to determine if a sexual encounter was rape. For a sexual aggressor and victim, this determination has immediate and long-term consequences.

No, reputation don't care in here. [They] don't care who you was in the world, you can be anything with a pistol, but if you don't fight, you're weak. If they retaliate [after sexual assault] they're viewed a little different, might just be a weak person that's just studding up, they're still weak. Your personality and character tells all of it. Everybody sees you as something weak, can't turn yourself around, once you get a [weak] jacket, it sticks with you.

Prison worldview conceptualizes any type of sexual violence as a set of actions by inmates, which are connected over time. The physical act of sexual violence is momentary, but to interpret that act we have to look at behavior other than the act. In order to interpret sexual violence (rape) as inmate culture does, we have to isolate and interpret particular actions of a prospective rapist and victim.

Prison rape is a social process with onset occurring days or weeks or months before the physical act. We call the period preceding sexual violence its pre-text. Subsequent to the act of sexual violence an aggressor and a victim go their different ways. We call the period subsequent to sexual violence its post-text. In the post-text, inmates interpret the physical act of sexual violence. Inmates decide if the sex act is rape and whether the aggressor or the victim is responsible for the act. Acts of sexual violence are not rape unless those acts meet particular conditions set by inmate culture's construction of rape.

The cultural schema in figure 6.1 identifies rapists' motives, the ways inmates get themselves into the position of a possible rape (in inmate view), and specific social mechanisms observable in inmate social life that work to prevent violence. Figure 6.1 does *not* predict when and to whom rape will occur. Inmate culture's depiction of prison rape has traits, and the identified traits are

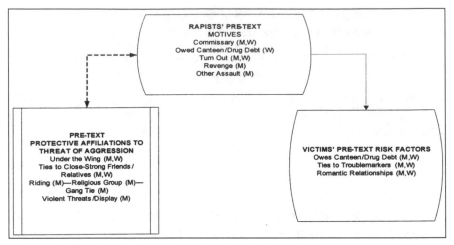

Figure 6.1. Prison Rape: Pre- and Post-Text Conceptualization

common patterns of behavior. Patterns of behavior specific to gender are noted with (M, W), that is, men's and women's prison, respectively.

Victims' Pre-Text Risk Factors

Among a range of inmate behaviors there are a finite number that increase the risk of sexual attack. These risk factors affect the nature of social contexts, by enabling a social context to shift from low risk to high risk of sexual attack. These are called pre-text risk factors. Pre-text risk factors that are especially important are debts, negative social attachments, and romantic relationships.

Debts. Of utmost importance to increasing risk, inmates say, are unpaid drug or canteen debts. Debts are likely to bring a debtor trouble. A debt could be overlooked by a creditor; however, overlooking a debt indicates a creditor's weakness and potential for additional economic exploitation. As a result, commissary, drug, or gambling debts or property theft leave a debtor vulnerable to acts of sexual and nonsexual victimization. As one inmate describes, *"A lot of people . . . use the word rape to administration, but it usually doesn't happen that way. They consent to sex to get out of debt."*

A violation of social protocol incurs if debts are unpaid. However, if a creditor interprets a debt as a public insult, the likelihood of violent retribution increases. Some inmates questioned the underlying motives of debt-related sexual violence, arguing that they may in fact be unrelated to the incurred debt.

> Never heard of anyone raped for owing money. Say if I owe someone money, they'll say "when am I going to get my money," we might fight for it, but unless it was all about sex to start with, that's not an issue.

Negative attachments. Secondarily, friendships can increase risk. Inmates say they need social ties for protection and social support, but on the other hand, social ties can bring trouble. They have to be careful about their choices of personal ties, which means a conscious awareness of manipulation scams and violent reputations (here, the lessons of prison rape lore have an important educational function). If, inmates say, they can't make good personal choices that won't lead to trouble; the best option is to stay away from the yard, avoiding mingling and gossip.

> I've noticed the young ones almost always get swept into the mix. There's more black women that are involved in it. The mix is basically your crowd, if you're in the mix you're in the "in" crowd for sexual activity, just like junior high, in the in-crowd; also more likely to do criminal behavior and fighting.

Romantic relationships. Stealing away with someone's lover, cheating on one's own lover, and public disrespect for one's lover—with the exchange of sexual favors for drugs or property, or verbally disobeying him or her in a public setting—can effect culturally sanctioned violent recrimination. As one inmate explained, "*Today it's more violent than back then. The yard is fighting all the time over girlfriends—you talked to my girlfriend or wife and they fight.*"

Relationships may also increase risk for sexual violence through a combination of sexual entitlement and withholding. As a male inmate described, "*[we were] in a relationship [and I] did not want to have sex and he took it upon his self to take it from me. That caused our relationship to end. He wants to get back with me.*" Similarly:

> I haven't never seen a man raped but I have heard of them happening. It's kind of like if you're with your wife and she doesn't want to do nothing but you do, dudes will do that to their boy and they take it, that's just it.

Additionally, drawing parallels to domestic violence on the outside, inmates report an increase in risk when ending a relationship. As one male inmate described, "*We don't call it rape. I seen situations where couples have been together forever and she wants to leave and he don't want her to, and he sexually rapes her.*" A similar sentiment:

> I know a couple together for 10 years, if she was to leave him, he might have her hurt and a rape could occur then, guys overdo things, they take it overboard. He'd just be ordering her to get hurt and they take it over the top.

Risk factors enable risky contexts, but do not guarantee harm. Although risk factors may facilitate the contexts in which sexual assault may occur, many inmates have debts without getting raped. Similarly, many inmates can easily navigate personal affiliations without ever getting into a scrap of any kind.

Pre-Text Protective Affiliations

Protective affiliations do not necessarily deter rape (noted in figure 6.1 by a dotted line). Knowing a lot of people, but not necessarily hanging out with them, creates social protection. Inmates say that "under-the-wing" relationships or close friends and relatives inside are the strongest forms of resiliency against any kind of social threats. There is protection in deliberate, systematic patterns of achieving personal safety through social affiliation.

Fighting against sexual aggression has long standing in prison research. The metaphor "fuck, fight, or hit the fence" (Eigenberg, 2002) captures the idea of three hypothetical types of self-protection against sexual aggression. "In the prison vernacular, [correctional officers] told them to 'fight or fuck.' At the same time, [correctional officers] would caution them that fighting was a rule violation and that they would be punished—possibly losing good time or parole dates as a sanction for 'their' violence" (p. 49). The statement indicates inherent checks and balances in prison culture, which was suggested decades ago by Sykes and Messinger (1960b). The excerpt below talks about retaliation in a broader context of prison justice.

> [Retaliation] depends on the crime. There is an odd sense of justice here. If [victim] didn't have that coming then there would be retaliation. If he did have it coming, like if he were a child molester or something, he would have to retaliate himself.

We emphasize that sexual-violence retaliation functions as a hypothetical cultural option. Figure 6.2 shows inmate perceptions of the likelihood of sexual victims' support by companions to retaliate against an assailant. These data do not indicate the prevalence of rape or "actual" rape retaliations.

Data indicate a strong perceived cultural agreement that a rape victim's companions will assist the victim in retaliation. Agreement about retaliation decreases among women inmates from 57 percent for inmates who have served less than 5 years to 42 percent for those serving 10 years or more. Among men inmates an agreement about retaliation follows an opposite pattern, increasing from 51 percent for those serving less than 5 years to 62 percent for those who have served 10 years or more.

The first years of women's imprisonment are a time of sociosexual unions and romantic breakups. More breakups cause more hostility, sexual aggression, and potential retaliation. As years pass, sexual adjustment grows less tumultuous as women establish a broad network of friends and lovers who can,

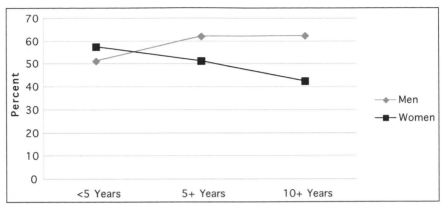

Figure 6.2. Inmates' Perceptions of Rape Victim's Companions' Retaliation by Gender and Time Served

if necessary, offer physical protection. More protection means less aggression and less retaliation.

Inmates reported an increase in men's rape retaliation over time. However, inmates also explained why rape retaliation is culturally *unlikely*. They said that if a man is weak, he will not violently resist an attack. He will "give in" and will then not exhibit the courage to retaliate. Inmates do not befriend weak men; if they did, they too would be considered weak.

We have a clear cultural argument explaining the absence of rape retaliation. How do we explain inmates' assertion that rape retaliation increases over time? There are two sociocultural explanations. The first explanation focuses on inmate social dynamics. The second explanation focuses on cultural dynamics.

Social dynamics. Young male inmates, so prevalent in modern prisons, perceive that older inmates are vulnerable to physical and sexual attack. An inflow of young, aggressive men into high-security prisons sets the stage for young inmates to aggress against older, prison-savvy inmates. In more than a decade inside, older inmates form a network of friends who help defend them. Young inmates who attack older men soon learn that aging inmates don't grow weaker and more vulnerable to assault.

Cultural dynamics. Three cultural characteristics of sexual behavior come into play. First, men's resistance to homosexual sex weakens over time. Second, real men can, if they choose to, prevent rape. Third, some men, even real men, enjoy aggressive sex. If we combine those cultural characteristics the result is an abstract conformation of cultural beliefs about men who practice homosexual sex. From an aggressor's perspective, he forces a man into sex, but the "victim's" resistance over time has weakened. With a weakened resistance, the victim fights back hard enough to avoid the label *punk*, but not hard

enough to prevent the sex act. That interaction between an offensive aggressor and a somewhat defensive victim elicits the cultural explanation that "you
can't rape the willing." Willingness to be raped is also exhibited, inmates
said, by a man's decision to remain in the general population, even though he
could request protective custody. Despite an inmate's cultural willingness to
be raped, inmate culture now requires rape retaliation. When we asked "will
friends retaliate?" an "ideal" cultural response is "yes." A response based on
actual behavior, however, is "no."

Retaliation accompanied by companions may be "culturally" dangerous for
victims' supporters. Victimization reveals mental and physical weakness. In
prison culture, weakness can be contagious and spread to otherwise nonweak
inmates who are publicly supportive of weak inmates. Too much support for
a sexual assault victim connotes supporters' weakness.

> Yeah, it depends on what the guy raped does, if he accepts it, it won't be an is-
> sue but if he retaliates his friends for real will ride with him. Someone who is
> raped is still looked at OK as long as he does something, they'll go with him.
> Only if he is involved in the retaliation, friends would never retaliate for a rape
> victim without him there.

Under the wing. Being "taken under the wing" places a weak inmate "under" the protection of an older veteran inmate who "schools" him in the ways
of the prison. As a male inmate recounts, "*After I got to [prison], they brought
this kid down there. When I come here I was an 18-year-old young white kid.
The older guys took me under their wing and schooled me.*" Although there
is no guarantee that "under-the-wing" relationships won't take a coercive
turn, protectors commonly said that a young inmate's fear reminded them of
their own anxiety and fear upon entering prison, causing them to reach out to
offer protection.

> They gave this kid [youngster new in prison] forever. The kid looked like he was
> 14 years old, was about 5'5", 120 pounds soaking wet, short hair, no facial hair,
> kid couldn't read or write. I took him up under my wing and tried to school him
> and told him this is what you got to do. Always talk back if you get pressed,
> fight, stab, kill, tell them "you have my word"—this means I'm protecting you.

Gang/group affiliation. The cultural logic for gang protection is paradoxi-
cal. Gang affiliation affords members the support of the gang group, but the
support comes only if members demonstrate personal strength and are well
liked; gang members need companions who will back them up. If a gang
member gets raped he clearly demonstrates weakness and doesn't deserve
gang-group support. Personal strength extends to owing debts. If a gang
member incurs debts, he should be strong enough to handle payment of the

debts on his own. If an indebted gang member fails to pay debts, he must be strong enough to cope with the consequences on his own. The paradox is that gang members must be strong, but strong men don't get raped or get into debt they can't handle. Strong men don't need gang-group protection. Our data include no examples of personal rape retaliation and retaliation by gang groups or groups of non-gang-affiliated inmates. The single-most common exception, inmates said, is affiliation with the Black Muslims. Inmates say if you fight one you fight them all.

> Some dudes are so weak to the point that the gangs don't even embrace them. They can be in the same gang but they're weak. A gang is based on strength, he can be a member if he got in on the street with a gun, here you got your hands. He's a weakback, not a fighter. He would be a target for rape or extortion or anything. It's not a safety protection. The only group that would protect even a gay or weak dude is the Muslims. They don't care what's wrong with their brother, you better not do nothing to them. They deep, there's repercussions behind that. . . . Your strength is important, not your gang membership.

Family/friends. The only instance when an injured party may seek assistance, and actually receive it, comes if he has relatives inside or "tight" street friends. But as inmates say, that too "depends." As one woman described, *"Yeah, my sister's here, she's taking me under her wing, she's looking out for me. She's there for me if I need somebody to talk to, just somebody who's there."* Similar protective affiliations may stem from close friendships or street ties.

> I took my codefendant under my wing when he came here, he didn't know anybody so I took him under my wing and introduced him to the people I'm familiar with and my crew so to speak and helped him get on his feet, send money to his people to send back to him if necessary.

Third-party obligations may provide a protective shield as well.

> Me and his father celled together in [other state pen] in the days. . . . He was in prison for stealing cars. I made him go to school and get his GED, I used to bribe him, bring him cigs and mags if he go to school every day and stuff. . . . I called the gang leaders out and told them, I don't care what you do to boys on the block, just stay away from little [PERSONAL NAME].

Friends, relatives, riding with a gang, and being under someone's wing are no guarantee of personal protection as a function of the relationship itself; wise inmates don't rely on others for their protection.

Violent display. One way to garner protective relationships is through a violent display. Inmates respect those who are not "weak" and who are willing to fight to protect themselves at any cost. As a male inmate explained,

"Ninety percent of the time you got to fight for yourself, then someone will help you. If you don't fight for yourself you don't get any help. If they don't deal with it themselves they lose respect." Self-protection through violence is considered an integral part of penitentiary life. As one inmate describes, regardless of the outcome, standing up for yourself is expected. *"It doesn't matter if you win or lose, you just have to stand up. As long as we see that you're willing to stand up then you're OK, even if you lose. In fact you usually do lose."* Similarly, a male inmate explains:

> One guy told me when you come on the yard you find the biggest guy on the tier and you go and sock him and people will never harass you for the rest of your time. I was 21 and small and a I'm thinking well, OK, if this is what I do, so I did it, just the point that I stood up.

Pre-Text Motivation: Rapist Motives

Rape motivations are integrally linked to risk factors and protective affiliations. The judgments inmates make concerning the rapists' motives play a strong role in deciding if an act of sexual violence is in fact a rape. Inmate culture examines motivation as a cultural explanation for a sexual act.

Commissary/canteen. Inmates say that rapists find only the easiest targets and that, because sex is so easy to get, a rapist seeks economic gain from the transaction. As one male inmate described, *"[a victim is] small, pretty, and [has] money and shows that he has money. Tennis shoes, watch, commissary, and that is your target."* Men or women who have a continuous supply of commissary goods may find themselves persistent rip-off targets from inmates who have little-to-no financial support.

Richer inmates believe canteen items are exchanged for protection, but canteen and drugs target indebted inmates for physical assault. Sexual exchange functions as part of the social and economic system of inmates. Economic indebtedness not only causes violence, but also causes a perpetrator to feel *entitled* to act out sexual violence. One woman remarked, *"When I think of rape, I think 'what does she owe?'"* Violence against the debtor doesn't absolve a debt. Victimization of a debtor is considered punishment for embarrassing the lender in public view of inmates. Embarrassment implies that the creditor is not strong enough or threatening enough to force payment of the debt. Beaten or sexually assaulted, the debtor must still repay the debt. If a creditor sexually assaults a debtor, the inmate audience decides if the assault was rape or if the assault was justifiable. If the assault was rape, the creditor is responsible. If the assault was justifiable, the debtor is responsible.

Turn-outs. Turning out an inmate can be quick and aggressive or slow and persuasive. If a turn-out target acts too slowly in turning over sex to his pursuer, his pursuer's strategy may shift from slow and persuasive to quick and aggressive. Inmates say that a "quick" turn-out looks like rape but isn't. For a variety of reasons, prison culture interprets a slow to quick turn-out as self-victimization. As one male inmate stated, *"Probably because they tried to turn out and the person wouldn't convert, so they got fed up with trying and they just took it."*

Figure 6.3 shows inmates' perceptions of whether a rape and a turn-out are similar sexual acts. Men's and women's thematic perceptions are consistent within gender but quantitatively different across gender. A much higher percent of men perceive rape and turn-out to be similar acts. *"Yes, it's the same. 'Cause they still taking advantage of you."* Or similarly, *"Yes. One used finesse, another can use strength, but the result is the same."* Among women who served less than 5 years, 16 percent classified the acts of rape and turning out as similar compared with 40 percent of men. The gender difference in dissimilarity and similarity in the acts of rape and turning out remained stable with 21 percent of women who served 5 years or more and 22 percent of women with 10 or more years incarcerated compared with 44 percent of men incarcerated for 5 or more years and 51 percent of men who served 10 or more years in prison.

Entitlement to sexual violence. "Entitled, yeah. People think that, yeah, to be a bully." Entitlement to commit a sexual assault either in fact or as a cultural option seems a persistent and especially violent theme in prison culture. Instigated by a victim's physical or mental weakness or by a victim's violation of inmate behavior protocols, more than a fringe percentage of both men

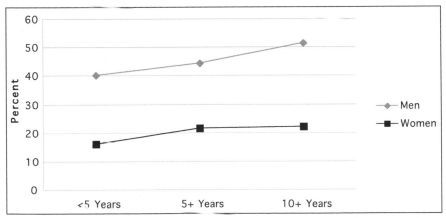

Figure 6.3.   Inmates' Perceptions of Turn-out vs. Rape by Gender and Time Served

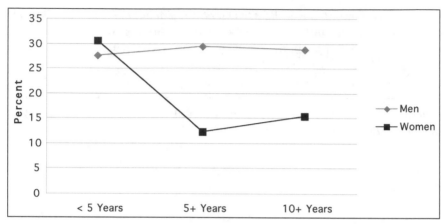

Figure 6.4.   Inmates' Perceptions of Rapists' Entitlement to Commit Sexual Assault by Gender and Time Served

and women inmates report perceptions of sexual assault as a form of entitlement. As one woman commented, *"she feels entitled to power. Because a victim owes the rapist, victim has debts, so the rapist can take what she wants."* Similarly, a male inmate explained, *"If I see someone just come into the system. I offer him a shot of coffee. I give him some shoes. If he accepts all this I would expect to get a paycheck."* A different take on entitlement involves the amount of time served; as one male inmate described, *"Dude might have a life sentence and he rapes somebody and they'll say, oh well, I don't blame him if I had that much time I'd be raping someone too."*

Figure 6.4 provides an empirical assessment of perceived sexual entitlement. Men inmates share a similar level of perception of sexual violence as an entitlement (28 to 29 percent), regardless of time served. Women inmates who served less than 5 years shared similar levels of agreement with male inmates; however, those serving 5 or 10 years or more who perceived a rapist's entitlement to commit an assault dropped to 12 and 15 percent respectively.

PRISON RAPE LORE'S INTERPRETATION OF A VIOLENT RESPONSE

Prison rape is a decision made by those who know or hear about the aggressor and victim. No matter how an institution treats a sexual assault, an aggressor, or a victim, inmate culture has its own method of determining the nature of the violence. Specific perceptions are used to determine if a victim was sexually assaulted, or if the assault was a type of "self-victimization" as defined by criteria specified in inmate culture. Inmates define a situation that is in effect self-victimization as violence occurring solely as an effect of something a victim did or didn't do. For example, "he shouldn't have used drugs."

Inmates decide a rapist's and victim's immediate and long-term social fate. Judgment rests on an interpretation of the sexual assault. Was it rape? Was an assailant *entitled* to take the sex? Was an assailant an impatient turn-out artist who pushed the victim into a quick contact with his inner homosexual, knowing he would be turned out anyway? A critical element in the judgment considers if, and if so how, a victim holds some or even all responsibility for the sexual assault. If so, the assailant has no personal responsibility in the sexual assault, freeing him of becoming a rapist.

Figure 6.5 is a concept flow illustration that captures the audience's post-text decision judging an incident of sexual violence. *Rape pre-text motives* show in rank order reasons a rapist would consider assaulting a victim. As noted earlier, gaining access to a source of commissary goods is the top reason.

Violent Response

Inmate culture interprets a violent sexual assault on the basis of how a victim responds to the assault, that is, a *violent response*. If a victim fought hard to

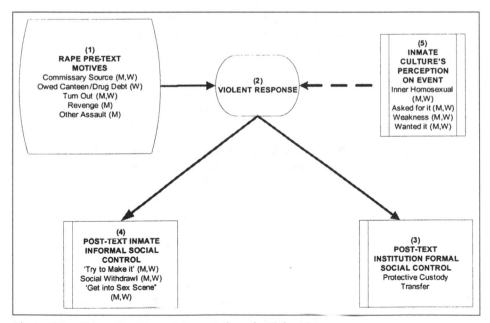

Figure 6.5.   Prison Rape Lore: Interpretation of a Violent Response

prevent being raped and was raped anyway, the audience judges the victim as a "man," and allows him to retain some, but not all of his reputation.

> If it was forced and if you fight it every time; pretty well tarnished but at least you better fight back. Best thing to do is just kill the guy if you can. Nobody going to mess with you again; beat him real bad or kill him. Never saw this happen.
> I feel like if someone is raped by force they have the right to come back and redeem themselves, like if someone pulls a knife with me or if I'm beat down and raped I have the right to come back right then and there and redeem. I won't be weak or scared if I redeem. If I was just straight talked into it there's no redeeming for that. I feel like it'd take a lot of confidence to redeem yourself after something like that happened so they'd be more respected.

Inmate Culture's Perception of the Event

There are many reasons an audience may use to explain a victim's role in an assault. The broken line connecting *perception of the event* to *violent response* indicates a degree of uncertainty about an audience's reaction to a victim's violent response. Even though a victim may have fought hard or even retaliated against an attacker, an audience does not completely absolve a victim from causing or setting the context for the assault.

Weakness. Weak inmates' physical or mental inability to protect themselves, to some degree, justifies their victimization and eliminates an assailant's full culpability in the act. If a victim strenuously resisted a sexual or nonsexual attack, and even if a victim retaliated against an assailant, an inmate jury might acquit a victim of some culpability, and to some degree lift a shroud cast by weakness and its incumbent negative social stigma. Nevertheless, the social consequences of the *weak* label and the effects of sexual victimization will never be fully escaped.

Fighting may impress bystanders who may decide to offer the victim a modicum of social support afterward. Talking to a victim or "checking" on him constitutes social support. Fighting back or not, in the end, however, the audience still sees a weak man who in some way permitted the rape. If a man had friends, inmates say, he wouldn't have been raped.

> If a friend of mine was raped, I'd help him, but I've never seen it. I'm sure some do. The problem is that most victims don't have any friends that would [help him], that's why they were a victim in the first place.

Weak inmates don't have friends. Since a weak inmate has no friends, there's no reason to bother with him. Whether a weak inmate is or isn't raped has the same social consequences in the eyes of an inmate jury. If a physically or sexually assaulted inmate fails to make an effort at self-protection, the inmate audience turns its back toward him. Bystanders, even a victim's partners, would not risk their own safety and reputation over someone else's suffering.

The inner homosexual. Inmates may perceive victims as homosexuals who are ashamed to come out of the closet (see chapter 5 for a detailed discussion). Men who were afraid or ashamed to be homosexual on the street can come to terms with their inner homosexual behind the prison walls.

> Most common and easiest is you got people who it's already in 'em to be gay and haven't run across the right person. You pull up on them and talk to him, and put him around another homosexual to turn him out and show him how to do it, then they start shaving their face and arching their eyebrows and all that other crap, changing their voice, they want someone to bring it out of them.

Con games. A sex victim may be perceived as running a con on his assaulter. An ostensible sexual victim may allow an assailant to believe he has the upper hand when in fact the act was instigated and controlled by the perceived victim who wants an instrumental outcome. For example, a sexual victim may receive protection or monetary remuneration in exchange for sexual services.

> They put their well-being in your hands. All you got to do is sit there and keep your mouth shut and they help you, if you're weak, you will meet them half way. You feel protected and your property isn't stolen, so you'll have sex with them, it's compensation.

> He was protecting me, he knew my first year was hard and told me he'd make sure no one would bother me anymore. We were friends, he was so nice and kind, and I really thought we were just friends. Then one day he came in my cell and said, [PERSONAL NAME], I have needs and you need to satisfy them. I've given you all this stuff, protected you. I told him I'd given him stuff too, and that I thought of him like an older brother. He said I could either do it or he'd take it. So I bent over and let him do it to me . . . Now I just find my own protection. Look for the downest, baddest motherfucker.

Wanted it. Two socially constructed categories of sexual behavior, which possess culturally abstract connotations, are labeled with the verbs "to want it" and "to ask for it." The semantic connotations of both verbs possess the concept of volition as an inmate accepts a passive role in an act of sexual aggression. Both of these sexual practices are sadomasochistic behavior. The use of these terms in a sociocultural context helps explain their connotations.

A prison worldview holds that a "real" man is incapable of sexual victimization unless he "wants it." To want it means that a real man assumed a passive role and was "voluntarily raped" in the attack. A male inmate describes the meaning of voluntary rape. *"The way I see it, he raped him but the dude he must have had it in his mind before, you just can't do that to someone who don't want it."* A real man embodies attitudes about men's defensive strength and gender identity. Inmates say real men aren't weak-minded, a real man stands up and fights. If a real man allows himself to be an ostensible sexual victim, then within prison worldview the act cannot culturally be labeled rape. In prison culture rape is unacceptable and unjustifiable; however, cultural conditions affect the interpretation of violent sex acts. Whether a violent sex act is interpreted as a rape depends on a victim's post-rape behavior.

Tough, strong-minded men who stand up for themselves in other situations but accept a passive role in sex fall in this category. A weak man's passivity isn't an expression of wanting it or asking for it. A weak man cannot physically and mentally defend himself. The cultural interpretation of a weak man's sexual victimization does not culturally assign blame to the aggressor, but rather the cause of the rape was the weakness of the victim. *"I look at it if a person do get raped he wanted it or he would have said something, just like in a man and woman relationship."* A man who gives up and gives in to physical force carries a damning label forever.

> Most definitely you turned them out no matter what. You violated the rules. You have no choice but to continue what you are doing. All it takes is one time and you [victim] will be labeled the rest of your life. You will be a dick sucker.

Asked for it. The second socially constructed category of sexual behavior is labeled "asked for it." To want it and to ask for it both refer to sexual aggression directed toward an ostensible victim. The victim voluntarily places himself in a passive role and willingly becomes the target of aggression. Some inmates, we were told, enjoy being beaten up while engaging in sex. As one male inmate describes, *"They just tell them how they like it, I want you to hit on me, to squeeze my arm or my neck, hit me in the sack, hit me in the chest."* Rough sexual activity may be misinterpreted as rape by prison outsiders and correctional officers. A female inmate recounts sexual aggression as part of a "normal" pattern of sexual interaction. *"Rough sex is very common, no one is gentle in cell block. Pulling hair, biting, punching each other out, using strap-ons."*

Previous victimization. Childhood sexual abuse precludes claims of rape victimization in adulthood. A rape worldview asserts that early-life experience with sexual abuse acquaints the subject with same-sex relations and therefore he cannot be raped again. Prison worldview asserts early-life abuse experiences should have provided knowledge and foresight sufficient to prevent rape. Inmate culture holds that an inmate should be strong enough to control his or her own destiny. As one male inmate describes, *"Guys who get raped in here were [rape] victims outside; they allow themselves to get into situations; they're molested and weak."* If rape happens, it occurs only because a victim wanted it to occur.

> Hear about homos being sexually abused, when she comes in she's now in control of her sexuality. I think it could be like I remember on the street. Most homos I've encountered when they came up, someone either a family member or close friend was a homo or in the closet and has molested them or they've seen something homo between two men, starts the process of curiosity or violence.

Post-Text Institution Formal Social Control

A sexual victim's plight continues even if the assault is reported. Figure 6.5 illustrates that a rape victim or victim of another type of sexual assault ultimately finds a wide variety of negative outcomes. Once assaulted, a sexual victim is met with cultural isolation. Victims are cultural castoffs to marginal social positions. Finding alliances of any type would be highly doubtful. Two institutional responses are available: protective custody or a transfer to another institution. Both options produce a victim's quick diminishment in quality of life.

Protective custody (PC). There are prisons inside of prisons. Prisons within prisons are called administrative detention and disciplinary segregation. These are two high-security cell blocks where inmates' lifestyle privileges are stripped away and replaced by 23-hour-a-day lockdown.

Disciplinary segregation houses inmates who violated rules in the inmate code of conduct and have been processed through the institution's judicial system. Administrative detention houses inmates who violated rules but have not been processed in the prison's judicial system and those whose rule violations are still being investigated. Inmates who were raped or fear they will be raped are housed in administrative detention. Even though raped or threatened inmates didn't violate institution rules, they are subject to the same conditions as those who did.

Figure 6.6 reports inmate perceptions of PC as a safety strategy. Less than 50 percent of male inmates believe protective custody is a positive safety option. The initial perception changes little with time served (41.4 percent of those serving less than five years compared to 45 percent of those serving 10 years or more). Female inmates have a slightly different trajectory. Over 80 percent of women who have served less than five years believe PC is a safe strategy. This number decreases to 67 percent for those serving 10 years or more.

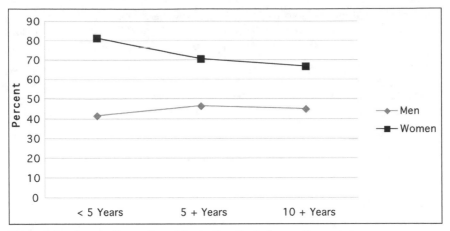

Figure 6.6.   Inmate Perception of Protective Custody as a Rape Strategy

Protective custody increases the safety of threatened and raped inmates, inmates said, but protective custody comes with a heavy price.

> Putting yourself in PC actually makes you more of a prisoner in prison than you already are. Right now, from my perspective, I can't go home and see my family but I've got a job, I work, I've got freedom. In PC, you're locked down, under constant supervision, you get a break in common area an hour a day. You just sliced your own freedom's throat.

> While they're on PC [they are safe]. The only bad about going on PC is the stigma of going into PC, whenever you come off PC then you're scared. That's like hanging a sign out saying take advantage of me. People try not to go into PC.

Transfers. Inmates can request a transfer to another prison. A transfer may help resolve the problem of an immediate threat, but inmates talk, and again a victim may be targeted. As one male inmate explained, *"Maybe temporarily [they will be safe]. If a person's real feminine looking or are just weak, they'll just be victims wherever they go."* In a similar description, an inmate reported, *"It solves the problem for that institution, but if he's being pressed for sex here he'll be pressed for sex there, you'll see his weakness and try to exploit him."* To compound that dilemma, a victim may be housed in protective custody before a transfer.

Figure 6.7 reports inmate perceptions of institutional transfers as a positive safety strategy. Men inmates report lower perceptions than women inmates as to the use of transfers. Approximately 30 percent of men and closer to 50 percent of women perceived transfers as a safe strategy for rape protection. Little change was noted in inmate perception across time served.

Post-Text Inmate Informal Social Control

Rape destroys inmates' reputation and increases their vulnerability. Informal social control lets inmates control their own safety. Despite obvious risks, three options are available for victims if they choose to remain silent: social withdrawal; making it as best they can; and moving into the sex scene.

Social withdrawal. Staying on the compound may show resilience and strength but nevertheless carry negative stigma and consequences. Victims may withdraw from compound social life, preferring to avoid unnecessary social contact, which ironically may publicly support the contention that a victim wasn't raped. As a male inmate describes, *"They tend to draw away from them; say 'they brought it on themselves; if they weren't weak it wouldn't have happened; say they are a turn-out, homosexual anyway so it doesn't matter.'"* Victims may remain in their cell or close to it, take "sink" baths, thus avoiding a shower area, and eat commissary goods instead of venturing to a dining hall. Social withdrawal may seem like a reasonable option; however, unless an inmate chose a solitary lifestyle and exhibited mental and physical strength to support such a social decision, withdrawal can increase a victim's risk of physical, sexual, and economic victimization.

> Most people try to stay away from them, they are definitely marked, cause most of the time people question whether or not they were really raped. They worry that they would try to entrap anyone else who would try to be nice to them. A

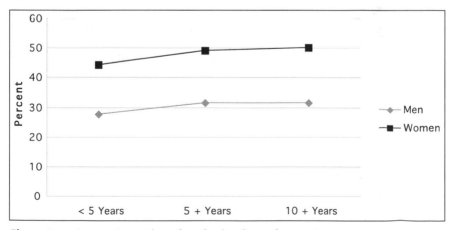

Figure 6.7. Inmate Perception of Institutional Transfer as a Rape Strategy

lot of times they're labeled mental. One instance where a snitch was accused of raping this one girl and they're both just bad news. You don't even want them sitting at your table, you don't want to know and you don't want to be drawn into the drama.

Making it as best as they can. Victims' best options, inmates say, are to *learn to accept sexual assault and move on as best they can* or *move into the sex scene.* Staying on the compound shows resilience and strength, and may eventually lead to a normal social life, but there may be bumps and bruises along the way as victims are "tested" for weakness. As one male described, *"No, you're not safe anywhere here, you cause yourself a problem, you're going to get it. Yeah but it sucks, because you're segregated in PC. Take a shower [if you've been raped] and try to cope with it."*

Moving into the sex scene. The alternative path moves victims into the sex scene. By analogy, this option hides a tree in a forest. The audience, no matter what victims did, will believe to some degree that victims contributed to their own victimization. As one male inmate describes, *"They would be a punk; that is something you can't do nothing about, once you are raped you are raped. They don't care if you fight or not. They look at it as he let that dude fuck him basically."* At this point, a public display showing that victims accept their inner homosexual and have come to terms with their sexual identity is a fairly safe option if victims can find social protection.

Sexual victimization may lead an inmate into full participation in gay subculture. This self-report highlights the cultural interpretation of his sexual victimization.[2] This narrative reveals the complex dynamic of a sexual assault and the mixed emotions and interpretations of its victim. The narrative expresses the victim's characterization of the rapist. The victim said his rape was not "aggressive" and that his rapist made him "feel comfortable." Here can be found the conceptual gray area between prison rape and prison sex as interpreted within prison worldview. In the eyes of an inmate jury, a nonaggressive sexual act, wherein a victim reported that he felt comfortable, would not be judged by an inmate jury as rape.

It was after the riot. My experience with the rape came when we came off the yard, and they put me in a cell with ten inmates who were naked. They left us in there for 24 hours with no clothing. They came and after about seven days with being in a cell with ten guys they moved everyone out and left two inmates in a cell with one bed.

I was in there with a big older dude and he was trying to explain to me that he wanted to have sex with me. I told him I wasn't feeling it and he came at me and tried to choke me, put his hands around my neck. I got him off of me and we started wrestling. I started punching him and we fought until we couldn't fight anymore. He called me [PERSONAL NAME], and said [PERSONAL NAME]

I'm not going to hurt you, over and over again. I was so tired, I was just like "fuck, OK." He went over to a little corner of the cell and got a piece of soap and washed hisself and me off. He inserted his penis in my butt; he was so gentle, he didn't aggressively take me. He was older and knew what he was doing. After he got finished he sat down and talked to me and stuff like that. I was so angry and couldn't do nothing about it; emotionally it really messed me up. It's still a rape, there's nothing I can do about it. When I got out in general population I was turned out. There wasn't no beating, he choked me at first to get me, but after I submitted the rape itself wasn't aggressive he didn't continue to choke me while penetrating or nothing like that, he made me feel comfortable.

PRISON RAPE LORE'S INTERPRETATION
OF A NONVIOLENT RESPONSE

If victims choose a nonviolent response to sexual victimization, inmate culture's interpretation of victims' behavior is clear. Figures 6.5 and 6.8 are identical, except for the victims' response. Figure 6.8 shows a nonviolent response. Based on a passive response, the link between inmate culture and a nonviolent response is no longer open to interpretation.

Figure 6.8 shows that inmate culture judges unambiguously victims' direct contribution to their own sexual assault. We wish to reinforce the central idea

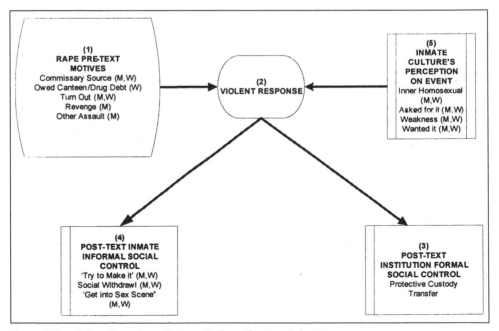

Figure 6.8.   Prison Rape Lore: Interpretation of a Nonviolent Response

of our research, that is, we have analyzed prison rape lore, not real-life responses to sexual aggression. Inmate culture doesn't find that reporting an aggressor isn't a prudent option. However, not reporting sexual assault does not necessarily imply that in real life all victims socially withdraw, accept their fate, or move into the sex scene. This also does *not* mean that all victims perceive protective custody and transfer as a negative option. It does mean that inmate culture via prison rape lore favors some options over others. *Inmates' actual behavior requires analysis of data other than prison rape lore.*

NOTES

1. This point becomes explicit when inmates differentiate a turn-out vs. a rape and coercive vs. consensual sex.

2. The term *rationalization* was avoided for a specific reason. The victim's characterization of the rape and rapist, and his response to them, is expressed uniformly throughout interview narratives. One might interpret uniform similarity as a set of rationalizations, but when inmates' self-reports are highly structured and uniform in content, independent of prison and geographic location, a strong argument can be made for cultural patterns rather than idiosyncratic interpretation.

Chapter Seven

Safe Zones

They can't really protect you in here from rape. They got their hands full. When you got 64 guys in one dorm and we're all moving around, one's in the shower, one's in the bathroom, one's talking to the free man, you know, by the time he'd know it's [rape] done. They do a good job at it, but there's always times they not around certain spots if someone's determined to do something like that.

CULTURAL FORMS OF SELF-PROTECTION

Inmates share a live-and-let-live attitude to prison social life. Social distance between inmates and staff creates social space. Operating in that social space are social arrangements that afford inmates safety. These are called safe zones; they are ways in which inmates take protection and safety into their own hands.

Some inmates deliberately create safe zones through self-protection. These safe zones are solitude; closeness to staff; violence; and physical strength. Other safe zones emerge from organic social forms that would be seen even without a potential for rape (religious groups, partnerships, families, gangs). Finally, some safe zones are created by establishing same-sex domestic relationships. However, these relationships can easily result in domestic violence.

Self-Protection

Personal safety lies squarely in the hands of inmates. Inmates aren't naive enough to believe that staff supervision and cameras in public spaces can prevent violence. They know that no matter how hard a prison administration works to keep them safe, safety procedures cannot keep them safe every-where at all times.

Inmates know that most of the time they will be safe if they follow the unwritten rules of inmate social life. Violence is instigated by a victim who has debts, insults someone in public, or congregates around others known for violent behavior. If an inmate doesn't violate rules of interpersonal protocol, stays away from gambling, drugs, and others' lovers, his chances of staying safe are optimistic. However, being hopeful that they'll be safe isn't enough. Personal preemptive safety precautions include avoidance, closeness to staff, and creating an aggressive posture, or a muscled physique.

Social isolation: Avoiding the sex scene. Inmate culture places blame on victims who do not actively avoid involvement in risky behavior. Inmates who choose involvement in prison sexual behavior are viewed as deserving of the collateral consequences they may incur. Trouble can be avoided if inmates do not put themselves in risky situations.

> Just don't get involved in the conversation. They have what they call games. They call them come-on games. They might grab the guy on the butt or say something sexual. You throw something at them to see how they react. Don't play the homosexual games, once it starts it gets out of hand. If a person is not like that then a fight will erupt. Main thing is how you carry yourself. If I go up to a man and tell him I'm gay, the next thing you know he's going to want me to do stuff for him, as long as I don't tell him, they'll leave me alone. If you feel they are trying to get you just stay away from that person.

Sexual involvement can lead to bitter jealousy, squabbles and fights, and their consequences—rejection and social isolation. Inmates report that a "just say no" outlook provides an accessible respite from many forms of violent behavior.

> Tell them that you don't mess around, and that you're not interested in it. If you isolate and do what you have to do for yourself, stay out of the way, you won't be involved. It's easy to stay to yourself. Read books, don't bother anybody, but I don't go out in the day room and socialize, I'm just doing my time and getting out. I see a lot of that.

Avoidance. Doing your own time, or keeping to yourself is a powerful protective charm for many inmates.

> Stay to yourself. Get you a book, get under your radio, get off into your own world. Here half the people I see stand to theirself. They [predators] pay that person respect, he don't want to be bothered.

Taking extra safety precautions through avoidance of risky behavior in settings that have a potential for violence provides a reliable safety buffer. Inmate examples include showering while wearing underwear or other clothing, or choosing to shower at times when others are unlikely to enter.

> We take showers with boxer shorts on. . . . If you see a guy naked in the shower you leave. Happened to me this morning some guy had his off and I waited for him to finish and went up on in there. There's a reason he didn't have his boxers in there, I don't know what he was doing, maybe no one was in there, and he wanted to be totally clean. If I walked up in there while he was naked I would have been telegraphing then.

Closeness to staff. New inmates move physically close to staff and cultivate relationships to encourage protection.

> To prevent being raped, some inmates get associated with staff early on, hang out in the chapels and officers lounges, volunteer for duties that will put them in contact with staff during the day, gardening and yard.

Staff relationships can be beneficial, but in prison, something good comes with a cost. Closeness to staff can set up an inmate as a snitch and weaken his ties to peers as they wonder why he spends so much time talking to "the man." *"Reporting to officials is another way to handle it, that's a safer way but in the long run it'll make you do hard time, the snitch label is hard to get rid of."*

Narratives report too that, despite the efforts of inmates to get close, some line staff avoid inmate relationships. As one inmate reported, *"Staff don't care—they make $10 an hour."* Inmates say many staff *"do their eight and go home."* As one woman described, *"Staff are usually in the cottages playing skip-bo or dominos or watching the game."*

Aggressive postures. "Victim [of violence] is a pussy; couldn't take care of himself. Lot of people who can look into someone's eyes and tell if someone's afraid. I don't look into people's eyes. I make up for it by trying to act like someone big." Inmates insist that an optimum form of safety requires skilled self-protection. Some do this with violence or the image of being violent. Narratives report that new inmates, especially whites, are "tested" soon after entering the compound. The excerpts below present examples of new inmates being tested. The context shows that a correctional officer watches but doesn't intervene. Allowing the situation to continue indicates the inmate's strength.

> Imagine a guy coming to penitentiary. The first time, child molester, or middle-age guys. They look at this place and say, where am I? They shrivel up and they jump when somebody says Boo. You don't have what it takes to be here. Everybody should come to maximum penitentiary first no matter what crime it is. Max

prison will make men change; smack a dude in the mouth; make him stand up
at chow; or make him wash your dirty draws because you think you're a piece
of shit. January '99 came into [UNIT NAME]. First dude said something I
smacked him in the mouth and got beat up. First time I put a shank in somebody,
dudes say, wow, he's bad. Word and respect are only things you have in here.

When I first took a shower here, three black guys surrounded me. One had a
broom; he told me "what you going to do, white boy"? There's an officer standing right there just watching it. I was scared but I kept making eye contact, said
I'm not going to swing first. I have no clue what to do, especially since the officer is right there, I just didn't back down.

Physical strength. A bodybuilder's physique may offer protection. Open
display of size and strength sends a powerful message. Many inmates work
to enhance their strength and ability as a protective facade against would-be
predators. Predators prefer an easy target and may be less likely to put in the
time and effort if they are unsure of the outcome. As one male explained,
"Youngsters are strong; after about 190 pounds rape gets very hard to do."
Physique is an important tool for many inmates, including homosexuals. As
one inmate reports, *"Back in the day, young victims were targets of sexual aggression, but now the game has changed. You got big muscle-bound dudes
wearing panties. Who is going to tell this big 6'5" guy he's not gay?"*

SOCIAL GROUP PROTECTION

What does the fag give a straight in return for protection? Sometimes there's just
cool guys in here [straights] that don't like to see people get taken advantage of,
it just felt like I wanted to, don't need nothing in return.

Prison life embodies social interactions. The formation of social groups or-
ganizes social interactions and creates inmate social structure.[1] Inmates on the
margin of inmate culture have few options to connect to inmates in groups.
Such a connection requires a link between them and the group. The most
common mechanism necessary to create a safe zone requires social ties to
partners. A new inmate needs a single social tie to slide into the mainstream
social culture. Social jostling symbolizes shifts in social ties. An affiliation
with other inmates or inmate groups happens in a variety of ways, including
sex. Partners may be crime partners, former cell mates, former street companions, and relatives—cousins and siblings or parents. If a young inmate can
quickly establish social affiliations, others do not perceive him to be weak.
Thus, his vulnerability decreases. *"There's no safe zone if a guy's got no part-*

ners. In a high-security prison if a guy wants you, you gonna be had. Max joint dudes [when they] first come in they look for someone they know. If they don't, they in trouble."

Recidivists have ready-made social networks upon reentry. As one inmate describes, *"Guy comes in and goes to reception. That's where they link up with other groups. He knows where he fits if he's a repeat offender."* New inmates are less likely to form immediate social ties upon arrival. The next excerpt illustrates that an absence of social relationships increases an inmate's risk of sexual violence. *"Certain things can make a guy focus on you. Not having, if people recognize that you're by yourself certain individuals will start targeting you to be their bitch. Being alone."*

Generally, physical safety cannot be guaranteed on a prison compound, but the acquisition of companions can afford inmates a sense of safety. Overall, an individual's safety depends on personal network size. However, other factors influence the potential effect network size has on safety. Direct social ties to groups, such as joining a religious group, may provide rape protection, but protection depends on the nature of the group and on the reputation of an inmate. Partnerships signal an inmate's sociability and strength, but no one wants to affiliate with a weak inmate.

[Rape is] trying to make a person do something they normally wouldn't do, mentally, physically, whatever. If he's not gay but is weak-minded he will go for anything to be welcomed into the utopia in [THIS PRISON]. Weak-minded guy will be gay or do sexual favors if they don't have extra money or commissary. [They'll do] anything so they'll be liked by a dude who's liked by a lot of dudes, but it don't ever really work like that. They're still seen as weak.

As this quotation illustrates, inmates' subjective perception of others' strength or weakness influences the nature of inmate social relationships. A culturally determined level of weakness and strength has direct effects on inmates' reputation. Social reputation influences social network formation, which in turn increases or decreases the risk of sexual violence.

Schooling. Coming under someone's wing puts a weak inmate "under" the protection of an older veteran inmate who "schools" them in the ways of the prison. A protector does not necessarily ask a young inmate to repay his protection debt with sex, commissary, cash, or stamps. Protectors said that a young inmate's fear reminds them of their own anxiety and fear upon entering prison, so they reach out to offer protection.

I'll give you an example of how [safe zones] works. After I got to [prison], they brought this kid down there. When I come here I was an 18-year-old young white kid. The older guys took me under their wing and schooled me.

Religious group affiliation. Religious group affiliation has a range of functions. The following excerpt shows that, in some sense, a tough public image and religious group membership are mutually exclusive.

> Some dudes put up that "I'm tough image," some guys go to religion, got the Muslims, the Christians, and there's a lot of them, been in the system a long time, not going to let nothing happen to another Christian.

Inmates may interpret religious affiliation as either a hustle for protection and easy access to the chapel or, more likely in women's than men's prisons, a true emergence of religious spirituality. Chapels are commonly cited places where homosexual relationships occur. Chapels have little supervision, thus easy access to sexual relations. What's more, inmates said, staff can't prevent inmates from attending chapel services.

> Safe haven for all of the sex offenders, convicted sex offenders. They flock to the chapel and religious services. A lot of sexual stuff takes place in the chapel, it's one of the foremost meeting places for sex, it's less patrolled by officers cause there's less violent offenders there. Not very many officers up there.

Interview data indicated that in order to publicly demonstrate a true religious calling, inmates must attend all services and Bible study groups, behave in religiously appropriate ways (accepting dietary restrictions), carry a Bible, and wear religious clothing even outside of public view. The devout inmate will behave this way over many years. Religious protection may extend to other inmates. As one woman describes, *"if you have a strong Christian, inmates will modify their behavior around that person, if you have several, the whole area will be less aggressive."*

No one confronts an inmate's religious hustle, inmates said, but these inmates acquire a hustler's reputation. They are now "fakers."

> A lot of people coming through the gate with the holy Bible in their hand thinking that's going to stop it, within a week you find out they're not Christians and they're not going to church they're using that to duck and they're going to flock on them. If you come in here and you're a religious person they'll leave you alone.

The misrepresentation of a religious life may be transparent to predators.

> Well, I heard a lot of times that most of them using the religion for protection from the rest of the guys. The predator can just about see through it, see who's really down with Christian life or using that Bible to protect them. If they are real Christians they are not bothered period, religion gets respect from them all.

A religious group may be a safe zone if the group has earned respect—
"true" Christians, for instance, and has membership sufficient to impose their
power. Religion may provide a spiritual foundation.

> If they see that you are going to church they will give you that respect, they will
> treat you with respect. They'll test you, ask you something about the Bible. You
> got some running with Bibles and still in homosexual activity. But they got old-
> school convicts that can spot a faker a mile away, so you got to be careful. Try-
> ing to remain strong and not succumb to gay behavior is a challenge. Some in-
> mates use spirituality to strengthen them.

Gays and weak men in religious groups won't be openly bullied, mocked,
or picked on. Respect comes to inmates deemed religious. *"The only group
that would protect even a gay or weak dude is the Muslims. They don't care
what's wrong with their brother, you better not do nothing to them. They deep;
there's repercussions behind that. You have white and black Muslims; they
was behind the riots [at some prison]."* For some inmates, religion affords a
protective sanctuary from the elements of prison life.

> Religion helps for anything if you have any type of problems. Like a gang mem-
> ber wants to get out of a gang, if you choose religion they don't mess with you,
> I guess religion is the powerfullest thing in the pen if you walk the walk.

Gangs. Prison gangs, like religious groups, afford a modicum of protection. However, protection depends on the behavior of the person seeking it.
Owing debts would not likely motivate gang or religious group companions
to risk their safety and "freedom" inside for someone's self-created problems.
Interview data show that religious group affiliation, particularly membership
in the Black Muslims, affords stronger protection than gangs. Inmates "ride"
in a gang, inmates said, or are protected "under a gang umbrella." *"He'll say
that dude there belongs to the Crips or the Folks or they'll even say well the
Aryan Nation is protecting him for financial reasons. They ain't messing with
him, but they protect him anyway."* Protection under a gang's umbrella, inmates said, often leads to unfortunate consequences for naïve inmates who
seek to or are drawn into gang affiliation in the hope of gaining protection.
Finding safety under a gang's umbrella depends on how well other members
like an inmate, how he "carries himself," and his fighting ability.

> A lot of gang members tend to put umbrellas on homosexuals and friends; same
> if on the street and I knew you, and because I know you if you had a problem
> and knew me, nothing could happen because you knew me. You'd tell me and
> I'd take care of it. They do that in here.

Assessing the benefits of gang affiliation can be deceptive. Group affiliation also brings exposure to sexual and economic risks. A weak inmate may look like he's riding, while in actuality he's providing sexual services for other members in return, or gang members are exploiting him for his commissary, cigarettes, soup, or money he receives from his family. *"White boy may be with Bloods today, and Bloods get tired of him and sell to Hispanics for $75. Boy is ripped off because he isn't being provided with any commissary: 'he paying his own commissary'"*

FAMILY, FRIENDS, AND LOVERS: SOCIAL AND INTIMATE RELATIONS

The social structure of inmate society is composed of a complex set of interlocking social relations. Above we described safe zones, which include group-level voluntary social affiliations and personal modes of protection. Inmates who create personal safe zones are not prevented from other types of relations. An inmate may be well schooled and rely on his fighting ability to stay safe.

There are social ties whose function is emotional attachment. We call these attachments *affective ties*. Affective ties extend beyond friendships and may function as a safe zone. These ties apply to family members and lovers. Women inmates are well known in the research literature for forming pseudofamilies. Our data show men form pseudofamilies as well, although they are less socially expansive than women's. In a men's prison a family may include actual biological relatives; we heard cases of cousins in the same prison and a son who shared a cell with his father. Fictive kin ties create domestic units. Domestic units illustrate that an inmate's gender and his or her sociosexual role are independent. In a men's prison a domestic unit might include a male-husband, male wife, and male son. In a women's prison a domestic unit might include a female sister and a female brother. In the next section we discuss social ties, friends, and lovers.

Friends and Family

There are a variety of reasons for establishing friendship ties. Close friendships may be labeled with kinship terms. Sex and protection may be associated with such ties. Kinship terms may initially create an emotional tie, but fictive kinship terms provide no guarantee of prevention against sexual aggression.

Pollock's (2002b) study illustrates the use of women's kin terms to create inmate pseudofamilies. Our data show that women's pseudofamilies have social "breadth" and "depth." A "daughter" may have a "brother." They are the focal points for kin terms. Social breadth comes with expansion on generational levels. The daughter and brother have a "mom" or a "mom" and a "dad."

Mom and dad may have brothers and sisters who expand the breadth of kin ties to their sons and daughters. Now, the daughter and her brother have cousins. Social depth is achieved when including multiple generations (grandparents). Some inmates said that sexual relations usually don't occur between close relatives, such as mother and daughter; however, the same inmate had examples of sex between cousins and an example of fictive family incest.

Our prison rape research identified men's use of kinship terminology to create fictive kin groups, such as daddies and boys. These fictive kin ties are sociosexual roles within prison culture (Fleisher, 1989). When these social roles join, they always include sex. To date, research has overlooked the socioemotional and protective functions of male fictive family formation.

> [Street] women leave when men come to the institutions and get locked up. The man caused problems to make her leave so when he comes to the joint, the women leave, and here's the homo coming in for [his] companionship. Homo is his mother, wife, queen, his everything, and he is to her too. Dude is the father, big brother, and best friend to the girl.

Figure 7.1 shows usage data on kin terminology. Women report high rates of fictive families, with numbers fluctuating from 95 to 97 percent over time served. Men report increased familial knowledge, increasing from 34 percent of inmates with less than 5 years incarcerated to 54 percent for those serving 10 or more years in prison.

Domestic relations. Men's family relations include daddy/boy or daddy/son, and husband/homosexual (wife). A boy and a son are under daddy's wing. This arrangement has economic implications. Man/boy or daddy/boy relationships

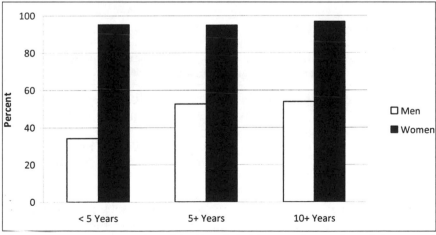

Figure 7.1.   Inmate Perception of the Use of Kinship Terms by Gender and Time Served

are not necessarily sexual, although personal ties can lead to sex. A daddy schools his boy and son in the ways of prison life and protects them. A daddy's protection requires compensation in the form of goods sent by a boy's or son's street family. The next excerpts show that the speaker refers to the daddy/son relation as a hustle; the daddy and son have a sexual relationship; and the daddy controls all property. Sometimes, the terms *son* and *boy* are synonyms; *boy* and *kid* are often interchangeable. Customarily, however, a son and his daddy have a nonsexual relation. This arrangement has an analogue in the mother/daughter relation in women's prison.

> Family units do exist here. An older guy befriends a younger guy, it's called a son; he'll be a guy that doesn't have much, is easily influenced. It's not a good title to have in the pen for someone to call you son. Don't have a mom though. [You] wouldn't hear the guy say "that's my dad."

> You don't have sex with your son, extort money though. The young guy is like a gopher and the older guy just uses him. Sometimes it's sexual; then you'd hear the older dude say "my boy." Majority of time it's not sex; but an older guy wouldn't call a kid his son.

> No one will hurt you if you're someone's son, respecting another man's hand, you got to respect what he's doing. It's [having a boy] another man's hustle. Women [queens] find weaker inmates and protect them; some mothers [queen playing mother to a boy] go for that. They'll [boy's family] send stuff from the outside to keep their son safe.

The next excerpt expands a daddy/son relation. The inmate daddy takes a wife (termed *fag*) and additional sons who are then brothers.

> Lot of guys have family that is dead or disowned him, so they get involved in a group and have [fictive] brothers and will have a fag and say this is my broad; the fag is the sister to his brothers. Most guys in here have compassion to kids and young people. There is no sex [among] brothers.

> A man and punk [fag] can adopt a son; he may be an older guy or younger guy. It's not a good title to have in the pen for someone to call you son. A man can turn him out [or adopt him] and have more sons and more wives depending on the initial situation. Some women can't stand their men going out with women. Some punks will allow their man to have other relationships but some won't.

Family members are *"less likely to be raped [by others], [be]cause they got a little family now, others will leave them alone."* Such ties don't, however, preclude intrafamily violence or, in extreme cases, intrafamily rape. As one man explains, *"Daddy keeps the kid around to just use them, whether for sex or extortion."*

A daddy-wife relationship permits sex. They are known to "set up house." Some men use the term *family*, some don't. Male domestic relations have complex internal dynamics; if serious family violence occurs, it would most likely be in a daddy/wife relation. A man's wife is often referred to as his fag, or his ho' or bitch. *"Daddy will call his wife my 'ho' or my 'mommie.' I've seen some pretty tough fellas, football players and wrestlers, have ho's and they [females] are [now] safe bitches."* Safety, mutual protection, support, and companionship are common functions of a daddy-wife relationship.

> A fag do what the women do; they like a stay-at-home mom. She take care of the cell, make a guy's food for him. Carry drugs and shanks if their dudes are in the business, like a mule in a sense, will do whatever to keep their man out of the hole. I've seen the homo stab someone just to go to the hole to be with their man, very loyal.

Husband-wife relations may evolve into a long-term relationship and last many years. In the initial dating stages, violence would be unlikely. But as a couple stays together longer, violence may become more likely as their emotional closeness transforms into an emotional entanglement of jealousy and anger. The longer a couple remains together the more likely a man considers his wife his "property."

> I seen a bunch of it; couple having they problems like you would [on the street]. It's strange, weird stuff. You got a homosexual who acts, looks, and talks like a female; he's [husband] calling her baby this and baby that and [she's] jealous about him talking to another female. They [husband] get the shit; she might throw a pot at him or something. I've seen weird domestic fighting. I seen a stabbing before. They [husband and wife] really fall in love. It's a heck of a thing.

Domestic violence. Fictive kinship denotes inmates involved in domestic relationships. Domestic relationships[2] are short and long term. Short-term unions usually don't end in violence or rape. Relationships begin with a "feeling out" period, inmates said. During this time, inmates decide if they want a long-term relationship. A breakup may occur within 30 or 60 days with no consequences. Such relations are considered short dating episodes like those on the street. Long-term relationships—a year or more—can turn sour. When they do, domestic violence or even rape can erupt. Sexual violence may be a cultural possibility, albeit rare, said inmates.

Figure 7.2 illustrates a comparison of inmates' perceived estimates of domestic violence among dating inmates. These data show that 96 percent of women inmates reported the process of inmate dating. Among those women, 80 percent report violence in dating relationships. Men inmates reported that 67 percent date. Among those men, 64 percent report date violence.

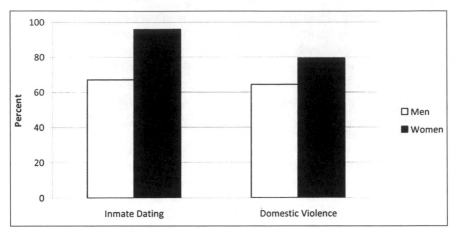

Figure 7.2.   Domestic Violence among Dating Inmates

Safe zones represent a cultural response to threats of dangerousness. Analysis reveals a variety of individual and group safety strategies. However, inmates are cognizant that safe zones do not guarantee protection.

Prisons are places of ultimate self-interest. It may sound ironic, but for an innumerable number of inmates, correctional institutions provide the ultimate self-interest—peace, comfort, and a regular lifestyle. The self-interest inmates seek we take for granted. It would be naive to think that prisons do not provide any type of social, emotional, material, and medical support for men and women whose lives were mired in drugs, abuse, mental illness, and loneliness.

Inmates seek peace and safety in simple things: a meal served three times a day; warm living quarters in the winter; dental care to repair teeth rotted by cavities and lost through violence and drug use; a social life absent of the hassles and dangers of street hustles.

Before you say it's ridiculous to think inmates find safety in prison, first ask yourself a few questions about your own early life. Were you always hungry? Were you warm in winter? Were your abusive parents alcoholics or drug addicts? Was your mother beaten by your father or stepfather or boyfriend in a drunken rage while you watched, hiding under a bed? Were you beaten with objects, punched with fists, and kicked by the people who were supposed to care for and love you? And as if those things aren't bad enough, were you sexually molested from early childhood into adolescence? Women readers, were you pregnant before you were a teenager? Ask yourself, how would such conditions shape your needs and desires for some type of ultimate comfort that might even for a moment relieve the pain buried inside your chest and the chaotic jumble of violent, twisted, destructive thoughts racing like a tornado and bouncing without end through your mind?

Inmates we interviewed provided graphic depictions of the pain of street fights and beatings; hangover after hangover; insecure places to sleep; filthy clothing; handcuffs binding wrists all too tightly and all too often; endless hours of interrogation; jail holding tanks where the stomach-churning odor of vomit falls out of the mouths of drunks and drug addicts; and months or years of waiting to go to trial, then more months waiting to be transferred to a prison. Eventually that chaos and pain ends upon arrival at the sally port of the prison they will inhabit for years, a familiar place providing peace, clean living quarters, food three times a day, clean clothing, medical help, and maybe a few friends with whom to stroll around the yard on sunny days. There's one way to understand inmates' life in prison. Meet Mary.

Mary

For many inmates, prison is an inevitable part of social life. Incarcerated women typically have a long history of past abuse before they ever set foot behind prison walls. Adults we meet in prison today grew up with mothers and fathers who also served time, with drug addiction and alcoholism running rampant through their family tree. When we met Mary, she was serving eight years for a drug conviction with a history of past convictions for prostitution, DWI, and theft. Mary lost four children to a tragic accident 10 years prior, and her two remaining children were currently being cared for by a close family member.

Mary typifies the characteristics of a female inmate. She has a history of arrests for common female crimes, she is a mother, and she has a lengthy history of abuse.

> I was mostly molested from the age of 5 until I was 16. I got pregnant at 11 and I had my first child at 12, by my older brother. My brother and my uncle were molesting me and a couple of my first cousins on my mom's side. No drug or alcohol [abuse in the home], my mom was a social drinker. She just drank with her boyfriends.

Mary's history of abuse defined many of her interactions prior to incarceration: "*I have had homosexual relationships on the street, but it was to get dope. I was a prostitute.*" She has never been married and her children have different fathers. Additionally, Mary reports a history of depression for which she is currently receiving treatment and medication.

For many inmates, incarceration is one of the few safe points in an otherwise tumultuous life. Mary describes the family roles she has created within the prison as a way to provide positive role modeling that she never received:

> I have a little girl, she calls me mom, and she is my daughter. The girl that I was going with, she called her daddy . . . I love her like my own child. I try to keep her out of trouble. That is it. I would like to see her in the world too.

She further explains how families provide a sense of safety and protection, *"They just watch out for you and make sure nobody hurts you. You are simply not by yourself."* A prisoner's ultimate self-interest finds satisfaction in a safe zone where she isn't by herself.

NOTES

1. This usage refers to regular patterns of interactions.

2. In prison speech community, the term *partner* has a range of meanings. For example, *partner* refers to inmates who regularly walk the yard together and to crime partners and other applications. *Partner* does not include lovers. Inmates do not refer to domestic partners. Partners are distinguished from those inmates involved in amorous relations.

Chapter Eight

Sex and Prison Safety

Everything is the prison's fault. They blame their behavior and their thoughts on the prison system. A lot of men here don't have remorse, you hardly hear that someone is sorry. They don't say, "oh man, I messed up." It is hardly ever heard here.

Inmates create and sustain safe zones, but they know safe zones aren't enough to maintain a safe environment. A sensitive balance exists between safe zones and a reliance on prison management. Inmates are aware of prison management aimed at institutional safety. They also know that prisons are massive organizations, which cannot, even under optimum conditions, provide 24/7 protection to an institution housing thousands of inmates.

Sykes and Messinger (1960a) reported that inmates perceive themselves as the major stakeholder in institutional peace and order. Our data show that inmates are keenly aware that institution safety depends as much on their behavior as it does on management practices. To that end, inmates consent to participate in informal and formal systems of correctional management. We hear their consent in expressions such as *"inmates run the joint," "there are more of us than them,"* and *"we can take over the prison anytime."*

INMATES' PERCEPTIONS OF THE
MANAGEMENT OF INMATE SEXUAL BEHAVIOR

Clemmer's (1940) prisonization theory argues that group association (prison gang vs. religious group), housing (segregation vs. open dorm), and work assignment (warden's clerk vs. food-service worker) influence inmates' perception of prison violence. What inmates know and the amount they know about sexual violence varies by experiences in those and other

119

prison surroundings. Despite living in massive correctional institutions and creating safe zones, inmates participate in formal and informal systems of prison social control. Inmates perceive some prison management tactics as more effective than others.

> Sex does not affect quality of life on the compound. [Inmates] play the staff and try to sue to get money. The inmates protect the COs [correctional officers] they like. They blame others [COs] to keep the ones they like out of trouble. Black girls typically play COs for money. Staff get paranoid about this and lose trust with inmates. Officers get put on administrative leave. Most officers that get accused are black. Staff will bribe inmates, threaten them. . . . Girls claim staff raped [them] to get money from him. COs has good relationship with girls; share candy, bring gum. Someone snitches off a nice CO but girls claim some other CO did it, the one who they didn't like. Black inmates step up COs claiming rape—staff then get paranoid and distance themselves from inmates. Black officers are targets of rape scams.

Staff Verbal Messages about Sexual Behavior and Sexual Violence

Inmate response to the management of sexual violence requires a statistical and cultural interpretation. When we ask, "do correctional officers try to prevent rape?" our interpretation of affirmative and negative responses depends on our mode of analysis. We asked inmates a series of questions about prison management's ability to control prison sex and sexual violence. Figure 8.1 compares the aggregate of men and women inmates on five management issues: Hearing correctional officers talk about prison rape; reporting rape to officers; knowledge of officer-inmate sex; knowledge of officer-inmate rape; and false rape allegations. Questions investigated the interaction of staff verbal and be-

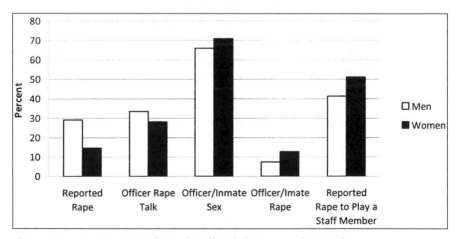

Figure 8.1. Inmate Perceptions of Staff Verbal Messages by Gender

havioral messages about inmates based on the assumption that staff behavioral and verbal conduct would influence inmates' behavioral and verbal conduct.

Rape reporting. Most inmates did not know cases of inmates reporting a rape to an officer. Only 30 percent of men and 15 percent of women reported knowledge of official rape reporting. Three common themes emerged from narrative data to account for the lack of rape reporting. Some inmates view a reported rape as an incident of snitching. To avoid the snitch label, inmates may be reluctant to discuss rape with correctional officers. As one male inmate explained, *"they're afraid of being labeled as a snitch or something like that."* Others rely on inmate protection. As one inmate describes, *"you don't do things like that, you wouldn't deal with a rape by telling an officer, you'd tell one of the dudes, we depend on each other, not an officer."*

Inmate culture prides strength. Handling a rape without official intervention allows an inmate to retain self-respect. Inmates report a low likelihood of rape reporting as a way to maintain a strong reputation. As one inmate explains, *"Nothing reported; nothing said about it. It's too embarrassing; you're admitting defeat and can't take care of yourself; you're like a little kid."* Finally, inmates may worry about the consequences of rape reporting. Some believe that officers share in the culture of inmate self-protection. A perceived lack of officer attention may also be a reason for not reporting. As one inmate reported, *"If you tell a guard, they say, you're a convict, deal with it."* Some also report a fear of being transferred to protective custody or to solitary confinement.

> Yes, I know someone who reported a rape to an officer. They reported it to the officer on the unit. They reported it to the officer on the unit and then went to a sergeant who took care of the rest of the problem, and both ended up in the hole.

Officer rape talk. If inmates hear staff talk or gossip about rape, they may be less likely to report a rape. Data show that 34 percent of men and 28 percent of women had heard correctional officers talk about prison rape. As one male inmate described, *"Yes, somebody that they don't like, if the person be raped and all that then they'll put him out there and say he was, they talk just like convicts. There ain't no secrets in prison."* Although data do not indicate the content of what inmates heard or where they heard it, verbal culture has the power to influence inmates' attitudes and beliefs.

> It's called putting you out there, they do that all the time, put it out there that you got raped. Say I cuss you out and they come back and say hey nigger, that's why you got fucked by so and so.

Officer-inmate sexual relationships. Men and women inmates reported sex with same- or opposite-sex staff as an opportunity for material gain and recreation.

A cute officer comes on, the inmate will immediately be at the desk, all up in his business and the officer will flirt back. Not all officers are fucking the inmates, but there have been several incidents where an inmate has got the officer fired and the officer sticks by the inmate and she goes home with him when she's done. It's usually black officers going with the white girls. It's inmate rumor. If the prison authorities are trying to prove it, it's really hard unless you can get the inmate to say it, but he's sending you money and giving you cigarettes. You not going to give it up. Inmate approaches the officer and the officer says "hell yeah, I'm the man, I'm the shit, all these bitches want to do it to me." In reality it's not really you, you just the only dick we have access to right now.

Sixty-six percent of men inmates and 71 percent of women inmates reported knowledge of sexual affairs between inmates and staff. Knowledge of staff-inmate sexual relationships may erode trust in staff, causing a lower likelihood of rape reporting.

Yes, I heard that the officer got fired. They investigated it; well he got suspended. She ended up copping from the hole and he never came back. They got into jack off in the closet. She had his cum to prove that.

Inmate narratives identified four main consequences of flirtatious and sexual affairs between staff and inmates. Each consequence results in decreased effectiveness of prison management practice. First, once inmates gain knowledge of a relationship between an officer and inmate, the door is opened for officer exploitation. As one woman described, *"If another inmate know they tell, they'd be jealous why you get to eat free food I want some too. You give me a chain I won't say nothing, they'll try to bribe or blackmail the person."* Similarly, a male inmate reported, *"If he's sharp enough, a dude could blackmail that officer to bring something to him. That's something I'd do."*

Second, inmates may become jealous when a staff member brings gifts to his/her inmate girl- or boyfriend. As one inmate explains, *"They talk a lot together with inmates, show favoritism. Favoritism causes problems."* Jealousy can engender open hostility between inmates and closed hostility toward the staff member. As one female inmate describes, *"They look down on the inmate, cause it wasn't them, they wanted to be in them shoes. That old whore, you're pissed off cause it wasn't you."*

Third, interview data suggest that inmates lose trust and respect for officers who violate conduct rules by engaging in illicit sex with inmates. Sexual and other types of misconduct weaken the trust between staff and inmates. As one inmate reported, *"Say about 30 percent of staff try to do the right thing but it's hard to do the right thing if others violate the rules."* The culturally prescribed "professional" social distance between staff and inmates increases, inmates reported, as trust decreases. Men inmates commented: *"I'm sure they must have rules on paper but it isn't worth a damn unless it's enforced."*

Fourth, inmates reported that honest and diligent line staff who are vested in their career drift away from "dirty" staff. Over time, inmates said, honest officers shift posts and move away from a dirty officer or officers. These post transfers, inmates said, likely result in a station with two, three, or four dirty officers as supervisors, making effective management less likely.

> I think they sort of turn on that officer. They'll talk openly about that officer, they lose trust in that officer, and they'll kid around with inmates about that officer. That officer is doomed in that prison if that goes on.

Officer-inmate rape. Inmates reported consistently low levels of knowledge of officer-inmate rape. Eight percent of men and 13 percent of women had heard about cases of officer-inmate rape. Interviews collected isolated examples of male staffers allegedly raping a male inmate.

> There was only one that I know of [rape] and that was at [OTHER STATE PRISON]. They tried to establish a relationship at first and the guy [inmate] wouldn't do it and then he [staff] tried money, and that didn't work so he went in there and raped him, while he was in the hole.

Although more female inmates reported knowledge of officer-inmate rape, most inmates had no knowledge of officers raping inmates. As one male inmate responded, *"No, staff don't rape inmates. There was a dude down here and he was sucking his [officer's] dick and he saved the sperm. That happened a couple months before I came down. I'd let a female officer rape me though."*

False rape allegations. Inmates' reports of rape, independent of staff conduct, may be forms of inmate-instigated staff manipulation. While inmates reported a consistently low level of agreement on correctional officers' sexual assault on inmates, data on false allegations of rape against staff emerge in stark contrast. Thirty-eight percent of men and 51 percent of women knew cases where false rape allegations were reported to officers. Women reported that false rape allegations may be perpetrated by women inmates who are jealous over a former male staff lover's admiration for another inmate, or jealousy caused by gifts given to some women but not others.

> A lot of [male] COs get walked because of relationships with [women] inmates, more men [staff] than women. If women has sex with a CO, the CO is getting played not the inmate. The girls tell on themselves. The girls tell another CO, the girl goes to the hole, the CO gets under investigation. Inmates initiate the relationship. Flirt with the COs. They tell a friend and the friend tells on them.

Hostility may lead to filing false rape allegations against the staff member who, an inmate believes, slighted or embarrassed her. As a female inmate described, *"They say they were raped by a staff member, they'd get locked up and do an investigation on a staff member, but it's consensual, when they don't get what they want, they tell."* Or similarly:

> Oh yeah. I've had friends I've known had sex with a guy [staff] and put it [semen] in something so he can bag it up and then he runs to the laws and claims rape. Having sex then [officers] don't like it anymore and [inmates] claim rape.

Table 8.1 examines the same five issues that influence prison culture and climate to assess differences in time served. The percentage of men and women inmates who heard officers talk openly about rape increased the longer they remained in prison. For men, the number jumped from 10 percent of those with less than five years served to 42 percent for those who served five years or more and 44 percent for those who were incarcerated for 10 or more years. Women's knowledge also increased over time; 11 percent of those serving less than five years heard officers talk about a rape compared to 20 percent of those with five or more years served and 21 percent of those with 10 or more years inside.

Both genders also report increases in hearing about inmates reporting rapes to staff. Although men and women with less than five years served reported 14 and 15 percent respectively, rape reporting increased by over 300 percent with an increase in time served. Forty-six percent of men and 48 percent of women serving five years or more knew of reported rapes. Those serving 10 or more years report further increases in rape-reporting knowledge, with 50 percent of men and 57 percent of women answering in the affirmative.

> Yes, to the lieutenant and then they'll let the unit manager know, they'll come and pull the guy out that reported it and talk to him and then would remove the rapist from the pod and take him to the hole, investigation, paperwork and highway patrol gets called.

Following the same pattern, increases in knowledge of officer-inmate sexual affairs occurred with time served. While 50 percent of men serving less than five years knew of inmate-staff sexual relationships, 80 percent of those serving 10 years or more shared that knowledge. For women, the numbers increase from 61 percent of those serving less than five years to nearly 90 percent of those serving 10 or more years.

> It is both men and women staff with inmates. I had a roommate that this officer, I had just left this unit. This officer would come and talk to my cell mate and say I love you and all that. She would take her out late at night and they would be together.

Knowledge of officer-inmate rape also increases with time served. Five percent of males with less than five years behind bars report knowledge of officer-inmate rape. This increases to 9 percent for those serving five or more

Table 8.1. Inmate Perceptions of Staff Verbal Messages by Gender and Time Served

	Men						Women					
	<5 Years		5+ Years		10+ Years		<5 Years		5+ Years		10+ Years	
	#	%	#	%	#	%	#	%	#	%	#	%
Have you heard officers talk about rape?												
No	117	90.0	116	58.3	73	55.7	70	88.6	40	80.0	23	79.3
Yes	13	10.0	83	41.7	58	44.3	9	11.4	10	20.0	6	20.7
Do you know cases of inmates reporting rape to an officer?												
No	107	85.6	105	54.1	65	50.4	59	85.5	25	52.1	12	42.9
Yes	18	14.4	89	45.9	64	49.6	10	14.5	23	47.9	16	57.1
Do you know cases of officers and inmates having sex?												
No	72	50.3	56	24.0	31	20.3	35	39.3	9	14.5	4	11.8
Yes	71	49.7	177	76.0	122	79.7	54	60.7	53	85.5	30	88.2
Do you know cases of officers raping inmates?												
No	127	94.8	181	91.0	117	88.6	75	90.4	48	82.8	26	81.3
Yes	7	5.2	18	9.0	15	11.4	8	9.6	10	17.2	6	18.8
Do inmates ever say they got raped just to play staff?												
No	99	79.8	106	52.0	67	48.2	38	52.1	25	44.6	15	48.4
Yes	25	20.2	98	48.0	72	51.8	35	47.9	31	55.4	16	51.6

years and 11 percent for those serving 10 years or more. For women, knowledge increases from 10 percent of those with less than five years served to 19
percent of those with 10 or more years served.

> It started out he was wanting to be a friend to me and it became flirtatious from
> both of us, and then I would say that we became kind of consensual, not in sex,
> but in kissing and hugging and things like that. Even though it wasn't sex, it was
> still forbidden. When it got crazy was when I tried to stop it. When I told him
> that I felt like it was a mistake and I wanted out he started threatening me. He'd
> hand me addresses to where my children were and said, "I know where they
> live," or tell me he would write me up for something I hadn't done and put me
> in segregation, and he got what he wanted by doing these things to me. I was
> scared to death of going to seg. I didn't hang around other inmates, so I really
> didn't know what prison was like. . . . They [the administration] came and talked
> to me and wanted to know if I knew anything about him and wanted to know if
> the rumors were true. I told them yes it was and so I wore a wire, I got him to
> talk and I got him removed. . . . Inmates hated me, he was a favorite, he let them
> get off with shit. They were all "You just got rid of a good one, thanks to you
> there's no telling what's going to happen."

Slight gender differences were noted with false rape allegations over time.
Male knowledge increased from 20 percent of those serving less than five
years to 52 percent of those serving 10 or more years. For women, however,
numbers increased less than 5 percent over the same time frame.

> Oh yeah, I'm sure; to transfer or move, they'll do a lot of things to try to get
> moved. They have a lover on another unit and want to get over there so they'll
> say anything. If they get off of enough units they usually wind up in the one they
> want. They file a Life Endangerment and all.

STAFF INFLUENCE ON SEXUAL CONDUCT AND
INSTITUTIONAL PRACTICES OF SOCIAL CONTROL

> I am not so sure that they specifically try to prevent rape. There is a real high
> degree of control. You are never without direct line of sight supervision. Other
> places I have been, there are anonymous kite boxes. I don't know. I don't know
> if there is a specific way they prevent rapes from happening.

Inmates perceive institutional prevention as a functional part of prison life.
They routinely report that staff take both preventative and reactive action
whenever possible. We asked inmates their perceptions of staff prevention for
both consensual sexual behavior and rape. Whether the actions taken have

any effect on inmate behavior is an area of contention. Many inmates report that there is nothing staff could do to prevent a rape or assault from occurring. Figure 8.2 examines how inmates perceive measures taken by prison administration to stop consensual and violent sexual behavior.

Officer supervision: prevention of inmate sex. Mixed agreement by gender was found for the active prevention of sexual behavior. Although most women (74 percent) reported that officers tried to prevent inmate sexual affairs, only 49 percent of men agreed. As one male described:

> They don't, not at all. The other day these guys are at [OTHER STATE PRISON], they get caught making out, they send them over here and put them in the same cell together. If you're trying to stop it, you don't put them in the same cell together, that's promoting. Officer will just walk away, won't say a word and keep walking, they're instructed to do that.

A female inmate offers a slightly different scenario:

> They separate them, like pulling a block from the wall. If it gets really bad they ship one off to another unit. It doesn't stop a lot of people, the chain keeps getting longer and longer and longer. They just sleep with more people wherever they go.

Officer supervision: prevention of rape. The majority of male (60 percent) and female (67 percent) inmates reported that officers tried to prevent rape. As one inmate explained, *"[Rape's] not even a threat no more, if it did happen the officers would stop it, the majority would. In the end, yeah. I don't think we*

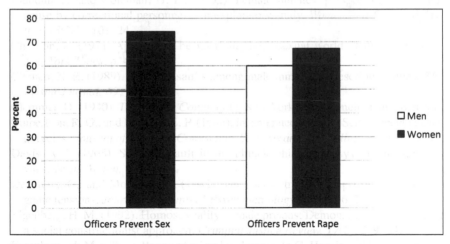

Figure 8.2. Inmate Perception of Management Response by Gender

have [officers] that would ignore it." Or similarly, *"[Administration] do take*
them [rapists] out if they catch them, they'll lock them up. The administration
will do something with a dude like that." Some inmates reported a lack of need
for active rape prevention on the compound. As one male describes, *"I don't*
think they too much worry about it happening now, nothing to prevent."

Table 8.2 reveals relatively stable perceptions of sex and rape prevention over
time served with some gender variation. Men reported subtle increases over time
in both sex and rape prevention. However, women's perception of sex prevention declined from a high of 76.8 percent (< 5 years served) to 63.3 percent (10+
years served), but women's perception of rape prevention was stable.

VISUALIZATIONS OF INMATES'
PERCEPTIONS OF KEY MANAGEMENT ISSUES

Although inmates are cognizant of preventative correctional practice, inmate
culture does not easily embrace officer action as a working preventative measure. As noted in Figure 8.3, there was agreement between the majority of male
(79 percent) and female (64 percent) inmates that "the correctional system," or
the nature of a correctional agency or institution, could not protect them from
rape. As one male inmate explained, *"[Rape] doesn't happen here. No one can*
prevent it but theyself, CO's can't watch you all day, they can't hold your hand,
if it's gonna happen it's gonna happen." Or similarly as a female inmate noted,
"No, how can they? They can't, it's like the only person that can protect a per-
son is God, have faith, they can't watch your every move."

However, many inmates did believe they could be protected inside and reported several strategies that institutions used to aid in prevention. As one female inmate described, *"A technique officers use to prevent rape [in women's*
prisons] is to put women officers with all men officers; they never have just
men; men can't do everything and go everywhere."

Clemmer's (1940) theory of supraindividual culture posits that inmates'
perceptions of management's attempts to improve institutional safety are unlikely to occur rapidly or at all, to any significant degree. Cultural attitudes,
beliefs, and perceptions change slowly. Seventy years of prison culture and
sex culture research has cited repeatedly a core array of findings about prison
culture and inmates' sexual behavior. Inmates too have reported similar beliefs and attitudes about prison sexual behavior over decades of research.
Such findings offered by both inmates and researchers support Clemmer's
theory of supraindividual culture.

Inmates' subjective impressions of prison sexual violence are embedded in
inmate culture. These impressions are transmitted from today to tomorrow to

Table 8.2. Perception of Management Response by Gender and Time Served

| | | Men | | | | | | Women | | | | | |
| | | <5 Years | | 5+ Years | | 10+ Years | | <5 Years | | 5+ Years | | 10+ Years | |
		#	%	#	%	#	%	#	%	#	%	#	%
Do officers prevent sex?	No	70	51.9	109	50.0	72	49.7	19	23.2	15	29.4	11	36.7
	Yes	65	48.1	109	50.0	73	50.3	63	76.8	36	70.6	19	63.3
Do officers prevent rape?	No	55	44.0	73	37.4	52	39.1	24	32.9	15	32.6	9	33.3
	Yes	70	56.0	122	62.6	81	60.9	49	67.1	31	67.4	18	66.7

generations of inmates. It seems that "new" information slowly enters inmates' transgenerational cultural system.

Inmates talk about past happenings as if those were happening today. Today's happenings slowly filter into and diffuse throughout inmate culture, creating a temporal continuum of knowledge. An inmate who's done 30 years does not share an equivalent body of knowledge with an inmate who's been inside 12 months. The time between "what was" and "what is" creates a time lag.

Cultural data are affected in subtle ways by a time lag. In a hypothetical example, let's consider physical innovations to prevent sexual violence. Cameras are visible. When cameras are installed in a dorm, in a flash every inmate knows. That innovation is visible, has direct effects on inmate behavior, and indisputably occurred yesterday. However, shifts in inmate culture's attitudes, values, beliefs, and norms slowly change. When we asked inmates if they knew for sure of a prison rape and the inmate responded affirmatively, we could not be absolutely certain of the point along the time lag represented by the inmate's affirmative response.

Old-schools love telling tales about the "the day before the day" when things were really bad in prison and only "real" men survived. If an inmate inside for six months hasn't seen or personally experienced sexual victimization, listening to old-schools tell tales day after day allows the new inmate to capture old-school knowledge and use it as his own. He then repeats and embellishes what he heard. Since the new inmate is a "real" man he (allegedly) watched firsthand—and exaggerated gory incidents. To be sure, he won't tell us that he really didn't see any gory incidents but instead learned "back in the day" tales from old-schools. But a "real" man wouldn't do that.

The new inmate internalizes old-schools' tales, and before long those tales are his own—his property that can be used to demonstrate his bravery and prison experience. To be most effective in social life, a new inmate reports his newly acquired tales as if they occurred in the most recent past. That process of learning culture from generation to generation is prisonization. The conveyance of similar tales from one to another generation causes generations' knowledge to overlap, so that independent of age, inmates share some part of a common body of knowledge. That intergenerational sharing is what Clemmer meant by supraindividual culture.

Figure 8.3 assesses inmates' perceptions of institution safety and rape protection among inmates over time served. Women's and men's levels of perceived agreement are similar controlling for gender and sentence length. Among men and women who have served less than five years, 35 percent of women and 30 percent of men agree that the correctional system can protect them against rape. As time served increases, so does agreement. Few

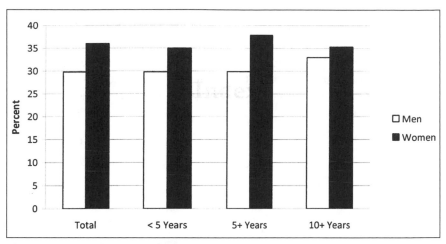

Figure 8.3. **Inmates' Perceptions of Correctional System's Ability to Protect Inmates from Rape by Gender and Time Served**

differences are seen between male and female inmates who have served less than five, five or more, or 10 or more years. A consensus, albeit low, controlling for time served and gender suggests a culturally influenced response: interpreted by Clemmer's supraindividual theory these responses suggest that, independent of correctional agencies' actual ability to protect inmates, inmate culture has low consensus of agencies' ability to protect them from rape.

Inmates create personal safe zones. They are also keenly aware that institution safety depends as much on their behavior as it does on management practices. Correctional institutions afford inmates a modicum of protection against sexual assault. Nevertheless, inmates learned in early life that adult caretakers charged with their care, safety, and protection often failed at those tasks and even became victimizers. Childhood victimization, social chaos of criminal street life, detention in juvenile facilities, and other terms of imprisonment in adult prisons taught inmates one valuable lesson: don't turn over personal protection to other people.

When inmates talk about personal protection they invoke an analogy to free-society crime prevention. In the free society, homeowners with burglar alarms didn't eliminate police protection through patrol cars, public-area cameras, good citizen rapport, and data banks on the street's high-risk criminals. Prisons have analogous protection systems, but inmates don't relinquish total control of personal protection to correctional management. They don't believe that institutional systems of social control can offer protection, night and day, month after month.

Common sense tells us inmates' balance of personal safe zones and institution safety seems rational and well reasoned. Better than anyone else, inmates know prisons are packed with violent offenders whose irrational behavior and high levels of anger led to homicide, assault, domestic violence, rape, and other heinous crime in the outside world. Inmates would be foolhardy if they put their personal safety solely in the hands of anonymous line staffers.

Epilogue

Everyone seems to know something about prison sexual violence. However, sexual violence is an act that inmates and citizens have rarely witnessed. Oddly, though, people are eager to believe what they hear in the media or read in tabloids about prison rape. Prison rape tales describe acts of such extreme violence that we wonder why anyone wants to think about, no less tell jokes about, "dropping the soap" in the shower.

Prison rape is publicly rationalized like other acts of horrific violence that exceed a rational vision of human behavior. American culture lightens the emotional load of extreme violence by diverting our eyes. We joke about prison rape, make movies about it, and pass along folktales of Boxing Betty and Purple Passion.

A "SHARED" VIEW OF PRISON RAPE

The concept of prison rape permeates American society. You don't need to know anything about prison rape firsthand to believe you know something about prison rape. Instead, all you have to do is peruse the multitudes of available films, newspapers, magazines, or websites and you'll find the best examples of prison rape's misinterpretation. You can watch graphic displays of prison rape in *The Shawshank Redemption* and *American Me*. However, if you haven't been a prisoner in an American prison, take with a grain of salt what you see and hear. Even if you were a prisoner, doing time doesn't ensure you'll learn anything firsthand about prison rape; but doing time does ensure you'll hear prison rape tales.

If we carefully study media articles, we see that reporters base their "knowledge" of prison rape on a publicly shared prison rape "prototype." The prison rape prototype forms through an integration of public sources (magazines, newspapers) with writers' and readers' active imaginations; learned and conjured expectations of prison life; sexual experiences of their own and others close to them; and personal beliefs, values, and norms. Given those means of acquiring a rape prototype we must necessarily conclude that every person uses a different prototype of prison rape, formed on different sets of life experiences.

Prison inmates too have a finite means of acquiring a prison rape prototype. If inmates allege rape, they have only two means to verify their allegation: material evidence (visual recording of the rape) and their own prototypical descriptions. Prison authorities investigate rape allegations to determine if they have some basis in fact (substantiated). Investigations of rape allegations show the statistical infrequency of sexual violence across the United States.

A National Institute of Justice Study conducted by James Austin et al. (2006) examined more than 2,000 rape allegations over four years in the Texas Department of Corrections (TDC). TDC had one of the nation's highest rates of alleged incidents of rape at 3.95 per 1,000 inmates and one of the lowest rates of substantiated cases at less than 3 percent. TDC's low rate of substantiated cases of prison rape falls in line with researchers' study of incidence and prevalence of sexual violence on a national scale.

A meta-analysis of published rape research found a 1.91 percent incidence of national prison rape (Gaes and Goldberg, 2004). In 2004 the Bureau of Justice Statistics (BJS) examined a national sample of correctional administrative records. BJS estimated that 0.005 percent of the total incarcerated population of males, females, and juveniles reported prison-based sexual victimization (Beck and Hughes, 2004). Recently the Bureau of Justice Statistics published a statistical analysis of the incidence of sexual violence in 146 state and federal prisons (n = 60,500 inmates). BJS determined a national estimate of 1.3 percent for nonconsensual sex acts and 0.8 percent for abusive sexual contact (Beck and Harrison, 2007).

Federal legislation to study prison rape. A strongly influential, political ideology emerged in America and found its outlet in the Prison Rape Elimination Act (PREA) of 2003 (Prison Rape Elimination Act, 2003). A careful reading of PREA shows it has a decidedly ironic anticorrections bias. PREA asserts that, by their inherent nature, American prisons are responsible and accountable for prison rape, sexual coercion, and sexual assault. Inherent nature implies that inmates' freedom has been stripped away, particularly inmates' control of personal decision making. The result is that inmates are at the beck and call of prison authorities who can inflict punishment at will.

PREA core assertions are that 13 percent of inmates in prisons and jails were victims of some type of sexual violence, and American prisons are violent and plagued by sexual coercion, sexual assault, and rape. Those two assertions clearly cannot be substantiated by quantitative or qualitative research. Prison culture researchers since the1950s have continuously reported that sexual violence is infrequent and that consensual sex dominates as the single most common type of homosexual sex (c.f. Davis, 1968; Struckman-Johnson and Struckman-Johnson, 2000). Inmates in our study self-reported the infrequency of rape and in fact, by filing false rape allegations, inmates overreported rape.

PREA's conceptualization of prison violence and rape relies on the veracity of the premise that prison staff members' indifference to inmates' well-being is a necessary *and* sufficient cause of prison violence and rape (PREA, 2003, Findings, paragraphs 12 and 13) (The Prison Rape Elimination Act, 2003). That premise is based on the assumption that conditions suitable to prison rape are the primary and overwhelming consequence of staff indifference, that prison inmates have no group-internal violence control mechanisms, that inmates' self-reports of sexual aggression are for the most part valid objective assessments of the causes and conditions of prison rape, and that prison inmates are for the most part sexually out-of-control, violent men and women who tolerate life in unpredictably violent surroundings.

In reality, inmates self-monitor their environment and try to control inmate violence. Staff members watch thousands of inmates who always watch one another and staff. There is always a good reason for inmates to snitch on inmates who have committed—or plan to commit—an act of sexual violence. Snitching, inmates think, will bring them favor and reward, such as a transfer, a cell change, a dismissed disciplinary case, or best of all, a good report in their central case file that will accompany them in the criminal justice system.

STRATEGIES FOR PREVENTION

We are compelled to accept inmates' words as they are reported. Inmates collectively told us that prisons cannot prevent sex acts of any type; but for reasons other than managerial malfeasance. First, prison management has significantly improved over the past several decades to produce relatively safe prisons. Second, no degree of prison staff supervision can prevent violent, mentally disordered inmates from committing violent acts. Third, prisons are big places inside and out, and there's always a dark corner or a dip in the ground on the compound where consenting inmates can hide for a few minutes.

Prisons rely on formal and informal systems of social control. Inmates self-police "their" community. No one, particularly inmates, wants violent prisons.

Peace is better than violence, life better than death, and freedom to walk about on a prison compound is far better than 23-hour lockdown. It is a reasonable assumption that if sexual violence were an epidemic, thousands of prison inmates would have been the first ones to yell at researchers, attorneys, judges, and anyone who would listen.

The PREA-estimated nonconsensual sex prevalence rate of 13 percent does not affect only a perpetrator and victim. We've demonstrated that sexual violence has a pre- and post-text, which directly affect other inmates. If we assume that a prison houses 1,000 inmates, a 13 percent prevalence rate yields 130 nonconsensual sex acts, which necessarily include at minimum 260 inmates (a rapist, a victim). If there are three rapists and one victim, then 520 inmates are involved in a rape. If we also assume that the pre- and post-text of one rape has a direct effect on three inmates, relatives and friends of a victim, in addition to one victim, then a 13 percent prevalence rate means that a single rape annually affects 910 out of 1,000 inmates. With that much violence and threatened violence surrounding them, even the most hardened correctional staffers would likely request early retirement.

Federal elected officials and private advocacy organizations distort and exaggerate scholarly research seemingly to support an anticorrections political agenda. If nothing else, inmate rape allegations capture the public attention and engender a constitutional if not moral argument that state and federal government has failed to meet its burden to protect the safety and well-being of prisoners. Private organizations' expression of anti-state and anti-federal government control over inmates is a philosophical position long extant in the literature. The federal government's support of an anticorrections stance is oxymoronic, since the federal government has statutory control of America's prisons.

Inmates' rights and improvements in prison quality of life have always been legislated by federal courts. If prison sexual violence is now at epidemic levels, federal elected officials were blind to sexual violence over decades and now find themselves behind in their legislative prison oversight responsibilities. So odd in today's cries of prison sexual abuse is that federal elected officials are overtly acknowledging their lack of knowledge of scientifically sound prison research. Quantitative and qualitative research, independent of its intellectual period in history and theoretical perspective of researchers, has found no credible, scientific support for PREA's assertion of a prison rape epidemic.

We find incredulous that anticorrections advocates ignore prison research in preference of a self-conceived perfect grasp of right and wrong. Advocates attack correctional officials and even refuse to accept decades of inmates' statements that rape is uncommon, rape is sick, rapists are sick, and rapists will be "taken off the count" if their sexually aggressive behavior persists. Similarly, anticorrections advocates refuse to think about inmates' reports that prisoners commonly issue false rape reports as retaliation against inmates, such as jealousy over an amorous affair with a generous staffer who brings gifts to his or her lover.

Prisons exist in a sociopolitical world. A full understanding of prison rape must necessarily go well beyond prison walls and the purview of correctional agencies. Correctional agency directors battle other government funding priorities, agency turf battles, and voters' opinions on inmate treatment and punishment. While prison funding gets cut, self-serving politicians who generally know little about crime, criminals, prison management, and inmate treatment proclaim they are "hard" on crime.

Prison staffers also suffer when funding gets cut. Staff members suffer maltreatment by maltreated inmates. Staffers are threatened; they are victims of physical violence; they are victims of distress caused by the level of hypervigilance required to work inside a penitentiary.

Clearly, prisoners are victims of political trends and public misunderstanding of prisons' role in modern society. Politicians and citizens don't consider the citizens who work inside prisons. Working in prison cell blocks tries one's patience and interpersonal skills in the best of times; however, when inmates are discontent, any inkling of a positive quality of prison life quickly diminishes and a potential for violence increases.

Inmates' world was designed for disorders left uncontrolled and untreated on the street. Inmates' thoughts and behavior are affected by PTSD, personality disorders, affective disorders, and addictions to alcohol, narcotics, glue and paint fumes, and any other type of noxious pharmaceutical they cram down their throat. Mental illness and their symptoms, such as drug abuse, alcoholism, and an inability to retain employment and maintain social relationships, effect higher levels of unemployment, poor literacy, domestic violence, child abuse, homelessness, and criminality. However, treatment programs are abruptly eliminated or shortened by too little funding to support well-trained professionals and best practices for treatment protocols.

In the absence of treatment, personality and affective disorders continue to cause family and community social problems, domestic and public violence, and criminality. Antisocial personalities make for poor students and chaotic schools. Borderline personalities create a swath of havoc. Depression glues people's feet to the ground and makes movement of the body and mind as difficult as crawling through liquid concrete.

The American prisoner population needs a serious proactive response to mental health treatment. If prison managerial malfeasance bares some burden for sexual violence, as PREA asserts, then state and federal government officials have a moral if not a legal obligation to fund necessary and sufficient programming to treat personal and affective disorders that would likely lead to prison sexual predation.

The Federal Bureau of Justice Programs reported on the state of mental health for prison and jail inmates. At midyear 2005, more than half of all prison and jail inmates had a mental health problem, including 705,600 inmates in state prisons, 78,800 in federal prisons, and 479,900 in local jails (James and Glaze, 2006). These estimates represented 56 percent of state prisoners, 45 percent of federal prisoners, and 64 percent of jail inmates.

Mental health data are shocking not so much for the high prevalence of inmate mental health problems but for the implication that these same inmates were not diagnosed and treated as children and adolescents by social service systems and community mental health organizations. Victims of sexual predators in prison are most likely mentally ill or intellectually impaired persons (Austin et al., 2006).

Prisons are our final chance to treat the medically and mentally ill. Correctional agencies need more psychiatrists, psychologists, and professionals skilled in the treatment of inmates who suffered childhood and adolescent sexual abuse and treatment of prison sexual predators. Disciplinary segregation, prison transfers, additional years on a sentence, and lockdown prisons don't resolve violence but only chill violent inmates on ice.

American culture so fondly embraces the punishment of wrongdoers. PREA mandates negative sanctions against correctional agencies whose prevalence of sexual violence falls within the top 10 prisons whose inmates are most likely to be sexually victimized. Punishing prisons in need of more funding to improve security and safety procedures, to enhance staff member training, to increase staff salaries to attract better-qualified applicants, and to increase correctional budgets in every correctional agency is no less an absurd solution to prison sexual violence than Karpman (1948) writing that prisons must punish homosexuality "out of" inmates.

In 2008, the federal government's operating philosophy of crime prevention mirrors Karpman's (1948) idea of 60 years ago: if criminals won't conform, then we'll punish criminality out of them. The burgeoning prison population clearly illustrates legislators' wrongheaded philosophy that if bad behavior is punished hard enough, offenders will miraculously become cleansed, law-abiding taxpayers.

No one doubts that penitentiaries house violent inmates. We expect occasional incidents of nonsexual and sexual violence. Multiple modes of research on sexual violence clearly indicate that American prisons have not reached epidemic levels of sexual violence. The federal government's national survey research shows that prison rape prevalence rates are low. The history of qualitative prison culture research over 60 years supports the federal statistical analysis.

Our nationwide, sociosymbolic study of prison sexual violence interpreted the sociocultural and psychosocial dynamics of inmate culture's myth of prison rape. Inmates above all others have a vested interest in the creation and maintenance of safe prisons. Despite our opinions of the moral character of prison inmates, their expertise and knowledge of prison life are sufficient to illustrate in the myth of prison rape a collective ethos of prison safety. Firmly embedded in nationwide inmate interview data we found that sexual predators are abhorrent and sexual predation a distinct threat to inmate peace and social safety.

Beyond the intellectual contribution of our research, we have shown that prison culture has an elaborate system of behavioral, psychological, and symbolic complexities. Whether or not you accept our argument about and interpretation of the myth of prison rape, you now recognize that prison culture and social life are far more sophisticated than you initially believed. Inmate society finds its complexity and interpretations from the men and women who live in prison. Prisoners don't "just" do time. Rather prisoners continually create, modify, and sustain internal systems in prison culture.

We've shown that a prison society isn't a territorial chunk of a community enclosed by a fence. Real live men and women, inmates and staff, live in prison. We don't mean to use the term *live* in a flippant manner. To live in prison means far more than doing a 60-month sentence while residing inside prison walls and fences. To live in prison means to become fully engaged and embedded in prison society's systems of social interactions and belief and value systems, and imbued with symbolic interpretations that strongly influence inmates' perceptions of the world around them.

Over decades of inmate imprisonment, prison culture knowledge and rules of behavior, beliefs and values, and social norms indelibly imprinted the "reality" of prison life on the consciousness of inmates. The realities of prison life cannot be overlooked when verbal tales of folkloric rapists and incidents of sexual predation are vividly conveyed by the Myth of Prison Rape.

Appendix: Lexicon of Prison Sexuality and Homosexual Sex

Generally speaking, a lexicon provides as much cultural and social information as possible so that a careful study of a lexicon would be a partial ethnographic study of a culture or a specialized domain of behavior and meaning within a culture.

A lexicon is more than a vocabulary list for common terms in a language, such as words and expressions for vegetables in Spanish. A lexicon provides a broader cultural and semantic perspective on a language's terminology, which necessarily includes denotative and connotative meanings and variations in meanings.

A lexicon conveys cultural meanings of terms and variations of meanings by sociocultural contexts as these meanings are compressed into verbal utterances. A lexicon represents what people think and vocalizations of those thoughts. This lexicon of prison sexuality and homosexual sex includes words and expressions collected during 564 interviews with men and women prison inmates.

A lexicon's words and expressions include those uttered by one, several, tens of dozens, or hundreds of inmates. A lexicon is a "slice" of vocal utterances of what inmates know about the culture of prison sex. By no means are single lexical entries representative of the entire social class of inmates in America. The meaning of words and expressions in this lexicon were not known by all inmates. We certainly would not expect that to occur.

Verbatim examples of inmate usage are italicized.

TERM	DEFINITIONS: DENOTATIVE AND CONNOTATIVE MEANINGS; *CONTEXTUAL USAGE*
ADOPT	TO ACQUIRE FICTIVE CHILDREN. *THE CHILDREN THE DADDY HAS ADOPTED ARE IN CAHOOTS WITH DADDY TO BREAK MOM, AND SOMETIMES THE DADDY IS DOING THE CHILDREN UP IN THE ROOM WHILE THE MOMMY IS IN THE OTHER BUILDING.* [FEMALE USAGE]
AGGRESSIVE FEMME	A FEMME WHO CAN FIGHT. ALSO A WOMAN WHO SHAVES HER HEAD OR WEARS MAKEUP, CAN PLAY EITHER MALE OR FEMALE ROLE. *AGGRESSIVE FEMME, THEY KIND OF LIKE DRESS UP LIKE GIRLS BUT DO THE MALE SEX STUFF. SHE'S IN BETWEEN, MORE DOMINANT THAN PASSIVE, SHE'S NOT BOY LOOKING BUT SHE WEARS THE PANTS, MAKES THE CALLS, RUNS THE RELATIONSHIP.*
AGGRESSOR	DOMINANT PARTNER IN A FEMALE SEXUAL RELATIONSHIP. SYNONYMS: DYKE, FEMME
ALL-OUT QUEEN	A HOMOSEXUAL WHO DISPLAYS AND EXTORTS FEMININE TRAITS OFTEN IN AN EXAGGERATED MANNER. MAY FASHION WOMEN-LIKE CLOTHING; WALK WITH SWINGING HIPS; TAKE ON A HIGH VOICE; DECORATE EYELIDS WITH POOL-CUE CHALK, SKITTLES, OR KOOL-AID. CHARACTERISTIC TRAIT: THEY ARE NOT WEAK. SYNONYM: ALL-OUT FUCK BOY *QUEENS CAN STAND UP AND FIGHT LIKE A MAN. QUEENS DON'T WANT TO BE ASSOCIATED WITH ANYTHING MASCULINE.*
ALL THE WAY OUT	AN INMATE WHO ONCE CLAIMED TO BE HETEROSEXUAL AND THEN SWITCHED TO HOMOSEXUAL. *ALL OF THEM [STUDS, DADDIES] TRY TO PLAY THE MAN ROLE UNLESS THEY'RE ALL THE WAY OUT.*
ARCH; ARCHIN'	EYEBROWS SCULPTED INTO THE SHAPE OF AN ARCH. MEN WHO ARCH THEIR BROWS TO LOOK LIKE WOMEN. *I GOT TREATED WORSE IN HERE, IN HERE OFFICERS ARE ALWAYS TELLING ME TO WALK LIKE A MAN, DON'T ARCH YOUR EYEBROWS, LIKE ONLY MY EYEBROWS ARE GAY, WHATEVER.*

ASS BANDIT	*SEE* BANDIT.

ASS CHASER	AN INMATE WHO PRESSURES SOMEONE FOR SEX. SYNONYMS: ASS BANDIT, BOOTIE BANDIT, PEANUT BUTTER CHASER *SOME [*BOOTIE BANDITS*] ARE CALLED ASS CHASERS . . . IT'S JUST A TERM, USED WHEN YOU'RE JOKING ABOUT IT. YOU WOULDN'T REALLY CALL SOMEONE THAT TO THEIR FACE, YOU'D JUST SAY THAT THERE'S A PEANUT BUTTER CHASER AND EVERYONE WOULD LAUGH.*

ASS PUSSY	MALE ANUS, ANALOGOUS TO A FEMALE VAGINA. SYNONYM: BUTUSSY

BAD BONE	A BAD RUMOR. A RUMOR THAT CAUSES WOMEN INMATES TO STAY AWAY FROM ONE ANOTHER; TO PUT A BAD BONE ON SOMEONE; A REPUTATION WORSE THAN A SNITCH; A BAD QUALITY IN A PERSON'S CHARACTER. EXPRESSION USED WITH OR INSTEAD OF SLURS. *SOMEONE LIKE THIS HAS TO EARN BACK REPUTATION. IF I CALLED SOMEBODY A SNITCH—SHE'S A SNITCH. SHE CAN'T RECOVER FROM A BAD BONE AS A SNITCH.*

BANDIT	INFREQUENTLY USED AS AN HONORIFIC FOR OLDER INMATES WITH SOCIAL STANDING BUT MAY NOT HAVE SEXUAL CONNOTATIONS. AN INMATE WITH *GAME* WHO TURNS OUT INMATES. AN INMATE WHO HAS THE REPUTATION OF PRESSURING INMATES FOR SEX. AN INMATE WHO HAS MULTIPLE SEXUAL RELATIONS OR *ONE-NIGHTERS.* DISTINGUISHED FROM A VIOLENT PREDATOR. SOME INMATES TAKE PLEASURE OR ENJOYMENT FROM BEING OR BEING KNOWN AS A BOOTIE BANDIT AND WILL TALK OPENLY ABOUT THEIR CONQUESTS. SYNONYMS: ASS BANDIT, ASS CHASER, SHARK *1. A BANDIT WON'T GET ALL MAD IF HE DOESN'T GET IT [*SEX*], BECAUSE HE'LL GET IT SOMEPLACE ELSE.* *2. THERE WAS SO FEW GUYS [*HOMOSEXUALS*] COMING INTO THE JOINT AT THE TIME, IT WAS MORE OF A COMPETITION [*FOR SEX*]. SO BEING A BOOTIE BANDIT WAS AN ART OR A SKILL, IT WAS LIKE A LIMITED COMMODITY. NOW THERE ARE SO MANY COMING IN WHO HAVE ALREADY BEEN EXPOSED TO IT [*HOMOSEXUAL SEX*], EASIER ACCESS TO IT.*

BEAST FUCKING	AGGRESSIVE OR ROUGH SEX. SYNONYMS: DICKING DOWN, BEAT IT
BEAT IT	SEXUAL RELATIONS SYNONYMS: FUCK, HIT IT
BELL PEPPER	A LARGE PENIS HEAD.
BICURIOUS	A *STRAIGHT* WHO IS CURIOUS ABOUT AND OFTEN TRIES A SAME-SEX RELATION. THE INMATE POPULATION DOES NOT CONSIDER BICURIOUS INMATES TO BE HOMOSEXUAL. SYNONYM: CURIOUS *IF YOU'RE NOT GAY OR A LESBIAN OR BISEXUAL AND YOU WANT TO TRY SOMETHING NEW, THEY CALL YOU BICURIOUS, SOMEONE WHO WILL DO ANYTHING TO SEE WHAT IT DOES.*
BIG DICK BOB	FICTIVE CHARACTER WHO "TAKES CARE" OF AN INMATE'S SIGNIFICANT OTHER WHILE THEY ARE IN PRISON. SYNONYM: OLD JOE
BIG MAMMA	*SEE* MADAM.
BISEXUAL	A MAN WHO ON THE STREET HAS SEX WITH WOMEN, BUT INSIDE PRISON PLAYS THE PASSIVE SEXUAL ROLE WITH HETEROSEXUAL MEN. ONCE THAT HAPPENS HE IS NOT CONSIDERED BISEXUAL. HE IS HOMOSEXUAL BECAUSE HE TAKES ON A FEMALE ROLE. BISEXUAL HAS SEVERAL CONNOTATIONS: 1. HOMOSEXUAL BEHAVIOR AFTER BEING TURNED OUT. *I'VE HEARD A LOT OF GUYS THAT ARE HOMOS SAY THEY ARE BISEXUAL, BUT THEY'RE ACTUALLY THE ONES WHO WERE TURNED OUT. THEY WERE FORCED TO BE A FAG. IF SOMEONE SAYS HE'S BISEXUAL IT MEANS HE'S A TURNOUT. IF HE SAYS HE WAS GAY, HE WAS ALWAYS GAY. I'D PUT THEM ON A DIFFERENT LEVEL.* 2. BISEXUALS CONTRAST WITH A SINGLE SEXUAL ROLE. *THEY GETS DOWN, IN THE GAME, YOU ARE EITHER THE BOTTOM OR THE TOP, THE MAN OR THE PUNK, NO BISEXUALS HERE, EVERYTHING IS BOLD.* 3. *THERE ARE NO TERMS FOR [*A HETEROSEXUAL INMATE*]. I NEVER HEARD OF THEM. A LOT OF PEOPLE WHO ARE FULL BLOWN [*HOMOSEXUALS*] IN HERE. WHEN HIS WIFE COMES TO VISIT, OFF COMES THE MAKEUP AND HE IS A MAN. HE IS GONNA TELL HER THAT HE IS A HOMOSEXUAL WHEN HE GETS OUT. HE WANTS TO SEE HIS KIDS STILL. HE SAID THAT SHE WILL NOT FORGIVE HIM. SHE WILL TAKE OFF.*

| BITCH | OFTEN USED AS A TERM OF REFERENCE OR ADDRESS TO DE-NOTE A TRUSTWORTHY FAG OR A MAN'S *WIFE*. ALSO USED AS AN INSULT. MULTIPLE MEANINGS IN A VARIETY OF CONTEXTS. |

1. *THERE IS PREJUDICE TOWARD THEM [HOMOSEXUALS] IN HERE, THEY'RE CONSIDERED, THEY'RE ABUSED, TALKED BAD ABOUT, CALLED BITCHES AND PUNKS, TREATED DISRESPECTFUL.*
2. *HER, WIFE, OR JUST HIS BITCH.*
3. *A LOT THINK THEY'RE IN THE CLOSET BUT PEOPLE TALK, A CLOSET BITCH.*
4. *BITCH AND PUNK ARE VERY SERIOUS WORDS.*
5. CONNOTATION IN DISTINGUISHING THE USE OF MONEY OR COMMISSARY IN A CONSENSUAL SEXUAL RELATIONSHIP. MALE INMATE: *IT DEPENDS, ON WHETHER YOU'RE HUSBAND AND WIFE, MAN AND MAN, OR GIRL AND GIRL. WE JUST CONSIDER OURSELVES, BABY. WE BOTH GET STUFF FOR EACH OTHER. IF IT'S HUSBAND AND WIFE IT'S JUST LIKE THE FREE WORLD. "GOD DAMN YOU STUPID BITCH SHUT UP I DIDN'T MARRY YOU FOR MONEY."*

| BLOW JOB | ORAL SEX.
SYNONYM: CAP, SKULL |

IT TICKLES ME TO DEATH. YEARS AGO IF YOU SAG YOUR PANTS THAT WAS ADVERTISING YOU WERE AVAILABLE. OVER THE LAST 20 YEARS, IT'S NOW THE COOL THING, AND THEY DON'T UNDERSTAND THAT THAT WAS ADVERTISING FOR SEX, THAT I'M FOR SALE. I'VE HEARD LOTS OF STORIES ABOUT PEOPLE SELLING THEMSELVES. THERE WAS ONE GUY IN HERE, BIG BLACK GUY WHO WOULD COME IN SOMEONE'S CELL, HE SAID EITHER YOU LET ME GIVE YOU A BLOW JOB OR I'M GOING TO WHIP UP ON YOU.

| BLOW JOB UNDER THE INFLUENCE | ON THE STREET "BLOW JOB UNDER THE INFLUENCE" REFERS TO INFLUENCE OF DRUGS AND ALCOHOL. INSIDE, THE EXPRESSION REFERS TO A BLOW JOB UNDER THE INFLUENCE OF PRESSURE, DEPRESSION, OR LONELINESS. |

| BODY FUCKING | TO RUB TOGETHER BODIES UNTIL ORGASM; BODIES ARE USUALLY CLOTHED. |

ORAL SEX AND BODY SEX [ARE MOST COMMON SEX ACTS]. THEY CALL IT BODY FUCKING. [FEMALE]

I SEEN SOMEBODY FUCKING BEFORE BUT NEVER SEEN A RAPE. SOMEONE HIT [OPENED] THEIR DOOR BY MISTAKE. I WAS LOOK- ING OUT MY DOOR AND I JUMPED BACK. IT FUCKED ME UP [SUR- PRISED]. I NEVER SEEN NO TWO MEN DOING SHIT.

BOO	TERM OF ENDEARMENT, "LOVE NAME" USED BY DOMINANT FE- MALE. *SHE'S MY BOO; SHE'S MY SHORTY.*
BOOTIE	ASS; CAN BE USED TO REFER SPECIFICALLY TO THE ANUS. *NO ONE MAKES YOU TAKE ANYTHING INSIDE BUT NO ONE STATES THAT YOU'LL HAVE TO GIVE UP THE BOOTIE WITHOUT REPAYMENT.*
BOOTIE BANDIT	*SEE* BANDIT.
BOTH WAYS	INMATES WHO SWITCH BETWEEN MALE AND FEMALE ROLE IN SEX ACTS. SYNONYM: FLIP-FLOP
BOTTOM HO	THE NUMBER ONE QUEEN IN A GROUP OF *HO'S* THAT IS OVER- SEEN BY A STRONG MAN. *IF THEY RUN ACROSS A STRONG DUDE AND HE TURNS THEM OUT TO THE GAME OF GETTING OTHER HO'S UP UNDER THEM, THEY BECOME THE BOTTOM HO, THE NUMBER ONE.*
BOXING BETTY	FOLKLORIC CHARACTER RECOGNIZED BY INMATES ACROSS A WIDE GEOGRAPHIC AREA. IF THE NAME BOXING BETTY DIDN'T APPEAR IN INTERVIEWS, INMATES KNEW THE TALE. AN INMATE, TYPICALLY A WEIGHT LIFTER OR BOXER, WHO LOOKED STRONG, BUT WAS HOMOSEXUAL. BOXING BETTY COMMONLY WOULD KNOCK OUT UNSUSPECTING INMATES ON THE YARD AND PER- FORM ORAL SEX.
BOY	USED BY A DADDY TO REFER TO HIS *SON*. SYNONYM: SON *HE COULD HAVE A BOY, PUT HIS BOY OUT TO MAKE MONEY OR GET COMMISSARY OR DOPE OR CIGARETTES, IT JUST DEPENDS ON THE INDIVIDUAL.*
BREAK YOUR BACK	VERY AGGRESSIVE ROUGH SEX. MAY CAUSE INJURY AND/ OR LOOK LIKE RAPE. ALTERNATIVELY: TO BREAK THE BACK DOOR *LET ME BREAK YOUR BACK*, MEANING I WANT TO PUT SOMETHING ON YOU THAT YOUR BACK CAN'T HANDLE.

BULL-DAGGER	[NOUN] FEMALE INMATES WHO PLAY MASCULINE ROLES. ALSO A DEROGATORY REFERENCE FOR A WOMAN WHO HAS SEX WITH BOTH *FEMMES* AND *DYKES*. [VERB] BULL-DAGGING OR BULL-DAGGERING. SYNONYM: BULL DYKE *BULL-DAGGERS ARE ALSO MASCULINE, MORE SO THAN JUST AGGRESSORS, LOOK MORE LIKE MEN, MASCULINE.* [FEMALE SPEAKER]
BULL DYKE	DEROGATORY. FEMALE INMATE WHO PLAYS A MASCULINE ROLE. SYNONYM: BULL-DAGGER
BULLY	TO FORCE AN INMATE TO DO SOMETHING HE DOESN'T WANT TO DO. COMMONLY USED IN REFERENCE TO SEXUAL ACTIVITY.
BUMPING PUSSIES	FEMALE SEXUAL CONTACT WHERE BOTH PARTICIPANTS RECEIVE SEXUAL GRATIFICATION. SYNONYM: FLIP-FLOP
BUSHWACKER	A PREDATOR. SYNONYM: TREE JUMPER *BANDIT IS MORE SOMEBODY WHO JUST THINKS ABOUT HAVING SEX ALL THE TIME WITH A BOY. THAT'S ALL HE WANTS TO DO IS SEX. A BUSHWACKER IS LIKE A STALKER OR ACTUAL RAPIST.*
BUST A 60	TO SPEND ALL YOUR MONEY ON SOMEONE FOR PROTECTION. *FIGHT, FUCK, OR BUST A 60* [COST VARIES BY LOCATION; COST MAY COME AS COMMISSARY ITEMS, STAMPS, DRUGS, OR ANY TYPE OF VALUABLE PROPERTY].
BUTCH	A FEMALE INMATE WHO IS MASCULINE IN APPEARANCE, DRESS, OR VOICE. *IF YOU TAKE ONE BUTCH AND FOLLOW HIM OVER 1 YEAR, I BET SHE'D BE WITH EVERY FEMME IN HERE. NO LONG-TERM RELATIONSHIPS; IT'S ALL FUN AND GAMES, I THINK.*
BUTTHOLE BANDIT	*SEE* BANDIT.
BUTUSSY	MALE ANUS, ANALOGOUS TO A FEMALE VAGINA. SYNONYM: ASS PUSSY *I DON'T SEE HOW THEY MISTAKE A BIG HAIRY ASS FOR A PUSSY . . . THEY CALL IT A BUTUSSY, IT IS A MAN'S BUTT.*

CAMP SNOOPY	A PENITENTIARY WITH A NONVIOLENT REPUTATION; USED FOR MALE OR FEMALE INSTITUTIONS. SYNONYMS: PRISNEYLAND, PRISNEYWORLD *THIS PRISON, IT IS LIKE CAMP SNOOPY, IT'S A COUNTY JAIL WITH MORE RULES AND MORE RESPECT, AND MORE FREEDOM.*
CANTEEN HO	AN INMATE WHO TRADES SEX FOR COMMISSARY. AN INMATE WHO *IS WITH SOMEONE BECAUSE THEY GOT CANTEEN.* ALTERNATIVELY: COMMISSARY HO, STORE-BAG STUDS, CANTEEN WHORE, BOX WHORE *CANTEEN HO'S ARE WITH SOMEONE ONLY BECAUSE THEY GOT CANTEEN.*
CAP	ORAL SEX. CAN BE A NOUN OR A VERB. SYNONYMS: BLOW JOB, SKULL *TO CAP A DUDE; DUDE GOT CAPPED.*
CAR WASH	A LARGE SHOWER AREA WITH MULTIPLE SHOWER HEADS; NO PRIVACY. TERM ISN'T RECOGNIZED IN A NUMBER OF STATES PROBABLY BECAUSE INMATES ARRIVED AFTER PRISON REMODELING AND DIDN'T EXPERIENCE A CAR WASH SHOWER. *BACK IN THE CAR WASHES, MULTIPLE NOZZLES WITH 20 GUYS, NOW YOU HAVE SHOWER DOORS AND ONE MAN SO IT [RAPE] DOESN'T HAPPEN ANYMORE.*
CARPET MUNCHERS	WOMEN WHO PARTICIPATE IN ORAL SEX WITH ANOTHER WOMAN.
CAVE MAN	A BRUTAL INMATE WHO TAKES SEX BUT WHO IS NOT PERCEIVED AS A RAPIST. INMATE WHO DOES IT REPEATEDLY HAS *CAVE MAN SYNDROME.* *SOME ARE JUST BRUTAL CAVEMAN TYPE PEOPLE THAT TAKE IT.*
CAVE MAN SYNDROME	A RATIONALE FOR MALE INMATES WHO TAKE SEX IN PRISON. *FRUSTRATION. NINETY PERCENT OF THE TIME [SEX IS] NOT BECAUSE THEY'RE GAY. IT'S BECAUSE OF CAVE MAN SYNDROME. A BASIC NEED, BASIC DESIRE, WANTING FULFILLED, AND GUYS WHO ARE LESS MORALLY STRUCTURED DON'T CARE ABOUT STUFF LIKE THAT, OR IN SOME CASES THEY ARE LEGITIMATELY GAY AND THEY WILL GO TO A GAY PERSON.*

CELLIE — CELL MATE.

THERE ARE A LOT OF HOMOSEXUALS THAT WILL CHOOSE YOU, FIND YOU ATTRACTIVE, OFFER YOU A CIGARETTE, THEN YOU TAKE TWO, THEN HALF A PACK, THEN YOU GET A JAR OF COFFEE, AND BEFORE YOU KNOW IT, YOU GOT A NEW CELLIE WHO JUST WANTS TO "BLOW YOUR SOCKS OFF."

CHECK IN — TO REQUEST PROTECTION IN A PRISON'S ADMINISTRATIVE SECURITY UNIT. OFTEN USED AS PART OF A HUSTLE.
SYNONYM: CHECK OFF

WELL, THEY STICK YOU DOWN IN THE HOLE AND IN SOME CASES, DUDE CONSENT AND HE CALL RAPE AFTERWARD, THEY SAY "I GIVE YOU SOME STORE GOODS IF YOU LET ME HIT THAT ASS." THEY GET THE STORE GOODS AND CHECK IN, THEY SAY IT'S RAPE.

CHECK OFF — TO TRANSFER OR CHECK INTO PROTECTIVE CUSTODY.
SYNONYM: CHECK IN

YO, "WHEN YOU GOING TO GIVE ME BACK FOR THAT STUFF I GAVE YOU?" YOU SAID YOU WAS LOOKING OUT FOR ME AND THEY LIKE, "NO MAN, NO ONE LOOKS OUT FOR YOU IN PRISON," AND HE LIKE "MAN YOU JUST GIVE ME A LITTLE BIT OF THAT ASS AND WE'RE EVEN." THEY DON'T WANT TO CHECK OFF OR YOU GOT THAT LABEL ON THEM.

CHILD MOLESTER — 1. AN INMATE WHO IS TOO PHYSICALLY WEAK TO HIT ON STRONG INMATES OR HAS A RAPE CHARGE OUTSIDE.
SYNONYM: CHO MO

[THIS PRISON] IS A RESCUE CAMP FOR CHILD MOLESTERS . . . NINETY PERCENT OF CHILD MOLESTERS ARE GAY THEMSELVES. THEY HAVE NO CONTROL OVER SEXUAL DESIRES.

2. WOMEN INMATES, TO REFER TO A STUD BROAD WHO PREYS ON MUCH YOUNGER INMATES.

[FEMALE INMATE] IN HERE RAPES OR IS A FAGGY. YOU ONLY HAVE 20 PERCENT IN HERE FOR DRUG DEALERS OR ROBBERY OR MURDER; 80 PERCENT IS [CONVICTED] RAPISTS OR CHILD MOLESTERS OR SEX CRIME. [CHILD MOLESTERS] PLAY ON THAT AND TRY TO ASSASSINATE YOUR CHARACTER AT ALL COSTS.

CHO MO	A CHILD MOLESTER. ALTERNATIVELY: C-MO, CHESTER THE MOLESTER *I HAVE A CHO MO ACROSS THE TIER. I TALK WITH THE GUY, I DON'T DISASSOCIATE MYSELF.*
CIVILIAN	A MALE INMATE WHO ISN'T *HOOKED UP*. AN INMATE WHO HAS PEOPLE SUPPORTING HIM AND DOESN'T NEED A SEXUAL RELATIONSHIP. CIVILIANS HAVE POTENTIAL TO COME TOGETHER AND BE A STRONG FORCE. *IF YOU NEED SOMETHING YOU CAN GET IT FROM A CIVILIAN AND GET IT WITHOUT HIM EXPECTING SOMETHING IN RETURN.*
CLOSET CASE	AN INMATE WHO DENIES HIS/HER HOMOSEXUALITY; A *STRAIGHT* GUY WHO PRETENDS TO BE STRAIGHT IN FRONT OF HIS FRIENDS, BUT PRIVATELY IS MORE ACCEPTING OF HOMOSEXUAL BEHAVIOR. SYNONYM: UNDERCOVER *CLOSET CASES, SOME CLAIM THEY ARE NOT GAY, BUT THEY GET CAUGHT HAVING SEX. ANYONE THAT MESSES AROUND. YOU ARE STILL CONSIDERED A HOMOSEXUAL OR A FAG EVEN IF YOU SAY YOU ARE A STRAIGHT. THE BIBLE SAYS THAT THERE IS NO BISEXUALNESS SO YOU ARE EITHER HETEROSEXUAL OR HOMOSEXUAL.*
CLOSET PUNK	AN INMATE WHO CONCEALS THEIR HOMOSEXUALITY. ALTERNATIVELY: CLOSET QUEEN, CLOSET FAG, CLOSET HO, CLOSET FREAK SYNONYMS: DOWN LOW, UNDERCOVER, UNDERCOVER PUNK *SOME GUYS THAT ARE LIKE THAT, CLOSET PUNKS, THEY TRY TO KEEP IT IN THE CLOSET, YOU KNOW, UNTIL A HOMOSEXUAL COMES INTO THE COUNT AND BRINGS THEM OUT OF THE CLOSET.* *CLOSET QUEENS, THESE DUDES THAT'S STRAIGHT, CALL THEMSELVES BEING STRAIGHT, THEY DON'T WANT NO ONE TO KNOW, THEY THINK THEY BEEN A REAL MAN BUT THEY SUCK PENISES ON THE SIDE.*
COCK BLOCK	AN INMATE WHO STANDS IN THE WAY OF A SEXUAL PREDATOR. AN OLDER INMATE MAY BE A COCK BLOCK FOR A NEW INMATE. *THAT'S WHAT I'M DOING TO BIG BUCK, HE'S TRYING TO GET THE BOY AND I'M IN THE WAY SO I'M A COCK BLOCK. SOMEONE WHO STANDS IN THE WAY BETWEEN A VICTIM AND PREDATOR. OR IF A MUSLIM BROTHER SEES SOMEONE WHO'S GOING TO FALL INTO THE WRONG GROUP.*

COCK SUCKERS	INMATES WHO PROVIDE ORAL SEX. ALSO A DEROGATORY TERM FOR A SEXUAL SNITCH.

IF [AN INMATE] GETS RAPED AND THEY REPORT IT TO THE AUTHORITIES [INMATES] CALL THEM A SNITCH, CALLED A COCK SUCKER OR A SLUT IF THEY REPORT IT. IF THEY DON'T REPORT IT THEY'RE VIEWED THE SAME WAY BUT LEAVE OUT THE SNITCHING WORD. IT GIVES EASY ACCESS TO OTHER PEOPLE. THEY'LL SAY "SHE'S EASY, GO DO HER," "SHE'S GOOD, SHE WON'T SAY NOTHING."

COCKGLAZER	AN INMATE WHO WAS FORCED INTO SEX AND ENJOYED THE EXPERIENCE.

COCKGLAZER WAS FORCED INTO SEX THE FIRST TIME THEN CONTINUED TO HAVE SEX VOLUNTARILY.

COMMISSARY QUEEN	AN INMATE WHO FORGES SEXUAL RELATIONSHIPS WITH OTHER INMATES FOR MONETARY GAIN, TYPICALLY THROUGH COMMISSARY GOODS. ALTERNATIVELY: COMMISSARY HO SYNONYM: CANTEEN HO

COMMISSARY IS NECESSARY	TO COMMIT AN ACT IN ORDER TO OBTAIN COMMISSARY. ACTION MAY OR MAY NOT BE SEXUAL. THIS PHRASE IS USED TO JUSTIFY SEX FOR MONEY.

WOMEN WHO CUT THEIR HAIR AND PRETEND TO BE BUTCH SO THEY CAN GET PAID WITH 25 CENT SOUPS. THEY CALL IT COMMISSARY IS NECESSARY—PEOPLE THAT DON'T HAVE MONEY AND ALL THEY WANT IS COMMISSARY.

CON	A STRATEGY OF MANIPULATION. SYNONYM: TO RUN A GAME

ALL YOUR RAPES NOW ARE CON GAMES, THEY CON THEM INTO OR LURE THEM INTO IT BY LOANING THEM STUFF, IT'S THE ONLY WAY.

COP, STOP, BLOCK, AND LOCK	A TURN-OUT STRATEGY; CONNOTES POWER IN A SEXUAL RELATIONSHIP; STAGES OF A CLOSE, DELIBERATE TURN-OUT; STRATEGY REQUIRES FINDING A TARGET (COP); STOPPING THE TARGET FROM THINKING ABOUT OTHER RELATIONSHIPS OR FRIENDS OR FAMILY (STOP); STOPPING TARGET'S INTERACTION WITH OTHER INMATES (BLOCK). ONCE THE TARGET HAS BEEN ISOLATED, THE AGGRESSOR HAS TARGET IN A SOCIAL AND PSYCHOLOGICAL STATE VULNERABLE TO SEX (LOCK).

*OLD SAYING, GOTTA COP STOP BLOCK AND LOCK. I GOT MY OWN PLAYER BOOK AND I DON'T LIKE GIVING UP MY SKILLS. WHEN YOU SEE A HOMO AND YOU LIKE WHAT YOU SEE YOU PRESENT SOMETHING FLASHY [*LET THEM KNOW YOU GOT MONEY OR OFFER TO BUY SOMETHING FOR THEM*]. THAT'S CALLED COPPING. BLOCKING IS WHEN YOU MAKE SURE THAT EVERY THOUGHT THAT SHE [*MALE INMATE*] HAD BEFORE YOU IS NOW GONE. IT'S ALL ABOUT YOU. NOW YOU GOT HER FOCUSED. STOP ALL OTHER MOTIONS PUT HER ON THE PATH. "I'M NOT GOING WITH NO ONE; YOU'RE NOT, IT'S ALL ABOUT ME AND YOU." I PUT A THOUSAND ON THEIR BOOKS. I'M GOING TO GET THAT BACK. IT'S NOTHING. THEY AIN'T GOT TO WORRY ABOUT WASHING OTHER DUDES' CLOTHES FOR A HUSTLE. THAT'S THE FLASHING. THEY KNOW THEY AIN'T GOT TO WANT FOR NOTHING OR SELL THEIR BODIES. BLOCK, I LET THEM KNOW YOU WANT TO STAY FOCUSED ON TRYING TO GET HOME, TAKE THEM AWAY FROM VIOLENCE AND STEER THEM TOWARDS THE RIGHT PATH. STOP PART ALL IS SHIELDED OFF AND FOCUSED THIS WAY. THEY THOUGHTS IS ALL ON ME. LOCKED IN AND IT'S OVER WITH.*

IN STREET TALK, *GET IT AND LOCK IT IN AND KEEP IT TO YOURSELF.*

CORNER PERSON	AN INMATE WHO HAS BEEN RAPED AND STAYS ON YARD. CORNER MEN HAVE ECONOMIC VALUE.

HE'S IN THE CORNER. NO ONE WILL HANG OUT WITH HIM. SOMEONE WOULD PICK HIM AND SAY, "MAKE ME SOME MONEY." THERE'S MONEY IN RAPED GUYS STILL ON THE YARD. HE'S PUSHED ASIDE. NOBODY WILL HANG WITH HIM.

CRAP ON	TO ASK A MALE INMATE IF HE IS INTERESTED IN HAVING SEX. A GAY MIGHT CRAP ON A GUY BY ASKING "*DO YOU FUCK AROUND?*"

CREEP	TO SNEAK BEHIND A LOVER'S BACK TO HAVE SEX WITH ANOTHER. ALTERNATIVELY: CREEPING, CREEPER
	SYNONYM: SNEAK TIP

[*PERSONAL NAME*] *ALWAYS HAD ONE CHICK IN THE OPEN AND THEN HAD TO CREEP ON THE DOWN LOW.*

CROSS OUT	TO CREATE A FALSE CASE ON AN INMATE OR OFFICER AND THEN TELL STAFF. EXAMPLE: TO SNITCH OFF THAT AN INMATE HAS ILLEGAL DRUGS, OR THAT A WOMAN HAS AN AFFAIR WITH A MALE OR FEMALE STAFF MEMBER.

THEY'LL GO AND EITHER FIGHT THEM, OR GO TO AUTHORITY, OR THEY WILL DO ANYTHING JUST TO CROSS THE PERSON OUT, TO MAKE THEIR LIFE MISERABLE.

CROSS-OVER HETEROSEXUAL HAVING HOMOSEXUAL SEX OPENLY.
SYNONYMS: KING CROSS-OVER, BISEXUAL

I GUESS IT'S WITHIN EACH INDIVIDUAL ON HOW FAR THEY'RE WILL-ING TO GO IN ORDER TO REACH THAT ULTIMATE LEVEL OF PLEA-SURE, THAT CLIMAX. FOR A WOMAN IT MAY BE CHEATING ON HER HUSBAND, FOR A MAN IT MAY BE CHEATING ON HIS WIFE, PLACED IN PRISON IT MAY BE MASTURBATION. IF THAT'S NOT ENOUGH, AND YOU GOT TO HAVE MORE, WHAT DO YOU DO? SOME PEOPLE MAY BE GIVING INTO LATENT HOMOSEXUAL TENDENCIES, FOR SOME THEY MIGHT BE ABLE TO CROSS OVER EVERY BOUNDARY.

CUM GUZZLER MALE INMATE WHO ENGAGES IN ORAL SEX WITH MANY PART-NERS.
SYNONYM: THIRSTY MCGURSTY

CUPCAKE AN INMATE WHO IS EASILY MANIPULATED. AN INMATE WITH FEMININE TENDENCIES.

MOST BLACKS THINK WHITE DUDES ARE GAY AND THAT SOMEONE JUST DIDN'T BRING IT OUT IN THEM YET. WE HAVE A DUDE THAT WEARS A BEARD BUT HE'S A CUPCAKE.

CURIOUS AN INMATE WHO IS CONTEMPLATING SAME-SEX RELATIONS. IN-MATES SEEN AS CURIOUS MAY BE *TURNED OUT*. CONNOTES A SEXUAL EXPERIMENT TO ENGAGE IN HOMOSEXUAL SEX RATHER THAN A NATURAL INCLINATION.
SYNONYM: BICURIOUS
NEAR SYNONYM: TENDENCIES

IF YOU'RE CURIOUS THEY'LL TURN YOU OUT.
I THINK THERE'S JUST THE NORMAL LEVEL OF CURIOSITY. WE HAVE A LOT OF YOUNG PEOPLE WHO'VE NEVER REALLY SEEN [HO-MOSEXUAL SEX] AND THERE'S A LOT OF OLD-TIMERS TOO. THE NEW KIDS SEE THE OLD-TIMERS WHO HAVE BEEN DOING IT [SEX] FOREVER. THEY'RE KIND OF LIKE TURNING OUT THE YOUNGER KIDS. IT'S A WHOLE NEW LEVEL OF CURIOSITY. I THINK IT HAS A LOT TO DO WITH WHEN YOU FIRST COME TO PRISON. YOU'RE NOT SURE OF WHAT IT IS [REFERENCE TO BOTH PRISON AND SEXU-ALITY]. I WAS REALLY SCARED. I HAD THIS IMAGE OF A HARD

CORE PEN WITH BIG BERTHA COMING IN AND TAKING ME. AND THIS PLACE AIN'T SHIT, BUT IT'S REALLY LONELY.

DADDY	AN OLDER INMATE WHO WATCHES OVER A YOUNGER INMATE; *DADDYS TAKE* CARE OF THEIR *SONS*. THEY WILL FIGHT AND PROVIDE FOR THEM, AND IN RETURN DADDY COMMONLY RECEIVES SEXUAL FAVORS. SYNONYM: FATHER 1. *THE REAL GAY GUYS WILL TRY TO FIND A DADDY FOR PROTECTION.* [MALE USAGE] 2. *[DADDY] CAN BE USED IN SEVERAL DIFFERENT WAYS. YOU GOT DADDY AS IN LIKE SOMEBODY LOOKS UP TO YOU BECAUSE YOU GOT THE FEMMES AND STUDS, THEY WILL CALL YOU DADDY. YOUR GIRLFRIEND COULD CALL YOU DADDY, YOU MIGHT BE BIG DADDY OR SOMETHING. IN A FAMILY SITUATION SOME PEOPLE CALL THAT'S MY MOMMA AND DADDY AND THEY DO BE IN BED WITH THEM. THAT'S SICK.*
DADDY GIRL	A YOUNGER DOMINANT HOMOSEXUAL IN A MALE RELATIONSHIP. A DADDY GIRL TYPICALLY DOESN'T PROVIDE SEXUAL GRATIFICATION; HE ONLY RECEIVES SEXUAL GRATIFICATION. *DADDY GIRL IS MOSTLY BOY, SHE DOES GAY THINGS BUT IS MOSTLY A BOY.*
DAGGING	TO HAVE SEX. [LIMITED GEOGRAPHICAL MALE USAGE] SYNONYM: FLIP-FLOP *DUDE WAS IN THE HOLE. HE WAS DAGGING LAST NIGHT. DAGGING IS SEX. SHAGGING.*
DAG PARTNERS	INMATES WHO SWITCH SEXUAL POSITIONS, WITH EACH GIVING AND RECEIVING SEXUAL GRATIFICATION. SYNONYM: FLIP-FLOPPERS
DATE	TO SHARE MEALS AND ACTIVITIES TOGETHER. *THEY DATE. THEY GO TO REC YARD TOGETHER . . . GO TO CHURCH AND I'LL SEE THE SAME DUDE WITH OTHER DUDES HOLDING HANDS, I GUESS IT'S LIKE GOING TO THE MOVIES.* CONSENSUAL SEX WITHOUT COMMITMENT.
DICK SUCKER	DEROGATORY TERM FOR A *DOWN LOW* INMATE. SYNONYM: CLOSET PUNK

*FIFTY PERCENT [*OF DOWN-LOW INMATES*] ARE COWARDS, DICK SUCKERS. THEY ALL COME FROM THAT CRIME DISPOSITION AND DRUG ABUSE, THE OTHER 50 PERCENT JUST HAD CRIME PROBLEMS.*

DICKING DOWN	ROUGH SEX. SYNONYM: BEAST FUCKING
DIESEL DYKE	DEROGATORY TERM FOR A MASCULINE-LOOKING WOMAN. SYNONYM: TOUGH DYKES
DOGGY STYLE	TO HAVE ANAL SEX FROM A REAR POSITION. *I HEARD A QUEEN SAY MY MAN WAS HITTING ME DOGGY STYLE AND FLIPPED ME ON MY BACK AND STARTED PUT IT IN ALL WAYS, HE TRIED TO PUT HER THROUGH THE FLOOR. THIS QUEEN HAD TO HAVE AN ASSHOLE THE SIZE OF A HALF DOLLAR.*
DOME RIDER	A FEMALE INMATE WHO RECEIVES ORAL SEX. *USUALLY THE FEMME SAYS, "LET ME RIDE YOUR DOME" WHEN THE FEMME WANTS THE BUTCH TO DO HER.*
DOMESTIC VIOLENCE	VERBAL OR PHYSICAL DISPUTES BETWEEN INMATES INVOLVED IN A DOMESTIC RELATIONSHIP. THE MAN DOESN'T CONCEPTU-ALIZE MAN-WIFE AGGRESSION AS DOMESTIC VIOLENCE. AMONG WOMEN INMATES MAN-WIFE AGGRESSION IS INTER-PRETED AS DOMESTIC VIOLENCE.
DOUCHE BAG MOUTH	INMATE WHO HAS HAD ORAL SEX WITH NUMEROUS FEMALE PARTNERS. SYNONYM: YUCK MOUTH *THAT DOUCHE BAG MOUTH JUST LIKES EATING WOMEN OUT.*
DOWN	1. TO HAVE SEX WITH SOMEONE IN A HATEFUL MANNER TO-WARD SOMEONE ELSE. EXAMPLE: WHEN A FEMME HAS SEX WITH ANOTHER BUTCH IN FRONT OF HER BUTCH. 2. SOMEONE WHO HAS BEEN IN PRISON A LONG TIME. *PROBABLY BEING DOWN A LONG TIME, DON'T HAVE NO COMPAN-IONSHIP FROM OUTSIDE, DON'T GO TO FUNCTIONS.*
DOWN LOW	TO KEEP ONE'S SEXUAL BEHAVIOR IN A SAME-SEX RELATION-SHIP HIDDEN; SOMETIMES THOUGHT TO BE DISRESPECTFUL TO OTHER INMATES; BEING HONEST ABOUT SEXUAL ORIENTATION INSIDE IS NOT DISRESPECTFUL AND WILL PREVENT HOSTILITY.

I WAS APPROACHED LAST MONTH BY A GUY WHO WANT SOME CAP, CAN I PAY YOU A FEW DOLLARS TO GO IN THE CLOSET AND GET SOME CAP, HE WANTED TO KEEP IT ON THE DOWN LOW. I SAID JUST GIVE ME 10 DOLLARS I WON'T TELL ANYBODY SO I WENT AND DID IT AND I SAID THIS IS A FAKE-ASS AB [ARYAN BROTHER], I LOST RESPECT FOR THEM.

DRIVE-BY	MASTURBATING ON SOMEONE, OFTEN IN THE SHOWER.

1. *NOW, NICE TO THEM. TELL THEM SAY LOOK HERE. WE GOING TO START OUT I'M JUST GOING TO GET DRIVE-BYS [EJACULATING ON SOMEONE] AND SWEET EYES [WATCHING THEM MASTURBATE], JACKING OFF IN THE SHOWER ON YOU.*
2. *I AM SITTING DOWN RIGHT HERE AND THIS OFFICER CALL ME BY MY NICKNAME. SHE SAY "WHAT YOU GOT ON YOUR MIND?" I SAY "I AM THINKING ABOUT MY WIFE ON THE STREET." I SAY "I WANT TO NUT" AND "I WANT A DRIVE-BY." SHE SAID "YOU SHOULD BE WITH A BLACK LITTLE SISTER LIKE ME."*

DRY SNITCH	TO FILE A GRIEVANCE AGAINST STAFF OR INMATES, OFTEN WITH THE INTENTION OF BREAKING UP COUPLES OR CAUSING STAFF TROUBLE. MAY REFER TO AN ANONYMOUS SNITCH NOTE PLACED ON A STAFF MEMBER'S DESK. DRY REFERS TO UNSPOKEN.
DUDE	MALE INMATE. SYNONYM: MAN

WHITE DUDES ARE MORE VULNERABLE AND LOOKS MORE WEAKER, IF A BLACK OR MEXICAN ARE MESSING WITH A DUDE IT'LL BE WHITE.

DYKE	1. DOMINANT PARTNER IN A SEXUAL RELATIONSHIP. [FEMALE USAGE]

I CALL THE CHURCH DYKE CENTRAL, I WON'T GO TO CHURCH ANYMORE, THEY ARE KISSING, DIGGING IN EACH OTHER'S PANTS, I WAS LIKE HELL NO.

2. A HOMOSEXUAL INMATE WHO IS CONTROLLED BY HER MAN. [MALE USAGE]
SYNONYM: FAG

FACE	ORAL SEX. [FEMALE USAGE] TURNING OUT MEANS THAT SOMEBODY THAT'S NEVER BEEN WITH A WOMAN GIVES YOU SOME HEAD. THEY CAN BE TURNED OUT LIKE SOMEBODY COULD DO IT TO THEM, BUT THAT'S NOT TURNING OUT, YOU JUST GIVING THEM SOME FACE.

FAG

A DEROGATORY TERM FOR A MALE INMATE WHO LOOKS AND BEHAVES LIKE A WOMAN AND IS WEAK AND WAS COERCED OR FORCED IN HOMOSEXUAL BEHAVIOR. A FAG PERFORMS STEREOTYPICAL FEMALE ROLES. THEY STAY AT HOME AND ACT AS A MOM, TAKE CARE OF CELL, CARRY DRUGS AND SHANKS, AND DO WHATEVER THEY CAN TO KEEP THEIR *MAN* OUT OF THE HOLE.
SYNONYM: MY BABY, MAMMA, MOMMA LARK; LITTLE MAMMA

THE FAG STAYS IN THE CELL ALL DAY AND DOESN'T DO ANYTHING, STAYS IDLE SO THEY WON'T BE EXPOSED TO ANYONE. MAN KEEPS HER CUT OFF, AND THE FAGS ARE LESS VULNERABLE.

FAG HAG

INMATES WHO ARE NOT HOMOSEXUAL BUT HANG OUT WITH HOMOSEXUAL INMATES.

FAGGIES

A GAY INMATE; MAY BE AN INMATE WHO CAME IN GAY OR WAS TURNED OUT INSIDE. FAGGIES IS USED WITH PARTICULAR LIMITED GEOGRAPHIC DISTRIBUTION.

IT'S DL. EVERYBODY SEE THEM TODAY BUT THEY DON'T SHOW IT IN PUBLIC. THEY MEN IN DAYTIME AND FAGGIES AT NIGHT.

FATHER

AN OLDER INMATE WHO WATCHES OVER AND PROTECTS A YOUNGER, PRISON-INEXPERIENCED INMATE. SEX DOES NOT NECESSARILY HAVE TO BE RETURNED FOR THE BENEFIT OF THE PROTECTION. DADDIES MAY TAKE ON SONS IF THEY MISS THEIR OWN SONS. A SON WOULD NOT CALL HIS DADDY, FATHER. DESPITE KIN TERM USAGE, MEN INMATES DON'T NECESSARILY CONCEPTUALIZE THE FICTIVE KIN RELATIONS AS A FAMILY UNIT.

MOST OF THE TIME THE SON IS WEAKER THAN THE FATHER OR IS NEW INTO THE PRISON AND DON'T KNOW ANYONE OR WHAT REALLY GOES ON AND IS JUST SCARED.

FEFE BAG

A DEVICE FILLED WITH CHICKEN FAT, VASELINE, OR LIVER DESIGNED TO FEEL LIKE A WOMAN'S VAGINA. COMMON FEFE BAG CREATION INCLUDES PUTTING A PLASTIC BAG INTO A SOCK FILLED WITH LOTION AND THEN PLACING RUBBER BANDS— AROUND THE SOCK TO CREATE A SUCTION-LIKE DEVICE; ALSO COMMON IS A WARM WASHCLOTH BOUND WITH RUBBER BANDS. SYNONYM: POCKET PUSSY

THEY USE FEFE BAGS. THEY MAKE IT WITH A GLOVE AND HOT WATER AND YOU GREASE IT DOWN.

FEMALE

A MALE INMATE WHO PLAYS THE ROLE OF FEMALE.
SYNONYMS: FAG, ALL-OUT HOMOSEXUAL

THEY GO TO CHOW TOGETHER, LUNCH, EVERYWHERE TOGETHER.
THEY LINE UP PARTNERS IN THE FIELD, THE FEMALE WILL GO GET
THE WATER FOR THEIR MALE.

FEMME

1. WOMEN INMATES WHO LOOK FEMININE BY USING LIPSTICK
   AND OTHER COSMETICS; REFERS TO THE PASSIVE PARTNER
   IN A COUPLE.

   SAY LIKE I'M CHILLIN WITH ANOTHER STUD, SOMEBODY THAT'S
   LIKE ME, AND THEY GET INVOLVED WITH A FEMME AND THEY
   GET TOGETHER AND I WAS ALREADY YOUR CHILD OR WHAT-
   EVER. IF YOU MY MOM, NOW THAT'S MY DADDY.

2. A MALE INMATE WHO IS HETEROSEXUAL BUT LOOKS FEMI-
   NINE. LIMITED GEOGRAPHIC USAGE.

   QUEENS USE THE WORD FEMME, A FEMME CAN APPLY TO A
   GUY WHO'S HETERO BUT ACTS FEMININE. AN ALL-OUT QUEEN
   IS A FEMININE WOMAN. A FEMME IS A HETEROSEXUAL GUY
   WHO LOOKS FEMININE.

FEMME-FEMME

TO LOOK AND ACT FEMININE INCLUDING MAKEUP, HAIRSTYLE,
LIPSTICK, AND OTHER FEMININE COSMETICS.
SYNONYMS: GIRLY-GIRL, TRUE FEMME

IF I'M GOING TO BE WITH A WOMAN I WANT HER TO LOOK LIKE A
WOMAN, A FEMME-FEMME.

FISH

AN INMATE WHO IS NEW TO PRISON; INEXPERIENCED.
SYNONYM: MEAT

EVERYBODY LIKES TO SMOKE, IF YOU CAN'T SUPPORT THESE
HABITS A PREDATOR MAKES SURE HE WILL. THIS IS THE WHOLE
GAME, HE'S BAITING THE FRESH FISH IN, WHEN IT'S TIME TO PAY
THE PIPER THEY CAN'T BRING NOTHING TO THE TABLE.

FISTING

TO INSERT A FIST INTO A WOMAN'S VAGINA DURING A CONSEN-
SUAL OR NONCONSENSUAL ENCOUNTER.
ALTERNATIVELY: FIST FUCKING
SYNONYM: POWER

COULD START AS A WILLING SEX ACT WITH A PARTNER USING TWO
FINGERS AND PARTNER DECIDES TO SHOW YOU "THIS IS HERS"
AND FIST HER.

FLIP-FLOP   1. INMATES WHO SWITCH SEXUAL POSITIONS, PARTICIPATING IN BOTH GIVING AND RECEIVING.

MOST GUYS WANT TO GIVE SEX; IF MEN INMATES ARE TOTALLY GAY FLIP-FLOP IS NOT A BIG ISSUE.

2. A SWITCH IN SEX ROLES; MALE TO FEMALE, FEMALE TO MALE.

WE GOT FAMILIES. SAY DAY-DAY [A QUEEN] IS MY HOMOSEXUAL AND I AIN'T GONNA FLIP FLOP. I WOULD LET DAY-DAY HAVE A KID. SHE CAN DO HER FREAKY THINGS WITH THAT KID. THAT IS WHAT YOU CALL A FAMILY.

SYNONYMS: MEAT MONSTER, PEANUT BUTTER CHASER, LIPSTICK LESBIAN
USAGE: A FLIP-FLOP, TO FLIP-FLOP; FLIP-FLOPPER

3. FLIP-FLOP ALSO USED IN A NONSEXUAL CONTEXT.

[PRISON IS A] FLIP-FLOP FROM SOCIETY. I'M A WHITE MAN LIVING IN A BLACK MAN'S WORLD. I WATCH WHAT I DO, WHAT I SAY.

FLY TRAP   TECHNIQUE TO DETERMINE IF A MAN IS SEXUALLY INTERESTED IN ANOTHER MAN. TO DEFECATE WITH TOILET STALL DOOR OPEN TO SPOT PASSERS-BY WHO LOOK AT THE MAN ON THE TOILET. IT'S BELIEVED THAT AN INMATE WHO LOOKS SHOWS INTEREST IN SEX. MEN DON'T LOOK AT ONE OTHER ON THE TOILET OR IN THE SHOWER. IF THEY DO, THE CONNOTATION IS THAT THE OBSERVER IS INTERESTED IN SEX.

FREAK   AN INMATE WHO EXHIBITS EXTREME SEXUAL BEHAVIOR.
SYNONYM: FREAK BOY

FREAK, LIKES TO BEAT GIRLFRIENDS OR HAVE FIGHTS THEN HAVE SEX. MAKE DILDOS AND STRAP ONS.

FREAK BOY   A FAG WHO HAS EXTREME SEXUAL BEHAVIOR, SUCH AS GOLDEN SHOWERS.
SYNONYM: FREAK

THERE'S CERTAIN LAWS YOU OBEY. THE SHOWER ON TOP YOU TAKE A SHOWER WITH YOUR UNDERWEAR ON, TO JUST GET IN THE SHOWER ANYTIME YOU WANT, NO PROBLEM. WHEN YOU TAKE A SHOWER ON THE BOTTOM THE RESPECT ISSUE COME IN. THE NEXT MAN WHO COME IN WILL HAVE TO SAY "SHOWER" AND I'LL PUT MY CLOTHES ON, OR IF HE'S A FREAK BOY AND I'M A FREAK BOY

I'LL INVITE HIM IN AND HE'LL GET BUTT ASS NAKED TOO, AND IT COULD JUST BE A SHOWER.

FREAKY ISLAND	A NONSMOKING RESIDENCE UNIT PREFERRED BY HOMOSEXUALS. LIMITED GEOGRAPHIC USAGE.

ONE BLOCK OVER HERE IS FREAKY ISLAND, THE NONSMOKING BLOCK, EVERYONE MOVED OVER THERE TO BE WITH THEIR PEOPLE AND COUPLES.

FREE-WORLD FAG/PUNK	FAG ON THE OUTSIDE AND INSIDE. FREE-WORLD FAG GETS MORE RESPECT THAN AN INMATE WHO WAS TURNED OUT.

HIGH OFFICIAL RANKS WILL TAKE INTEREST IN FREE-WORLD PUNKS, THEY GOOD MANIPULATORS AND SNITCHES, GETTING PEOPLE OFF OF COMMISSARY.

FUCK	SEXUAL PENETRATION.

I'VE SEEN SOME OF THESE GUYS SAY IF THEY'RE FUCKING THEM IN THE ASS THEY'RE NOT TAKING ON THE FEMININE ROLE, THEREFORE THEY'RE NOT A FAG. I'M LIKE WAIT A MINUTE, IF YOU'RE SCREWING A GUY IN THE ASS, YOU'RE A FAG.

FUCK BOY	A MALE INMATE WHO ISN'T *ALL THE WAY OUT*; FUCK BOYS DON'T LOOK GAY. TARGET OF SEXUAL VIOLENCE IF HE DOESN'T DO WHAT HE IS ASKED TO DO; WEIGHT LIFTERS WHO GET "FUCKED" ARE FUCK BOYS. MINOR USAGE AS SYNONYM OF PRESSURE PUNK, EMPHASIZING THAT HOMOSEXUALITY IS NOT ALL THE WAY OUT. SOME USAGE OF FUCK BOY TO REFER TO A YOUNG TURN-OUT WHO IS PIMPED; SOME USAGE AS SYNONYM FOR TURN-OUT. SOME USAGE FOR DRUGGED-OUT BOYS WHO'LL DO ANYTHING FOR DRUGS. ALSO REFERS TO HETEROSEXUALS WHO WILL HAVE SEX FOR DRUGS AND DON'T CONSIDER THEMSELVES HOMOSEXUALS.

1. A FUCK BOY IS SOMEONE WHO CAN BE TAKEN TO A CLOSET AND ALLOW AN INMATE TO HAVE SEX, PENETRATION, THEY MORE MALE THAN FEMALE, THEY TRY TO PLAY THE MALE CHARACTER, AND SNEAK AND DO IT ON THE SIDE.
2. SINCE AIDS AND ALL THAT, YOU STILL HAVE SOME OLDER HOMOSEXUALS WITH SAME PARTNERS BUT YOU GOT A WHOLE LOTTA UNDERCOVER DUDES, FUCK BOYS, AROUND, THEY ON THE DOWN LOW.

FUCK THE SHIT OUT OF	USED TO INDICATE A MORE LENGTHY SEX ACT THAN A QUICKIE; OFTEN TWO TO THREE MINUTES.

FULL LOCKER	A LOCKER FULL OF COMMISSARY ITEMS; FULL LOCKER MAY RESULT FROM BEING A *COMMISSARY QUEEN*, TRADING COMMISSARY ITEMS FOR SEX.
	THERE'S A DUDE WHO RECENTLY GOT BUSTED FOR GIVING A BLOW JOB AND HE HAD A FULL LOCKER.
GANGSTER BITCH	STREET TERM, *HOMOSEXUAL WHO TAKES NO SHIT*. HOMOSEXUAL WHO GOES UNACKNOWLEDGED BY INMATES BECAUSE "SHE" HAS A VIOLENT REPUTATION. A BITCH THAT'S EDUCATED AND CAN BE TRUSTED.
	GANGSTER BOOTIE OR GANGSTER BITCH, BOTH ARE COMPLIMENTS IN THE SEEDY UNDERWORLD KIND OF WAY. I'M CLASSIFIED AS A GANGSTER BITCH QUEEN. I'LL STAND UP TO GUYS ON REAL STUFF LIKE DRUGS OR MONEY. A LOT OF LITTLE GANG BANGERS TRY TO TAKE MY STUFF. I TELL YOU WHAT. I'LL GET MY DOOR POPPED OPEN, YOU TAKE MY STUFF AND WE'LL HANDLE IT. TO THE HOODLUMS AND SHIT THAT'S GANGSTER FIRE IF YOU'RE WILLING TO BE STUPID ENOUGH TO SACRIFICE MY LIFE OVER A CASSETTE PLAYER.
GANGSTER BOOTIE	LIMITED USAGE TO MEAN *NICE ASS*.
GARBAGE DISPOSAL	A WOMAN INMATE WHO GIVES ORAL SEX TO MULTIPLE INMATES. SYNONYM: HEAD HUNTER, PAC-MAN
	WE CALL THEM GARBAGE DISPOSALS, THEY SLEEP WITH ANYTHING.
GAY	GAY HAS A CONNOTATION DIFFERENT FROM HOMOSEXUAL AND FAG. A GAY IS FLAMBOYANTLY HOMOSEXUAL. A GAY MAY *FLIP-FLOP* WITH A HOMOSEXUAL, PLAYING THE FEMALE AND MALE ROLES.
GAY BOY	A FEMALE INMATE WHO DOESN'T DRESS IN DRAG BUT TRIES TO ACT LIKE A MAN. A YOUNG MALE HOMOSEXUAL.
	GUYS IN POPULATION WILL LOOK FOR THE LITTLE GAY BOY ILLUSION, THEY'LL GIVE HIM A SANDWICH AND MEET HIM SOMEWAY AND MAYBE NOT EVEN DO NOTHING WITH HIM.
GAY FOR THE STAY	FEMALE INMATES WHO PARTICIPATE IN HOMOSEXUALITY WHILE INCARCERATED BUT RETURN TO HETEROSEXUAL RELATIONSHIPS ON THE STREET.

SOMETIMES THEY'RE JUST GAY FOR THE STAY, THERE'S NOTHING BETTER TO DO.

GEORGIA	PIMPING A STRAIGHT INMATE FOR HOMOSEXUAL SEX. LIMITED GEOGRAPHIC USAGE. *A DUDE CAN BE PIMPED MEANING YOU CAN PIMP YOUR DUDE. A MAN CAN BE PIMPED AND HE AIN'T GOT TO BE A HOMO TO BE GAY. IT'S CALLED GEORGIA.*
GETBACK	TO RETALIATE FOR A VIOLENT OR DISRESPECTFUL ACT. *GET HIS GETBACK.*
GET DOWN	A PROPENSITY TOWARD HOMOSEXUAL OR NONHOMOSEXUAL BEHAVIOR. *THE DUDE DON'T GET DOWN LIKE THAT.*
GET ON THE WAGON	TO ENTER A PRISON AS A NEW INMATE.
GIRL	MALE INMATE WHO BEHAVES LIKE OTHER INMATES OUTSIDE THE CELL, BUT ADOPTS FEMALE CLOTHING INSIDE THE CELL; COOKS AND CLEANS; MAY WEAR BRA AND PANTIES INSIDE CELL. FORM OF ADDRESS: *"HEY, GIRL." THEN TRICKERY STARTS. IF A STRAIGHT GUY CALLS A GAY "SHE," YOU'LL BEGIN TO THINK SHE CAN SATISFY YOU LIKE A BITCH.*
GIRL BOY	A VICTIM OF SEXUAL ASSAULT WHO DOES NOT *HANDLE HIS BUSINESS* [RETALIATE]; MAY BE AN OLD TERM.
GIRLY GIRL	A COSMETICALLY EXTREME VERSION OF *FEMME*; WEARS HEAVY MAKEUP, LIPSTICK, AND OTHER COSMETICS. SYNONYM: FEMME, FEMME-FEMME *A LOT OF WOMEN HERE THAT CUT THEIR HAIR SHORT AND SHAVE THEIR HEAD, COME INTO RECEIVING A GIRLY GIRL AND THEN HIT THE YARD AND BECOME A BOY.*
GIVE IT UP	TO GIVE IN TO SEXUAL PRESSURE. *IF YOU SEE SOMEONE YOU WANT AND YOU KNOW THEY GOT IT IN THEM, BUT THEY WON'T GIVE IT UP, YOU MIGHT JUST TAKE IT.*
GOLDEN SHOWER	URINATING ON A PARTNER DURING A SEXUAL ACT.

GORILLA PIMP	AN INMATE WHO FORCES INMATES TO HAVE SEX WITH HIM. A GORILLA PIMP *TAKES PUSSY*; UNLIKE THE STREET, A GORILLA PIMP DOES NOT *SELL PUSSY*. LIMITED USAGE REFERS TO OLD-SCHOOL INMATES. OLDER USAGE: TO FORCE SOMEONE TO GET SOMETHING; GAYS ARE GORILLA PIMPED. ALTERNATIVELY: GORILLA HAWK *OLD SCHOOL GUYS, JUST TAKING WHAT YOU WANT. USED TO HAVE A DIFFERENT MEANING. USED TO MEAN MAKING A MOTHER-FUCKER GOING TO GET WHAT YOU WANT, NOT EVEN SEXUAL, JUST MATERIAL. PEOPLE WHO GET GORILLA PIMPED ARE THE HOMO-SEXUAL, MAKING A HOMO GET SOMETHING FOR THEM.*
GOT SUGAR IN YOUR TANK	REFERS TO MAN WHO IS GAY THOUGH HE MAY NOT RECOGNIZE IT. *SOME INMATES RUN AROUND LIKE THEY REAL THOROUGH. TAKES ONE PERSON AND "YOU GOT SOME SUGAR IN YOUR TANK. HE JUST PULLED IT OUT OF YOU."* *DUDES ARE GAY INSIDE AND [PRETEND TO BE] TOUGH IN VISIT-ING.*
GRAVEYARD LOVE	TO PRESSURE SOMEONE FOR SEX WHEREIN THE OUTCOME IS SEX OR DEATH. 1. *YOU ARE GOING TO BE WITH ME OR BE WITH THE DIRT.* 2. *KILLING, BECAUSE ONE INDIVIDUAL, THE HOMOSEXUAL, WAS AC-TUALLY GOING HOME AND THE GUY, THE HUSBAND, MAN WAS STILL HAVING TWO OR THREE MORE YEARS LEFT. HE DIDN'T WANT HER TO LEAVE AND HE KILLED HER. WE CALL THAT GRAVE-YARD LOVE; ONCE THEY LOCKED IN THEY CAN'T SEPARATE.*
GRINDING	FEMALE SEXUAL BEHAVIOR WHERE BOTH WOMEN PROVIDE SEXUAL GRATIFICATION TO EACH OTHER. SYNONYM: BUMPING PUSSYS
GUMBY	AN *OLD SCHOOL* TERM FOR A HOMOSEXUAL INMATE. SYNONYM: FAG, PUNK
HARD ADDICTION	INMATE WHO HAS AN ADDICTIVE NEED FOR DRUGS, SEX, OR COMPANIONSHIP.
HATE ON	AN INTENTIONAL ACT OF HATRED TOWARD SOMEONE. NONVI-OLENT ACT OF DISLIKE. TO HATE ON SOMEONE.

HEAD	ORAL SEX; MALE OR FEMALE. SYNONYM: BLOW JOB *I'VE HEARD ABOUT PEOPLE GIVING HEAD TO THIS PERSON, "IF YOU GIVE ME A NOODLE I'LL GIVE YOU SOME HEAD."*
HEAD HUNTER	WOMEN INMATES WHO CONTINUOUSLY LOOK FOR ORAL SEX. *COCK SUCKERS ARE PEOPLE WHO LIKE TO RIDE (GIVE) HEAD, A HEAD HUNTER TRIES TO HUNT FOR A PERSON'S MOUTH.*
HE-SHE	DEROGATORY TERM USED BY HETEROSEXUALS FOR GAY INMATES. HE-SHE HAS A NON-NEGATIVE CONNOTATION.
HETEROSEXUAL	A MALE WHO HAD SEX ONLY WITH WOMEN OUTSIDE PRISON. HE MAY HAVE SAME-SEX RELATIONS INSIDE PRISON. HETEROSEXUALS ARE VIEWED AS STRONGER AND ABLE TO PROTECT OR PROVIDE SECURITY TO A HOMOSEXUAL.
HIT IT	1. TO HAVE SEXUAL RELATIONS. WOMEN'S USAGE INCLUDES SELF-PENETRATION WITH A DILDO. SYNONYM: FUCK *THEY'RE LONELY, THEY JUST WANT TO HAVE SEX, "HIT IT AND QUIT IT," KIND OF LIKE A ONE-NIGHT THING.* 2. TO HAVE SEX IN AN AGGRESSIVE WAY. *HE'S HITTING IT FROM THE BACK.* 3. MASTURBATION. *HE WAS HITTING IT ON THE STREET AND GOT ARRESTED.*
HO	1. A HOMOSEXUAL ONE CAN TRUST IN; FOR EXAMPLE, TO SELL DRUGS. DIFFERING FROM THE COMMON STREET DEFINITION, A HO DOES NOT NECESSARILY *SELL ASS.* A HO HAS *POLISH AND GAME.* *BACK IN THE OLD DAYS IF I RIDE [GET SENT TO ADMINISTRATIVE SEGREGATION] MY HO COMING BEHIND ME. A HO WILL HUSTLE, WASH CLOTHES, MAKE MONEY FOR HER MAN.* 2. AN EXPRESSION OF ATTACHMENT BY A MAN TOWARD HIS FEMALE (MALE) PARTNER. A TERM OF ENDEARMENT. *THOSE IN A RELATIONSHIP USUALLY CALL THEIR MATE A HO IF THEY SPEAK TO ANOTHER DUDE.*

3. DEROGATORY CONNOTATION: WHORE; CONTEXT DETERMINES MEANING.

YOU'RE A HO OR WEAK IF YOU GET TURNED OUT WHEN YOU GET HERE.

HOGGING	TAKING SOMEONE'S PROPERTY, MONEY, AND POSSESSIONS; PRESSURING AN INMATE TO DEVELOP A RIDING RELATIONSHIP. ALTERNATIVELY: BULL HOG *THEY ARE OUT TO HOG YOU OR GAME YOU.*
HOLE	A SEGREGATION HOUSING UNIT. *THEY WILL NOTIFY RANK AND LOCK YOU UP IN THE HOLE 9 OUT OF 10 TIMES.*
HOMOSECTING	TO HAVE SEX WITH ANOTHER WOMAN. RESTRICTED GEOGRAPHIC USAGE. *I THINK HOMOSECTING IS A 115. IT'S A SERIOUS WRITE-UP IF YOU GET CAUGHT.*
HOMOSEXUAL	1. A SEXUAL PREFERENCE. A PERSON WHO HAS NO DESIRE TO BE WITH THE OPPOSITE SEX. *IF SOMEONE COMES IN WHO HAS HOMOSEXUAL INCLINATIONS IT'S GOING TO COME OUT.* 2. A MALE HOMOSEXUAL ENGAGES IN SEX WITH MEN INSIDE AND OUTSIDE PRISON AND HAS RESPECT AMONG INMATES. HOMOSEXUAL MAY HAVE RESPECT AMONG INMATES FOR HIS STRENGTH, FIGHTING ABILITY, OR WILLINGNESS TO KILL. SEE FAG. SYNONYM: GAY, FAG *THE HOMOSEXUALS HERE, YOU KNOW WHO THEY ARE, BECAUSE SOME OF THEM HAVE BREASTS, YOU KNOW THE STATE LET IT GO BECAUSE THEY GIVE THEM HORMONE PILLS HERE.*
HOOKED UP	A WAY OF BONDING WITH ANOTHER INMATE WHO SHARES SEXUAL PREFERENCES. A GAY MAY APPROACH AN INMATE AND ASK, *DO YOU FUCK AROUND?* *IF POPULATION DUDE HOOKS UP WITH ONE OF THE GAYS, PURPLE PASSION HAS TO DEAL WITH THE POPULATION, SO PURPLE PASSION MAKES SURE THE VICTIM ISN'T HOOKED UP WITH A POPULATION DUDE.*

HOOKER	A PASSIVE PLAYER IN A SEXUAL RELATIONSHIP. SYNONYM: WIFE, MAMA, HO, BITCH

THAT'S MY HO, THAT'S MY HOOKER, THAT'S A TERM OF ENDEARMENT IN HERE. A HOMOSEXUAL WOULD SMILE AND ACCEPT THAT AND BLUSH.

HOT-PARTNER	A FEMALE INMATE WHO TAKES CARE OF OLDER INMATES. FOR EXAMPLE, HELPING THEM IN THE SHOWER. IN RETURN, A HOT-PARTNER MAY RECEIVE A LETTER FOR HER FILES AND THE RESPECT OF OTHER INMATES.

HOUSEWIFE	A *FAG* WHO CARES FOR A *MAN'S* CELL. *HOUSEWIFE* IS OFTEN USED IN A DEROGATORY WAY TO CONNOTE THAT THE FAG IS NOT RELIABLE OR WON'T OBEY HER MAN'S COMMANDS TO PROSTITUTE HERSELF FOR DOPE, CASH, OR COMMISSARY.

A HO IS WAY UP AND A HOUSEWIFE IS DOWN LOW. A HO WILL HUSTLE, WASH CLOTHES, MAKE MONEY, IN A HOUSEWIFE RELATION THE HUSBAND IS THE PROVIDER, IT'S A WHOLE DIFFERENT RELATIONSHIP.

HUSBAND	MALE INMATE WHO PLAYS A MAN'S ROLE IN A LONG-TERM, *MAN-FAG* RELATIONSHIP, OR MARRIAGE. NEAR SYNONYM: DADDY

HUSTLE	AN ACTIVITY THAT PRODUCES VALUABLE RESOURCES. SELLING DRUGS OR SEX IS A HUSTLE. AN INMATE WHO GIVES COMMISSARY IS ON THE HUSTLE.

I PUT $1,000 ON THEIR BOOKS. I'M GOING TO GET THAT BACK IT'S NOTHING, THEY AIN'T GOT TO WORRY ABOUT WASHING OTHER DUDES' CLOTHES FOR A HUSTLE.

INTO THE COUNT	AN INMATE WHO ENTERS A SOCIAL SCENE OR COMES INTO THE INMATE POPULATION.

SOME GUYS ARE LIKE THAT, THEY TRY TO KEEP IT IN THE CLOSET YOU KNOW, UNTIL A HOMOSEXUAL COMES INTO THE COUNT AND BRINGS THEM OUT OF THE CLOSET.

JACK BOOK	PORNOGRAPHIC MATERIALS USED TO MASTURBATE TO.

THEY'RE TAKING ALL THE JACK BOOKS AND YOU SEE THAT'S GOING TO BRING BACK A LOT OF SEX ABUSE.

JACK BOYS	PUBLIC MASTURBATORS WHO SIT TOGETHER AND TALK ABOUT FEMALE STAFF. [MALE USAGE]

THAT'S LIKE A JACK BOY KILLIN' ON A BOSS MAN.

JACK TICKET	AN INCIDENT REPORT ISSUED FOR MASTURBATION, OFTEN MASTURBATION IN A PUBLIC PLACE.
JACKET	LABEL OR REPUTATION. ALSO AN INMATE'S CRIMINAL OR INSTITUTIONAL HISTORY.
	THEY HARDER THAN ME AND THEY FOOLISH AND THEY GOT MURDERS UNDER THEIR JACKET AND THEY NOT AFRAID OF ANYTHING.
JACK-OFF	MASTURBATE
	SOME DUDES JACK OFF ON FEMALE COS. THAT WOULD HAVE NEVER HAPPENED BEFORE. THE COS WOULD HAVE KILLED SOMEONE.
JACK-OFF ARTIST	A COMPULSIVE MASTURBATOR. MASTURBATES IN PUBLIC WHILE LOOKING AT A FEMALE OR MALE STAFF MEMBER. HE MAY STAND IN A SHOWER AND MASTURBATE FOR HOURS IF A FEMALE STAFF MEMBER IS PRESENT. ALTERNATIVELY: JERK-OFF ARTIST SYNONYM: FREAK BOY
JOHN	AN INMATE WHO BUYS SEX. SYNONYM: TRICK, TREY
JUICY	A TERM OF ENDEARMENT FOR A MALE PASSIVE HOMOSEXUAL. SYNONYM: FAG
JUMP-AROUNDS	HOMOSEXUALS THAT MOVE FROM LOVER TO LOVER. [FEMALE USAGE]
K-DADDY	AN INMATE WHO PAYS ANOTHER INMATE FOR SEX. SYNONYM: TRICK
	A K-DADDY PAYS A BOY FOR SEX.
KICKING IT	HANGING OUT. USED IN DATING AS GOING TO THE YARD OR BINGO WITH A DATE.
	SAY THEY DON'T MESS WITH A DUDE BUT THE NEXT DAY THEY KICKING IT AND PLAYING B-BALL.
KILL	1. TO MASTURBATE IN PUBLIC (*KILL ON SOMEBODY*) OR LOOK AT SOMEONE WHILE MASTURBATING. CAN ALSO BE A NOUN (A KILLER) OR AN ACT (KILLING). SYNONYM: JACK BOY
	A COUPLE OF TIMES I'VE SAID HEY GIVE ME A KILL SHOT AND I MASTURBATE, AND HAVE THEM HAVE ON PANTIES AND STUFF, OR YOU MIGHT RUB ON THEIR LEGS OR ASS, THAT'S MORE COMMON THAN ACTUAL SEX, AND SAFER.

2. A TERM OF REFERENCE USED TO IDENTIFY A NONHOMOSEX-
UAL INMATE WHO WAS *RIPPED OFF* (SEXUALLY ASSAULTED)
AND THEN IS ABOUT TO OR HAS VIOLENTLY RETALIATED
AGAINST HIS RAPIST. TERM DOES NOT REFER TO AN INMATE
WHO COMMITTED HOMICIDE FOR OTHER REASONS. [LIMITED
USAGE]

*IF A PERSON IS RAPED AND THEY'RE NOT A HO AND RETALIATE
THEY'LL BE KNOWN AS A KILLER.*

KING CROSSOVER	HETEROSEXUAL WHO SWITCHES TO HOMOSEXUAL SEX IN PRISON. [MALE USAGE]

*A GUY WHO'S HAVING SEX WITH OTHER GUYS, HE'S BEEN BUSTED
OUT, HE WAS TRYING TO HIDE IT BUT NOW THAT HE'S OUT IT'S A
KING CROSSOVER*

KINKIN' — WOMEN'S PRISON USAGE REFERS TO WOMEN WHO ARE DATING.

KNOCK OFF — RECEIVE ORAL SEX.
SYNONYM: BLOW JOB

WANT HIM TO KNOCK ME OFF.

LEAVE IT AT THE GATE — PARTICIPATION IN SAME-SEX RELATIONS INSIDE PRISON AS A *HUSTLE*, BUT REMAINING HETEROSEXUAL UPON RETURN TO THE COMMUNITY; APPLIES EVEN IF A MAN WAS TURNED OUT.

AS LONG AS YOU LEAVE IT AT THE GATE, IT'S JUST A HUSTLE.

LIPSTICK LESBIAN — A FEMALE INMATE WHO SWITCHES FROM FEMININE TO AGGRES-
SIVE SEXUAL ROLES; ONE DAY A *STUD BROAD*, ANOTHER DAY A *FEMME*.
SYNONYM: FLIP-FLOP

A LIPSTICK LESBIAN IS A STUD WHO WEARS LIPSTICK ON VISITING DAY.

LION — AN INMATE WHO CAN PROTECT HIMSELF. A GENERIC TERM TO
CONNOTE AN AGGRESSOR BUT NOT NECESSARILY VIOLENT OR
SEXUAL. USED AS A METAPHOR FOR A STRONG INMATE.
SYNONYM: WOLF, STRONG

*YOU OFFICIALLY COULD CHECK INTO PC, COULD BUDDY UP WITH
A CORRECTIONAL OFFICER AND MAKE SURE HE'LL BE CLOSE BY
YOU, OR BUDDY UP WITH A LION TO PROTECT YOU.*

LOCK UP	TO TAKE REFUGE IN PROTECTIVE CUSTODY. *IF THEY DON'T LOCK UP AFTER A RAPE, THEY BECOME A BITCH, NEXT THING YOU KNOW THEY'RE OUT WALKING AROUND TALKING HIGH.*
LOVER'S LANE	A PRISON THEATRE. A POPULAR LOCATION OF HOMOSEXUAL SAME-SEX RELATIONS.
MADAM	NUMBER ONE QUEEN AMONG A GROUP OF *HO*S WHO ARE PROSTITUTES; CHARGED WITH MANAGING THE PROSTITUTION BUSINESS. [MALE USAGE] SYNONYM: BIG MAMMA
MAMMA	1. PASSIVE PLAYER IN A SEXUAL RELATIONSHIP. ALSO LITTLE MAMMA OR MAMMA LARK. SYNONYM: WIFE, HO 2. FEMALE INMATE ACTING IN A MOTHERLY ROLE IN A FICTIVE KINSHIP RELATIONSHIP. SYNONYM: STATE MOM *I HAVE 8 STATE CHILDREN, 13 STATE GRANDCHILDREN, AND A HOST OF STATE NIECES. "THEY COME TO ME AND SAY, "YOU SO NICE, WILL YOU BE MY MAMMA?"*
MAN	DOMINANT PARTNER IN A MALE SEXUAL RELATIONSHIP. *THAT'S MY MAN.*
MANHOOD	A MAN'S ANAL VIRGINITY. *YOU CAN DO ANYTHING BUT GIVE YOUR MANHOOD UP. IF YOU GOTTA GET BEAT UP, OH WELL, GET BEAT UP. IF YOU STAND UP FOR YOURSELF AND GET BEAT, THEN IN TIME YOU'LL GET HELP. SOMEONE WILL INTERVENE IF A DUDE IS GETTING BEAT UP.*
MARK	A RAPE VICTIM OR TARGET.
MARRIAGE	A LASTING SAME-SEX RELATIONSHIP OFTEN IDENTIFIED BY THE WIFE (MALE OR FEMALE) WEARING A WEDDING RING. MAY HAVE A PUBLIC CEREMONY IN A CELL HOUSE OR ON THE COMPOUND, PROCLAIMING THE PERMANENCE OF A RELATIONSHIP. GUESTS ARE INVITED, VOWS ARE EXCHANGED; RICE MAY BE THROWN, CAKE EATEN IF PURCHASED IN COMMISSARY. BRIDE MAY WEAR A SELF-FASHIONED WEDDING DRESS.

MARRIAGE OF CONVENIENCE	A MAN AND HIS HOMOSEXUAL SHARING THE SAME CELL.

MEAT	AN INMATE NEW TO PRISON. USAGE: FRESH MEAT; NEW MEAT; YOUNG MEAT SYNONYM: FISH *A LOT OF PEOPLE LIKE VIOLENT SEX AND LIKE FRESH MEAT AND FRESH PRISON PUSSY.*

MINUTE MAN	TO HAVE SEX QUICKLY. *MAKE LOVE, THIS IS RARE IN A CELL. THEY HAVE TO BE A MINUTE MAN. FOR SOME DUDES IT'S KIND OF HARD IF YOU IN THE PORTA CLOSET. IF YOU NEED 45 MINUTES TO MAKE LOVE IT HAS TO BE WITH A CELLIE.*

MISS THING	A MEAN QUEEN. [LIMITED GEOGRAPHIC DISTRIBUTION]

MIX	SOCIAL LIFE ON A WOMEN'S COMPOUND. COMMONLY CONSIDERED A NEGATIVE OR DANGEROUS WAY OF PRISON LIFE. *THE PERSON WHO GETS INTO THE MIX IS MOST VULNERABLE. MIX IS CLIQUES. YOU KNOW WHO NOT TO MESS WITH SO YOU STAY AWAY FROM THEM.*

MOMMY	1. FICTIVE FAMILY NAME. *SOMETIMES THE DADDY IS DOING THE CHILDREN UP IN THE ROOM WHILE THE MOMMY IS IN THE OTHER BUILDING. IT'S A GAME, EVERYTHING'S A GAME.* 2. TERM OF ENDEARMENT FOR MALE HOMOSEXUAL. *THAT'S MY MOMMY, MY WIFE.*

MORNING BOYS	RAPISTS WHO STRIKE INMATES EARLY IN THE MORNING. ALTERNATIVELY: THREE-FOUR-FIVE O'CLOCK IN THE MORNING BOYS *MORNING BOYS DO IT EARLY IN THE MORNING CAUSE THE DOORS IS JUST OPENING.*

NASTY HO	INMATE WHO TRADES SEX FOR DRUGS. ALTERNATIVELY: NASTY TRICK SYNONYM: STRAWBERRY *PAYING A BOY FOR SEX IS MORE LIKE A SLUT, A NASTY HO.*

NEW BOY	NEW INMATES ON THE CELL BLOCK; PRISON-INEXPERIENCED INMATES. SYNONYM: NEW MEAT, FRESH MEAT, FISH *THE VICTIMS ARE NEW BOYS AND YOUNG FISH, CAN VISUALLY PICK THEM OUT EASILY. IT'S A GAME WE PLAY WHEN WE SEE THEM IN RECEPTION.*
NIGHT CREEPERS	INMATE ON THE DOWN LOW. DURING THE DAY A NIGHT CREEPER PRETENDS TO BE STRAIGHT, BUT AT NIGHT LOOKS FOR SEX. SYNONYM: DOWN LOW *THEY FAKE LIKE THEY DON'T MESS AROUND IN THE DAYTIME, BUT THEY NIGHT CREEPERS.*
OFF THE RIP	QUICKLY; RAPID SOCIAL BONDING. TWO MEN WHO BOND QUICKLY AND FORM A LASTING RELATIONSHIP. *SEX HAPPENS QUICKLY IF MEN GET TOGETHER OFF THE RIP.*
OLD JOE	FICTIVE CHARACTER THAT "TAKES CARE" OF AN INMATE'S WIFE WHILE THEY ARE INCARCERATED. SYNONYM: BIG DICK BOB
OLD-SCHOOL	1. AN OLDER, EXPERIENCED INMATE. *I THINK EVERY OLD-SCHOOL HAS STORIES TO TELL.* 2. A SLOW COVER TACTIC TO TURN OUT A YOUNG INMATE BY CREATING A FRIENDSHIP BOND THROUGH ATHLETICS, SHARING MEALS, AND LETTING THE YOUNG INMATE BELIEVE THE OLDER INMATE IS HIS FRIEND. *RAPE, THAT'S OLD SCHOOL, THAT DON'T HAPPEN, MAYBE IN THE '80S AND MID-'90S, BUT NOWADAYS IN THE NEW MILLENNIUM IT AIN'T REALLY JUMPING OFF LIKE THAT.*
OLD THINGS	TRUSTWORTHY HOMOSEXUALS; MAY BE IDIOSYNCRATIC USAGE. *OLD THINGS CAN TAKE CARE OF MOVES. HE'LL GET $50 TO MOVE SOMEONE.*
PAC-MAN	WOMAN INMATE WHO PROVIDES ORAL SEX TO MANY FEMALE PARTNERS. SEX ROLES ARE NOT SWITCHED. *A PAC-MAN, THEY EAT ANYTHING OR EVERYTHING.*

PANCAKE	A HOMOSEXUAL WHO VOLUNTARILY SWITCHES SEX ROLES FROM MALE TO FEMALE, FEMALE TO MALE. [MALE OR FEMALE USAGE] SYNONYM: FLIP-FLOP
PARTNER	1. COMPANION. SOMEONE AN INMATE BELIEVES HE CAN RELY ON. *FIND THE LEADER OF THE WHITE GUYS AND BEFRIEND HIM, BECOME ONE OF HIS PARTNERS, LITERALLY KEEP TO YOUR OWN TYPE.* 2. MEMBER OF A COMMITTED SEXUAL RELATIONSHIP. *THE REAL WAY YOU CAN FIND OUT IF YOUR PARTNER IS CLEAN YOU CAN GO TO THE CLINIC AND FIND OUT. ME AND MY PARTNER BOTH ARE NEGATIVE SO WE CLING TOGETHER.*
PAYBACK	RETALIATION FOR A VIOLENT OR DISRESPECTFUL ACT.
PAYMASTER	TO BUY SEX AS ONE WOULD ON THE STREET. ALSO USING AN INMATE ONLY FOR THE PHYSICAL ACT OF SEX. SYNONYM: TRICK, SUCKER FOR LOVE, THIRSTY
PC PUNK	DEROGATORY. A WEAK INMATE WHO CHOOSES PC AS AN ALTERNATIVE TO THE GENERAL POPULATION. *SEE* PUNK CITY.
PEANUT BUTTER CHASER	*SEE* ASS CHASER.
PECKERWOOD	A WHITE SUPREMACIST. *A PECKERWOOD IS A STAND-UP WHITE GUY.*
PENITENTIARY SLICK	INMATE WHO CONS PEOPLE OUT OF SEX WITH SLICK TALK. *A LOT OF GUYS CALL THEMSELVES PENITENTIARY SLICK, THEY CON ARTISTS AND GET ON THE PHONE AND HAVE RELATIONSHIPS LIKE THAT. PUT THEM ON YOUR VISITING LIST AND THEY COME DOWN AND SEE YOU, SEND YOU LITTLE CARE PACKAGES.*
PILLOW PRINCESS	AN INMATE WHO RECEIVES ORAL SEX WITHOUT ANY RECIPROCATION. SOMETIMES ASSOCIATED WITH THE TERM *WIFE*. *SOMEONE WHO JUST LAYS BACK ON THE PILLOW AND RECEIVES ORAL SEX.*

PIMPING	MANIPULATION WITH OR WITHOUT SEX.
	A MAN CAN BE PIMPED, AND HE AIN'T GOT TO BE A HOMO TO BE GAY.
	[FROM OUR] STANDPOINT IF YOU PIMP ANOTHER DUDE YOU USING A MENTAL GAME. SEE GEORGIA.
PIRATE	TO STEAL. CONNOTATIONS IN SEXUAL USAGE INCLUDE A *PREDATOR* PIRATING A NEW INMATE'S ASS.
	WE FIGURED OUT A WAY TO GET CINEMAX, HBO, AND STARZ FREE, WITH WIRE AND A PEN AND A MAGNET AND IT'LL COME IN. WE FIGURED OUT HOW TO DO THAT. YOU JUST GOTTA FINESSE THEM AND YOU GOT SNITCHES THAT GO AND TELL ON US AND THEY'LL COME AND FEEL AROUND THE TV FOR THE CABLES. WE CAN PIRATE ANYTHING.
POCKET PUSSY	CREATING AN ARTIFICIAL VAGINA FOR SEXUAL RELEASE. SYNONYM: FEFE BAG
	THEY MIGHT USE POCKET PUSSY, CHICKEN FAT TO FEEL LIKE A WOMAN. MORE DUDES THAT AIN'T HOMOSEXUAL DO THIS.
POWER	INSERTING A FIST INTO A FEMALE'S VAGINA. *SEE* FISTING.
	THEY GIVE EACH OTHER THE POWER IN HERE . . . WILL SAY I DON'T MESS WITH WOMEN WHO DON'T TAKE THE POWER.
PREDATOR	AN INMATE WHO HAS THE INTENTION OF ENGAGING IN VIOLENT SEX. A PREDATOR IS SEEN AS A *STRONG* INMATE. A PREDATOR MAY TURN OUT AN INMATE, IN WHICH CASE, THE RAPE DOES NOT OCCUR. A PREDATOR MAY STALK AN INMATE AND RAPE HIM.
	PREDATORS ARE SNEAKY AND DANGEROUS. HE'LL JUST GET [SEX].
PRESS	REPEATED MENTAL MANIPULATION TO GAIN SEXUAL ACCESS. SYNONYM: SWEAT, PRESSURE
	MOST OF THE TIME DUDES JUST LOOK AROUND AND THEY'LL SEE SOMEBODY THEY ATTRACTED TO AND SEE HOW THEY CARRY THEMSELVES IF THEY WEAK MINDED THEY PRESS UP ON THEM, OFFER THEM MONEY, FOOD, IF THEY DON'T GET MONEY FROM THE OUTSIDE.
PRESSURE	VERBAL OR PHYSICAL FORCE USED TO GAIN SEXUAL ACCESS. TERM USED INSTEAD OF *RAPE.* AN INMATE IS PRESSURED INTO

SEX BUT NOT RAPED. IF AN INMATE CAN BE TALKED INTO SEX THEN HE'S NOT RAPED.

THEY GOING TO BE PRESSURED SOMEWHERE ELSE, YOU GOT PREDATORS EVERYWHERE, YOU MOVE THE CRACK TO THE OTHER NEIGHBORHOOD IT'S SOMEWHERE ELSE, YOU CAN'T RUN FROM IT, YOU GOT TO DEAL WITH IT.

PRESSURE PUNK   AN INMATE WHO AT FIRST REFUSED SEX BUT WAS LATER *PRESSURED* INTO SEX. A PRESSURE PUNK YIELDS TO SEXUAL PRESSURE AND PLAYS THE FEMALE ROLE. PRESSURE PUNKS ARE TARGETS FOR VIOLENT SEX IF THEY DO NOT DO WHAT SOMEONE HAS ASKED THEM TO DO. A PRESSURE PUNK DOES NOT TELL ANYONE HE HAS BEEN RAPED OR FORCED INTO SEX.

IF HE DIDN'T TRY TO RETALIATE, THEN HE'LL GET A REPUTATION AS A PERSON WHO ACCEPTED IT. HE'LL BE A PRESSURE PUNK 'CAUSE HE'S FORCED INTO PARTICIPATING IN HOMOSEXUAL ACTIVITY. IF HE FOUGHT BACK THEN HIS REPUTATION AS A MAN CAN STILL STAND. IF HE TRIED TO TAKE SOME RETALIATION OR TRIED TO SHOW HE DIDN'T WANT TO PARTICIPATE YOU KNOW.

PRISNEYLAND   A PENITENTIARY WITH A NONVIOLENT REPUTATION; USED FOR MALE OR FEMALE INSTITUTIONS.
SYNONYM: CAMP SNOOPY

PROOF OF LOVE   PERFORMING DEGRADING TASKS AS A WAY TO PROVE LOVE AND COMMITMENT.
EXAMPLES: SUCKING ON TAMPONS, DRINKING *RED TEA*, EATING *SHIT SANDWICHES*.

I'VE SEEN PEOPLE PEE INTO A WATER BOTTLE AND SEND IT TO THEIR GIRL TO DRINK. THEY SUCK ON EACH OTHER'S TAMPONS, TO PROVE LOVE . . . IN CLOSE CUSTODY THEY CAN'T GET OUT TO EACH OTHER, SO IT'S A PROOF OF LOVE.

PROTECTIVE   PROTECTED HOUSING UNIT IN THE PRISON. TYPICALLY HAS A
CUSTODY (PC)   NEGATIVE CONNOTATION. *SEE* PC PUNK OR PUNK CITY.

PULL UP   TO AGGRESSIVELY CONFRONT SOMEONE; TO PULL UP ON SOMEONE IN AN EFFORT TO PRESS SOMEONE FOR SEX.

DUDES WILL PULL UP ON A HOMO, ESPECIALLY IF THEY HAVE A FAT ASS, WILL CHASE THEM AROUND THE YARD, NO DIFFERENT THAN THE STREET.

PUNK

1. A WEAK INMATE. AN INMATE WHO CANNOT DEFEND HIM-
SELF OR TRY TO DEFEND HIMSELF. WOMEN WHO ARE
TURNED OUT ARE NOT CONSIDERED WEAK OR PUNKS.

IT'S WHAT YOU DO, THAT'S HOW IT IS. PUNK IS A WEAK DUDE
WHO HAVING SEX INSTEAD OF PROTECTING HIMSELF.

2. TO *TURN OUT* ANOTHER INMATE.

PUNK THEM OUT, MAKE THEM A BITCH.

PUNK CITY

PROTECTIVE CUSTODY.

THE ONLY THING THAT HAPPENS IS THAT PUNK GOES TO PUNK
CITY AND THE OTHER ONE WOULD GO TO SEG FOR A WHILE. THE
GUY WILL BE IN PUNK CITY FOR THE REMAINDER OF HIS SEN-
TENCE. I WOULDN'T RECOMMEND BEING IN PC.

PURPLE PASSION

FOLKLORIC FIGURE WHO RAPES VULNERABLE MEN. CHARAC-
TER IS HUGE AND EXCEPTIONALLY STRONG. SOME SAY HE ONLY
RAPES GAYS; SOMETIMES CALLED A BOOTIE BANDIT. HE WILL
RAPE ANYONE INDEPENDENT OF THEIR *QUALITIES*.

HE GETS YOU WHILE YOU'RE SLEEPING. HE HAS SOMEBODY WITH
HIM AND YOU CAN'T DO NOTHING BECAUSE HE'S SO BIG.

PUSSY

A MAN'S ANUS USED FOR SEX.

THAT PUSSY WAS GOOD. [MALE USAGE]
I CAN'T WAIT TO GET A HOLD OF YOUR PUSSY. [MALE USAGE]

PUSSY ALL
THE TIME

REFERENCE TO A MAN INMATE WHO WAS SEXUALLY ASSAULTED
AND DOES NOT RETALIATE; DENOTES A GIRL-BOY.

HE WAS PUSSY ALL THE TIME.

QUEEN

A COMPLEX CULTURAL CATEGORY WITH AT LEAST THREE DIS-
TINCT MEANINGS DETERMINED BY SOCIAL CONTEXT.
1. MALE INMATE WHO ADOPTS FEMININE TRAITS; SAME AS
QUEEN ON THE STREET BUT NOT THOUGHT OF AS A STREET
DRAG QUEEN, ALTHOUGH MAY BE REFERRED TO AS ONE.

ONE TIME I SLEPT ABOVE A DRAG QUEEN AND HIS HUSBAND,
AND THE DRAG QUEEN FLIRTED WITH EVERYBODY.

2. HIGHER STATUS THAN A HOMOSEXUAL. QUEEN HAS BEEN IN
PRISON LONGER AND HAS MORE EXPERIENCE IN SAME-SEX
RELATIONSHIPS. A *HO* IS HIGH STATUS BUT LOWER THAN A

QUEEN. QUEEN IS HIGHEST STATUS AMONG FEMALE-ACTING INMATES. STATUS DOES NOT REFER TO STRUCTURAL HIERARCHY. RATHER IT REFERS TO SOCIAL PRESTIGE, STRENGTH IN BEING OUT (THE STRENGTH IT TAKES TO COME OUT), WILLING TO BE WHO YOU ARE DESPITE OBSTACLES.

QUEEN SETS THEIR OWN RULES, THEY DON'T ALLOW A MAN TO DOMINATE THEM THEY HAVE RESPECT BY BEING OUT IN THE OPEN.

3. TOTAL HOMOSEXUAL, THROUGH EXTERNAL APPEARANCE AND BY PERSONAL DEFINITION. A QUEEN DOESN'T ACT LIKE A WOMAN, RATHER A QUEEN BELIEVES SHE *IS* A WOMAN.

THEY [QUEENS] HAVE LONG BEAUTIFUL BLONDE HAIR WITH BREASTS AND YOU'RE AROUSED IN THE SHOWER AND YOU HAVE CHOICES.

QUEENDOM — METAPHOR USED TO DESCRIBE THE PROCESS OF BECOMING A TOTAL HOMOSEXUAL. AN EMOTIONAL STAGE THAT DENOTES UNDERSTANDING OF ONE'S INNER SEXUAL IDENTITY.

THE GUYS WON'T ACKNOWLEDGE MY QUEENDOM, AND CALL ME TAMIKA. [I'M] ALL THE LADY THAT I AM. IT'S A QUEENDOM IN ME.

RANK — A CORRECTIONAL ADMINISTRATOR. A DIALECT VARIATION. SYNONYM: WHITE SHIRT

RANKS WILL TAKE INTEREST IN FREE-WORLD PUNKS, THEY GOOD MANIPULATORS AND SNITCHES.

RAPE — A FORM OF *TURNING OUT* AN INMATE. INMATES SAY 10 OR MORE YEARS AGO, RAPE WAS A WAY TO PROVE TOUGHNESS AND WAS MORE COMMON THAN TODAY. INMATES RARELY USE THE WORD RAPE. AS ONE FEMALE INMATE EXPLAINS, *RAPE IS WORD USED COMMONLY ON STREET SO THEY USE IT IN HERE.*

RAPIST — AN INMATE WHO TAKES SEX BY FORCE. A RAPIST MAY BE THOUGHT OF AS A *COWARD*. A RAPIST DOES NOT IMPROVE HIS SOCIAL EVALUATION.

RAPISTS WOULDN'T BE ALLOWED IN MY GROUP, RAPISTS ARE FRINGE PERSONS, OTHER GROUPS AREN'T GOING TO TAKE THEM.

RAPPIES — FRIENDS.

IT [TRANSFER] CAN, BUT THEN THE GUY MIGHT SEND WORD TO ONE OF HIS FELLOW RAPPIES IN ANOTHER JOINT. EVERYONE KNOWS EVERYONE, IN ANY JOINT.

RAPO	A RAPIST.

IF A RAPO RAPES SOMEONE WHO HAS FRIENDS OR IS A RELATIVE, THEY WILL GO AFTER THEM.

RASPBERRY	AN INMATE WHO EXCHANGES SEX FOR DRUGS OR MONEY. SYNONYM: STRAWBERRY

RASPBERRY TRADES HER BODY FOR CANTEEN.

RECRUIT	TO CAJOLE AND ENCOURAGE AN INMATE INTO A SEXUAL RELATIONSHIP.

MEXICAN GANGS HAD A RULE YOU COULDN'T DO IT, NO SEX. THEY DIDN'T TOLERATE HOMOSEXUAL ACTIVITY TILL A FEW YEARS WENT BY AND THEY STARTED RECRUITING GAYS, BUT THE CRIPS AND BLOODS ALWAYS RECRUITED HOMOSEXUALS. DON'T CARE AS LONG AS YOU'RE DOWN WITH FAMILY.

RED TEA	PLACING A USED TAMPON INTO A GLASS OF HOT WATER AND GIVING IT TO A SEXUAL PARTNER FOR THEM TO DRINK AS A PROOF OF THEIR LOVE. [FEMALE USAGE]

RENEGADE	AN UNATTACHED HOMOSEXUAL. ALTERNATIVELY: RENEGADE PUNK

THEY'RE ADDRESSED AS A RENEGADE HO, THEY DON'T HAVE A MAN.

REP	REPUTATION; TO HAVE ACQUIRED A REPUTATION FOR VIOLENCE.

IF THEY MOVE YOU TO ANOTHER UNIT YOU MIGHT HAVE YOUR REP BACK BUT WORDS GET AROUND.

RIDE	1. TO SEEK PROTECTION FROM A *STRONGER* INMATE, USUALLY INVOLVES A CASH EXCHANGE. SYNONYM: UNDER MY WING, HOGGING

IF IT'S A LITTLE BITTY DUDE AND HE DON'T GET DOWN OR RIDE WITH NOBODY THEN SOMEBODY MIGHT TRY TO PICK HIM UP LIKE THAT.

2. A NEW BOY WHO CAN BE USED FOR SEX.

THE FIRST DAY YOU GET HERE THEY ASK YOU IF YOU WILL FIGHT OR RIDE. THE ONLY WAY TO PREVENT IT IS TO FIGHT. OTHERWISE YOU BECOME SOMEONE'S RIDE.

3. TO HAVE SEX (*TO RIDE SOMEONE*).

> *THEY'D RIDE ME ALL DAY IN THE KITCHEN, WE HAD A BALL.*
> *GOT THAT BITCH TO RIDE MY FACE.*

RIP OFF	TO VIOLENTLY TAKE *BOOTIE*.

> *DUDE WAS RIPPED OFF.*

ROCK UP	TO STAND BEHIND AN INMATE AND PRESS CLOSE TO THEIR BODY.

> *WE HAVE TO BEFRIEND THEM AND GIVE THEM THINGS, JACK OFF*
> *ON THEM, ROCK UP ON THEM, TELL THEM HOW SWEET THEY IS.*

ROLLER	A CORRECTIONAL OFFICER.

> *GAYS HAVE A LOT OF WHAT YOU WOULD SAY PULL IN CERTAIN AR-*
> *EAS, LIKE CLOTHES WASHED OR PRESSED, MIGHT HAVE A GAY*
> *THAT'S COOL WITH A UNIT STAFF OR ROLLER THAT CAN GET A PER-*
> *SON MOVED FROM HERE TO THERE.*

RUN IN	TO HAVE A GRIEVANCE FILED ON A PRISON OFFICER BY AN IN-MATE, ALLEGING MISBEHAVIOR. [FEMALE USAGE]

> *SHE GOT JEALOUS, I WAS GIVING HER THE JEWELRY AND STAMPS*
> *THAT THE MAN WAS GIVING ME. SHE TOLD ME IF I DIDN'T GIVE*
> *HER HALF I'LL RUN IT. I TOLD HER TO RUN IT IN, THEY CAME AND*
> *HANDCUFFED ME, SHOT ME OFF THE UNIT, WENT TO RECEPTION,*
> *PUT ME IN TRANSIT LOCKED DOWN UNDER INVESTIGATION.*

RUNNING A GAME	TERM REFERS TO A PASSIVE PROCESS OF TURNING OUT SOMEONE. MAY ALSO HAVE NONSEXUAL USAGES.

> *YOU NOT GOING TO LET NOBODY RUN GAMES ON ME. YOU CAN'T*
> *TELL ME JUST DO ANYTHING. I BEEN HERE TOO LONG TO JUST DO*
> *ANYTHING. ALL THE GAMES THEY TRY TO PLAY NOW I PLAYED*
> *THEM 20 YEARS AGO. AS MY MOMMA USED TO SAY, THERE AIN'T*
> *NOTHING NEW UNDER THE SUN. YOU GET SOMEBODY JUST COM-*
> *ING IN, THEY DON'T KNOW ALL THE GAMES AND THEY GET*
> *TWISTED AND TURNED AROUND.*

SAFE ZONE	A SELF-CREATED SOCIAL CONTEXT IN WHICH AN INMATE FEELS MORE SECURE AND LESS THREATENED. EXAMPLES: MEMBER-SHIP IN A RELIGIOUS GROUP; GANG AFFILIATION; MAINTAIN SO-CIAL TIES TO OTHER INMATES FROM HIS NEIGHBORHOOD.

SERIAL KILLER	AN INMATE WHO CONDUCTS SERIAL INCIDENTS OF PUBLIC MASTURBATION.
SETTING UP HOUSE	A *GAY* AND HIS *BOY* CELLING TOGETHER OR FORMING A CLOSE RELATIONSHIP. THIS RELATIONSHIP IS ONE *GAY* AND ONE *PUNK* OR BOTH *GAYS*. IT IS NOT A *MAN-BOY* OR *MAN-WIFE* RELATION. GAY IS DOMINANT, BUT THEY MAY DECIDE WHO IS PLAYING MALE AND FEMALE ROLES.
SHARK	AN INMATE WHO IS LOOKING FOR SEX. AN INMATE WHO *SWEATS DUDES FOR SEX* IN THE SHOWER. SYNONYM: BOOTIE BANDIT

*WE HAVE SHARKS, YOU COME IN HERE AND YOU GO TO [*UNIT NAME*] UNTIL YOU ARE MEDICALLY CLEARED. THEY WALK UP AND DOWN AND SEE THE NEW RECRUITS. THE SHARKS WILL GIVE YOU STUFF AND THEN YOU OWE THEM.* |
| SHIT SANDWICH | HUMAN EXCREMENT WRAPPED IN BREAD. EATEN BY A FAG OR FEMME TO PROVE THEIR COMMITMENT TO THEIR MATE. *SEE* PROOF OF LOVE. |
| SHOE | A MAN'S ANUS. TO BE THE RECIPIENT IN ANAL SEX. USAGE: TO TAKE IT IN THE SHOE SYNONYM: PUSSY, ASS PUSSY, BUTUSSY |
| SHOOT | TO MASTURBATE WHILE LOOKING AT ANOTHER INMATE OR STAFF. SYNONYM: KILL

I SHOT HIM DOWN. I'D LIKE TO SHOOT HER DOWN. |
| SHOP 180 | TO SPEND THE MAXIMUM AMOUNT MONTHLY ON COMMISSARY.

I'M ONLY WITH YOU CAUSE YOU SHOP 180 AND DON'T FORGET MY CANDY. |
| SHORTY | A TERM OF ENDEARMENT OR "LOVE NAME" APPLIED TO A LOVER.

SHE'S MY SHORTY. |
| SHOT SWALLOWER | INMATE WHO SWALLOWS SEMEN AFTER GIVING ORAL SEX. SPECIFIC ROLE IN A GAY GROUP. A SHOT SWALLOWER IS A HOMOSEXUAL WHO DECLARED HIS SEXUAL PREFERENCE AS GIVER OF ORAL SEX ON MEMBERSHIP TO THE GROUP. GAYS USE SHOT SWALLOWER IN JOKES: *III, I'M CHRIS. I'M THE SHOT SWALLOWER FOR THE GAY CAR.* |

SILVER-TONGUE HAWK	AN INMATE WITH SMOOTH VERBAL SKILLS WHO TALKS OTHER INMATES INTO SEXUAL RELATIONS. ALTERNATIVELY: SILVER-TONGUE MONSTER SYNONYM: TURN-OUT ARTIST *THE SILVER-TONGUE MONSTER TAKES A GUY INTO HIS CONFIDENCE, TELLS HIM I GOT YOUR BACK, AND DON'T WORRY ABOUT THOSE GUYS, BUT IF I CUT YOU LOOSE THEY GOT YOU.*
SISTERS	TERM OF ADDRESS AND REFERENCE USED AMONG *ALL-OUT* HOMOSEXUALS. MINOR USAGE BETWEEN "GIRLFRIENDS" (MEN IN WOMEN'S ROLES) OF INMATES IN THE SAME GANG. *ALL THE QUEENS USED TO GET TOGETHER LIKE THAT AND WE WERE LIKE A FAMILY, WE CALL THEM SISTERS AND LOOK OUT FOR EACH OTHER.*
SIX-FIVE	TO WATCH OUT FOR THE POLICE (CORRECTIONAL STAFF). *THE SIX-FIVE GIRL—THE WATCH AND WHISTLE WHEN THE CO IS COMING LOOKOUT.*
SKEEZER	AN INMATE WHO JUMPS FROM PARTNER TO PARTNER TO GET MONEY. A GOLD DIGGER; HAS A POOR SOCIAL EVALUATION. *SKEEZER IS A FEMALE [*MALE IN FEMALE ROLE*] THAT JUST IN THE WAY, JUST WANT TO JUMP FROM MAN TO MAN TO MAN AND GET MONEY . . . BUT SHE AIN'T WORTH A SHIT.*
SKULL	TO RECEIVE ORAL SEX. SYNONYM: BLOW JOB, CAP (MALE), DOME RIDING (FEMALE) *LET ME GET SOME SKULL.*
SLOW TURN-OUT	A PROCESS OF *TURNING OUT* AN INMATE THAT TAKES A MONTH OR LONGER. OFTEN USED IN REFERENCE TO *TURN-OUTS* IN MINIMUM- AND MEDIUM-SECURITY PRISONS, WHOSE INMATES ARE NOT VIOLENT OR DON'T WANT TO COMMIT A VIOLENT ACT AND BE SANCTIONED AND TRANSFERRED TO A HIGH-SECURITY PRISON. *NOT MUCH FORCE GOING ON IF IT'S A SLOW TURN-OUT THE FRIENDLY WAY. HOMEBOY COME UP IN YOUR CELL TALKING, THEY GET TO WRESTLING AND THEN IT LEADS TO SEX.*
SNEAK TIP	1. A RELATIONSHIP BETWEEN A WOMAN INMATE AND MALE OR FEMALE STAFF MEMBER.

2. TO SNEAK BEHIND A LOVER'S BACK TO HAVE SEX WITH AN-
OTHER.
SYNONYM: CREEP

SNITCH	TO REPORT INFORMATION TO PRISON AUTHORITIES THAT MAY HARM AN INMATE. CAN BE A NOUN (A SNITCH) OR A VERB (TO SNITCH).
SON	FICTIVE NAME USED IN DADDY/CHILD RELATIONSHIP. SON HAS A NARROW RANGE OF MEANING. SON OFTEN USED TO DENOTE A NONSEXUAL RELATIONSHIP BETWEEN DADDY/SON, BUT DADDY COMMONLY EXTORTS MONEY FROM SON.

MOST OF THE TIME THE SON IS WEAKER THAN THE FATHER OR IS NEW INTO THE PRISON AND DON'T KNOW ANYONE OR WHAT RE-ALLY GOES ON AND IS JUST SCARED.

STABLE	MULTIPLE FEMMES CONTROLLED BY A STUD BROAD. THEY MAY RESIDE IN DIFFERENT HOUSING UNITS AND BE UNAWARE OF ONE ANOTHER. ALSO APPLIES IN MEN'S PRISONS.

1. *SOME GUYS HAVE A STABLE WITH TWO OR THREE PUNKS. THEN THE PUNKS HAVE SWAP-OUT BETWEEN ONE ANOTHER. THE MAN WOULD BE AN UNDERCOVER FAG OR FUCKBOY IF HE EVER TOOK A SUBMISSIVE ROLE.*
2. *HAVING 5 OR 6 HOMOSEXUALS AND THEY ALL PLAYED DIFFER-ENT ROLES. ONE COOKED AND ONE MADE MONEY AND ONE WENT TO WORK AND MADE MONEY. ONE RELIEVED TENSION. NOT COMMON ANYMORE, BUT BACK IN THE DAY. A LOT OF PEO-PLE DON'T PLAY THAT. I DON'T KNOW IF IT'S A PHOBIA OR DIS-EASES, BUT A LOT OF PEOPLE AREN'T INTO THAT. IT DEPENDS ON WHO I'M HANGING WITH. SAY I'M HANGING AROUND WITH [PERSONAL NAME] AND I KNOW THIS IS HIS THING, HE'LL SAY GO AHEAD, TAKE ONE, AND GIVE ONE TO ME.*

STALKER	RAPIST OR PREDATOR.

SHE'S ONE OF THE STALKERS WHO PREYS ON YOUNGER PEOPLE WHO JUST COME TO PRISON AND CONSTANTLY BRAGGING ABOUT HER CONQUEST OVER THE WEEKEND. I DON'T KNOW WHAT THEY DO IN THEIR CELL.

STATE	REFERS TO PSEUDOFAMILY RELATIONSHIPS FORMED IN PRISON. EXAMPLE: STATE DAUGHTER OR STATE MOTHER OR STATE FAMILY

	SOME SUPPORT EACH OTHER WITH MONEY. IF IT'S THE MOM, YOU'D GO TO YOUR STATE MOM FOR STUFF.
STAY ALL THE WAY AWAY	TO AVOID INTERPERSONAL CONTACT WITH HOMOSEXUALS. A STRATEGY TO AVOID BEING DRAWN INTO A SEX ROLE.
	STAY ALL THE WAY AWAY FROM HOMOSEXUALS, WHICH IS HARD BUT LIKE I TELL MOST YOUNG DUDES, GAMBLING, HOMOSEXUALITY, AND DRUGS, THAT'S ALL AROUND THAT, IT'S LIKE A REVOLVING DOOR.
STAY OUT OF THE WAY	TO AVOID INVOLVEMENT IN THE SEX SCENE.
STIFF GUY	TO HAVE SEX WITH MEN, BUT RETAIN A *STRONG* LABEL.
	I GOT IN A FEW FIGHTS WHEN I GOT HERE AND PEOPLE TOOK ME UNDER THEIR WING, WHEN THEY SEE YOU HANGING WITH PEOPLE WHO ARE STIFF THEY LEAVE YOU ALONE.
STORE-BAG STUD	*SEE* CANTEEN HO.
STRADDLE THE FENCE	A BISEXUAL INMATE.
	THEY JUST BISEXUAL, SAY THEY STRADDLE THE FENCE.
STRAIGHT	AN INMATE WHO IS BELIEVED TO BE HETEROSEXUAL.
	STAFF ALWAYS GAVE HOMOS MORE THAN PEOPLE WHO ARE STRAIGHT.
STRAIGHT-UP RAPE	FORCED SEX.
STRAIGHTENER	A BLOW JOB; TO HAVE A DESIRE FOR A BLOW JOB. ALSO USED TO DESCRIBE A VERY SATISFYING BLOW JOB (SO GOOD IT STRAIGHTENED THE CURLS OUT OF HIS HAIR — A STRAIGHTENER).
	A DUDE WANTS A STRAIGHTENER.
STRAWBERRY	A PROSTITUTE OR HOOKER WHO EXCHANGES SEX FOR DRUGS. COMMONLY BLOW JOBS ARE EXCHANGED FOR COCAINE, HEROIN, OR MARIJUANA. STRAWBERRIES ARE DRUG ADDICTS. REGIONAL VARIATION IN DEFINITIONS FOR STRAWBERRY AND SKEEZER; SOMETIMES THE TERMS ARE INTERCHANGEABLE. IF NOT INTERCHANGEABLE, SKEEZERS OCCUPY LOWEST STATUS.
	A STRAWBERRY IS EASY TO PICK.

STREET BISEXUAL	AN INMATE WHO WAS BISEXUAL ON THE STREET, BUT MAY OR MAY NOT PARTICIPATE IN SEXUAL ACTIVITIES INSIDE PRISON.
STRETCH	TO MASTURBATE. *TO STRETCH OUT [*HIS PENIS*]. A MASTURBATOR STRETCHES OUT.*
STRICTLY DICKLY	WOMEN INMATES WHO ARE CELIBATE IN PRISON, PREFERRING ONLY SEX WITH MEN.
STRONG	AN INMATE WHO CAN PROTECT HIMSELF; A MAN WHO CAN BE TREACHEROUS AND TOUGH. SYNONYM: LION, WOLF *PEOPLE RESPECT ME CAUSE I'M STRONG, AND I SEEN WHAT'S GOING ON FROM BACK IN THE DAY . . . I DON'T GET EXTORTED. I DON'T HAVE NO PROBLEMS.*
STUD	FEMALE INMATE IN A DOMINANT SEXUAL ROLE. SYNONYM: DYKE, STUD BROAD [REGIONAL USAGE] *IF YOU ARE A STUD AND YOU'RE DATING A FEMME IT'S DIFFERENT, CAUSE YOU'LL GIVE YOUR ALL TO THE FEMME, YOU'LL SEX HER UP. STUDS DON'T LIKE TO BE TOUCHED IF YOU'RE A TRUE STUD.*
STUD BROAD	A FEMALE INMATE WHO ADOPTS A MALE PERSONA. SYNONYM: DYKE, STUD, BULL-DAGGER, BUTCH *A STUD BROAD IS A MAN; TALKS, ACTS, THINKS LIKE A MAN.*
STUD UP	WHEN A *FAG* OR OTHERWISE WEAK INMATE BREAKS ROLE AND ACTS LIKE A *MAN,* TYPICALLY THROUGH FIGHTING OR OTHER PHYSICAL DISPLAY. CAN BE A TEMPORARY OR PERMANENT TRANSFORMATION. *THE ONLY WAY TO EVER GET OUT OF THAT JACKET IS TO STUD UP AND HANDLE THEIR BUSINESS AND PROVE TO ANYBODY THAT THEY'RE A MAN NOW.*
STUPID	TO BE UNAWARE OF SOCIAL GAMES OF INMATES, PARTICULARLY THOSE THAT LEAD TO UNWANTED SEX OR RAPE.
SUCKER	A HIGHLY VULNERABLE WOMAN INMATE. DENOTES A PROCESS OF SLOWLY MANIPULATING A NAIVE AND PERHAPS OVERWEIGHT, UNATTRACTIVE YOUNG WOMAN WHO IS WORKED TO PERFORM SEX ACTS ON A DOMINANT FEMALE INMATE WHO ALSO TAKES HER COMMISSARY.

	AGREE TO HAVE SEX WITH PEOPLE BECAUSE THEY LIKE THE AT-TENTION. SHE WOULD BE CALLED THE SUCKER.
SUCKER FOR LOVE	AN INMATE WHO PURCHASES SEX. SYNONYM: TRICK
SUGAR DADDY	A FINANCIAL SUPPORTER, PRISON OR STREET, OF A MALE OR FE-MALE INMATE. ALSO FOR AN INMATE WHO TAKES CARE OF HO-MOSEXUALS JUST FOR FUN. YOUNG WHITE GIRL IS FRESH MEAT. NINE TIMES OUT OF 10 SHE GOT A HUSBAND, BOYFRIEND, OR SUGAR DADDY TO MAKE SURE SHE HAS MONEY.
SUPER FREAK	AN INMATE WHO ENJOYS EXTREME SEXUAL BEHAVIOR. EXAMPLE: TO TAKE ON FOUR DUDES AT ONCE OR TAKE ON THE INMATE WHO PURPORTEDLY HAS THE BIGGEST DICK IN THE JOINT.
SWAP ARTIST	AN INMATE WHO SWAPS SEX ROLES FOR MONEY. AN INMATE WHO WILL HAVE ANY KIND OF SEX AS LONG AS THEY'RE PAID. SYNONYM: TO GO BOTH WAYS RELATED TERMS: SWAPS, SWAP-OUTS, SWAP-OUT PARTNERS
SWAP-OUT PARTNERS	INMATES WHO TRADE ONE SEXUAL FAVOR FOR ANOTHER. IN-MATES WHO WILL BOTH GIVE AND RECEIVE SEXUAL PLEASURE. SOME GUYS WILL TRICK THEM [SWAP-OUT PARTNERS] INTO GIV-ING UP SEX BY PERFORMING AN ACT ON THEM FIRST AND THEN LET THEM DO IT TO THEM. SYNONYM: FLIP-FLOP
SWEAT MASTER	AN INMATE WHO AGGRESSIVELY PRESSURES SOMEONE FOR SEX.
SWEET EYES	WHEN A MASTURBATOR HAS SOMEONE WATCH HIM MASTUR-BATE. I'M JUST GOING TO GET SWEET EYES.
TAKE IT TO YOU	TO HAVE SEX WITH SOMEONE.
TAKE ON	TO HAVE SEX WITH SOMEONE VOLUNTARILY. A RAPE VICTIM IS NOT TAKEN ON.
TAKE SOME ASS	TO TAKE SEX FROM ANOTHER INMATE. TO RIP SOMEONE OFF.
TAP OUT	TO SUCCUMB TO SEXUAL PRESSURE. DUDE HAD TO TAP OUT.

TEAR IT UP	TO HAVE SEXUAL INTERCOURSE WITH THE CONNOTATION OF AGGRESSIVE SEX. USED BY AN AGGRESSOR (*I TORE UP THAT ASS*) AND RECIPIENT TO AGGRESSOR (*I WANT YOU TO TEAR IT UP*).

THEY DONE TORE UP MY ASS.

TENDENCIES	TO EXPRESS A NATURAL DESIRE, EVER SO SLIGHTLY, TO ENGAGE IN HOMOSEXUALITY. ALSO USED AS *TENDENCIES TO BE WEAK* THAT LEAD TO HOMOSEXUALITY. CONNOTES AN INMATE WHO MAY LIKELY CHOOSE A HOMOSEXUAL LIFESTYLE WITHOUT A PREJUDICIAL RESPONSE FROM OTHER INMATES, IF THE INMATE DID NOT EXPRESS WEAKNESS BUT NATURAL DESIRE; ALSO CONNOTES THAT A NATURAL DESIRE TO BE HOMOSEXUAL IS BEING RECOGNIZED. TERM HAS A NATIONAL DISTRIBUTION; USED COMMONLY IN MEN'S AND WOMEN'S PRISONS.

IT'S LIKE SAY, I'M GAY AND THIS GUY'S NOT GAY, BUT I THINK HE'S GOT HOMOSEXUAL TENDENCIES. I START TALKING TO HIM, PUT MY ARM AROUND HIM, JUST SHOW HIM GENERAL AFFECTION BUT NOT GAY. THEN SAY MAN, YOU MISS WOMEN AND ALL THAT, SAY, WHY DON'T YOU GO AHEAD AND GIVE ME A BLOW JOB.

THIRSTY	1. TO PRESSURE SOMEONE FOR SEX.

DESPERATE OR THIRSTY ARE THE TERMS FOR HOW INMATES GET OTHER INMATES TO HAVE SEX WITH THEM EVEN IF OTHERS DON'T WANT TO HAVE SEX.

SYNONYM: BOOTIE BANDIT

2. HAVING A NEED FOR SEX. A THIRSTY INMATE MAY PAY FOR SEX TO QUENCH THEIR THIRST.

IF YOU GOT A BOYFRIEND AND YOU FEEL THIRSTY OR SOMETHING HE'LL TRY TO GO IN THE GYM OR REC AND HE'LL GIVE IT TO YOU.

THIRSTY MCGURSTY	MALE INMATE WHO PERFORMS ORAL SEX ON MANY PARTNERS SYNONYM: CUM GUZZLER
THOROUGH	A TOUGH, *STRONG* INMATE WHO IS ABLE TO HANDLE HIS BUSINESS. ALTERNATIVELY: PENITENTIARY THOROUGH

MIND YOUR OWN BUSINESS. GET THOROUGH FRIENDS. THOROUGH TO KEEP MOUTH SHUT. FRIENDS WHO DO WHAT THEY HAVE TO DO. YOU CAN TRUST THEM.

THUNDERCAT	A YOUNG FEMALE INMATE IN THE *MIX*.
	ALTERNATIVELY: THUNDERKITTEN *NO, NOT UP IN HERE. THESE WOMEN ARE WILLING. I COULD PROBABLY HAVE 10 OR 15 OF THEM IF I CHOSE TO BUT I WOULDN'T. I DON'T LIKE HURTING PEOPLE. THE ONE I GOT IS A THUNDERCAT; ONE THAT IS LIKE A TIGER OR LION OR LEOPARD OR BEAR. THEY WILD. THEY GET WITH YOU REAL QUICK. I ALSO USE THUNDERKITTEN. IT'S THE SAME BUT MILDER, BUT STILL SASSY OR JAZZY.*
TIP	TO HAVE PREFERENCE.
	HE'S ON THE FEMININE TIP.
TIE UP LOOSE ENDS	TO PAY BACK; RETALIATION.
TOSSING SALAD	LICKING IN OR AROUND THE ANUS. [MALE USAGE]
	I'M BISEXUAL, I LIKE WOMENS OK, BUT YOU STILL LIKE SALADS TOO.
TRANSFORMER	*QUEENS* OR *PUNKS* THAT TRANSFORM TO MEN WHEN NEEDED. NEAR SYNONYM: STUD UP
	A COUPLE OF WEEKS AGO ONE [HOMOSEXUAL] *GOT SMACKED IN THE YARD AND IT BROUGHT THE MAN OUT OF HIM.*
TREE JUMPER	A SEXUAL PREDATOR.
	SOMEBODY THAT THINKS ABOUT NOTHING BUT BOOTIE, LIKE A RAPIST. WE CALL THEM TREE JUMPERS. SYNONYM: BUSHWACKER
TREY	INMATE WHO BUYS SEX. SYNONYM: JOHN, TRICK
TRICK	INMATE WHO BUYS SEX. SYNONYM: JOHN, TREY
TRUCK- DRIVING DRAG HEAD	APPLIES TO MALE INMATES WHO CHANGE THEIR SEXUAL APPEARANCE. ALTERNATIVELY: TRUCK-DRIVING DRAG QUEEN SYNONYM: FLIP-FLOP
	TRUCKDRIVING DRAG QUEENS LOOK LIKE MEN SOMETIMES AND QUEENS OTHER TIMES. THEY WALK BOTH SIDES.

TRUE GUYS	INMATES WHO FEEL THAT OTHERS ARE TRYING TO ATTACH THEMSELVES TO THEM IN ORDER TO STAY SAFE.
TRY	TO TRY SOMEONE; TO CHALLENGE SOMEONE.
	DUDE WALKED RIGHT UP AND TRIED ME.
TRY SEXUAL	AN INMATE WHO WILL HAVE SEX WITH ANYONE.
TURN-OUT	1. A HETEROSEXUAL ON THE STREET WHO IS PRESSURED INTO SEX INSIDE PRISON.
	IF HE GOT RAPED AND HE ACCEPT IT, THEN HE A TURN-OUT.
	2. TO RELEASE SAME-SEX DESIRES. THERE ARE MANY FORMS OF RELEASING INSIDE SAME-SEX TENDENCIES. IN THE PROCESS OF COVERTLY PRESSURING SOMEONE FOR SEX, THE AGGRESSOR RELEASES A TARGET'S SAME-SEX DESIRES. AN INMATE IS TURNED OUT BY, FOR EXAMPLE, COVERTLY PUTTING THE TARGET INTO DEBT TO HIM, BY SHARING CIGARETTES OR CANDY OR BEFRIENDING HIM AND OFFERING PROTECTION.
	IF YOU TURN OUT AN INMATE, THAT MEANS YOU MADE HIM WANT IT.
TURNED OUT ALL THE WAY	TO HAVE A NEW EMOTIONAL AND PHYSICAL INVOLVEMENT IN HOMOSEXUALITY; INMATES WHO WERE FORCED THE FIRST TIME AND NOW DO IT WILLINGLY.
	[PERSONAL NAME]'S BEEN TURNED ALL THE WAY OUT. SOMEONE TOOK IT FROM THEM AND AFTER THAT HE HAD NO PROBLEM GIVING IT UP. HE STARTED SHAVING HIS LEGS AND WEARING MAKEUP.
UMBRELLA	PROTECTION FROM SEXUAL ASSAULT BY ASSOCIATION WITH A STRONG PERSON OR GANG.
	IF A DUDE AIN'T IN A GANG, AND THERE'S A LOT WHO ARE NOT, THEY WILL HAVE FRIENDS WHO ARE IN GANGS THAT TALK TO THEM IN A REGULAR BASIS. THEY ARE STILL PROTECTED BY THE GANG UMBRELLA. YOU ARE AFFILIATED BY ASSOCIATION EVEN IF YOU'RE NOT A GANG-BANGER. BUT ONLY IF YOU'RE STRONG. ALSO: GANG UMBRELLA, TO BE PUT UNDER AN UMBRELLA
UNDER YOUR WING	TO PROTECT SOMEONE.
	I GOT HIM UNDER MY WING.

UNDERCOVER   TO HIDE ONE'S SEXUALITY.
               SYNONYM: CLOSET, DOWN LOW

               [SEXUALITY] IS PRETTY OPEN AROUND HERE, EVERY ONCE IN A
               WHILE YOU GET SOMEONE WHO IS UNDERCOVER.

VETERAN, VET   AN OLDER INMATE WHO HAS BEEN IN (THE HOMOSEXUAL
               LIFESTYLE OR PRISON) A LONG TIME.

               TODAY, THIS KIND OF SUBPOPULATION ISN'T COMMON. SOME GOT
               OUT; SOME DIED; SOME GOT OLD AND RETIRED. THEY VETERANS
               AND DON'T WANT TO BE WARRIORS ANYMORE.

VIRGINITY   TO HAVE NEVER PARTICIPATED IN ANAL SEX.

               ONCE YOU GET PENETRATED YOU LOST YOUR VIRGINITY, ONCE
               YOU BREAK THE BACK DOOR, THE MANHOOD, YOU NO LONGER A
               MAN ANYMORE.

WAR PLAYING   AN INMATE WHO PLAYS THE MALE ROLE ONE DAY AND THE FE-
               MALE ROLE THE NEXT.
               SYNONYM: FLIP-FLOP, SWAP-OUT

WATER HEAD   AN INMATE WHO PROVIDES ORAL SEX.

WEAK   UNABLE TO PROTECT ONESELF FROM THE PRESSURES OF
               PRISON LIFE.

               IF A PERSON CAN'T TAKE CARE OF THEYSELF AND IF HE WEAK AND
               DON'T HAVE NO OTHER WAY OUT AND IF HE FEEL HIS LIFE IS IN
               DANGER HE MAY WANT TO TRY TO GET HIMSELF MOVED.

WEAK MINDED   SOMEONE WHO WILL HAVE SEX OR PROVIDE COMMISSARY OR
               MONEY IN ORDER TO ESTABLISH A SOCIAL TIE TO AN INMATE
               WHO HAS MANY FRIENDS. WEAK-MINDED CONNOTES THE IN-
               ABILITY TO SOLVE, OR THINK THROUGH, A PROBLEM. WEAK-
               MINDED REFERS TO AN INABILITY TO CONTROL EMOTIONS.
               OPPOSITE: STRONG-MINDED

               IF YOU HAVE A PRETTY BIG ANGER PROBLEM, YOU'RE WEAK-
               MINDED. IF YOU'RE IMPULSIVE AND CAN'T THINK OF WHAT
               YOU'RE GOING TO SAY BEFORE YOU SAY IT, YOU'RE WEAK-
               MINDED.

WHITE SHIRT   INSTITUTION NON-UNIFORMED STAFF, COMMONLY MANAGERS
               AND ADMINISTRATORS.
               SYNONYM: RANK

THE OFFICERS REALLY THEY CAN'T DO TOO MUCH, BUT BREAK IT UP, THEY WOULD HAVE TO CALL A WHITE SHIRT AND SAY THIS DUDE WAS SCREWING A DUDE AND A WHITE SHIRT WOULD LOCK THEM UP.

WIFE	MALE INMATE IN A FEMALE ROLE IN A LONG-TERM *MAN-FAG* MARRIAGE. SYNONYM: HO, MOMMY A DEROGATORY TERM IDENTIFYING A FEMALE PARTNER WHO WILL NOT OBEY "HER" MAN'S COMMANDS. CONNOTATION OF A WIFE APPROACHES THAT OF STREET PROSTITUTE. *DUDES DON'T WANT A PROSTITUTE. THEY WANT A HO WHO WILL DO ANYTHING FOR THEIR DUDE. A HO IS WAY UP [HIGHLY VALUED, PRAISED]. A HOUSEWIFE IS DOWN LOW.*
WING GIRL	A *FEMME* WHO IS THE OBJECT OF SEX ONLY IN A HOUSING UNIT. A WING GIRL HAS SEX WITH A *STUD BROAD* ONLY INSIDE A HOUSING UNIT. THE STUD BROAD HAS SEX WITH OTHER *FEMMES* ON THE COMPOUND WITHOUT THE WING GIRL'S KNOWLEDGE. *THAT FEMME IS A WING GIRL. SHE'S THE OBJECT OF SEX INSIDE THE UNIT BUT NO PLACE ELSE.*
WOLF	AN AGGRESSIVE INMATE. USED AS A METAPHOR FOR PREDATORS SEARCHING FOR PREY; A SEXUAL PREDATOR. SYNONYM: LION *YOU COULDN'T MIX THE CAMP GUYS WITH US, IT WOULD BE LIKE SHEEPS IN THE WOLF PEN.*
WOODPILE	A GROUP OF *PECKERWOODS*. *IT'S A VERY RACIST PLACE HERE, BUT PEOPLE DON'T SEEM TO REALIZE THAT THERE'S A NIGGER IN THE WOODPILE SOMEWHERE.*
WORKED	VICTIM OF MANIPULATION. FEMALE INMATES AND STAFF ARE COMMONLY WORKED FOR SEX. *THIS IS A HORRIBLE, DISGUSTING, AND DEPRESSING LIFESTYLE. STAFF GET WORKED AND DON'T KNOW IT.*
YUCK MAN, YUCK MOUTH	TO HAVE MANY FEMALE PARTNERS IN ORAL SEX. SYNONYM: DOUCHE BAG MOUTH

References

Alarid, L. F. (2000). Sexual assault and coercion among incarcerated women prisoners: Excerpts from prison letters. *The Prison Journal, 80*(4), 391–406.

Austin, J., Fabelo, T., Gunter, A., and McGinnis, K. (2006). *Sexual Violence in the Texas Prison System* (No. NCJ 215774). Washington, DC: U.S. Department of Justice

Beck, A. J., and Harrison, P. M. (2007). *Sexual Victimization in State and Federal Prisons Reported by Inmates, 2007* (Special Report No. NCJ 219414). Washington, DC: Bureau of Justice Statistics.

Beck, A. J., and Hughes, T. A. (2004). *Sexual Violence Reported by Correctional Authorities* (No. NCJ 210333). Washington, DC: U.S. Department of Justice, Bureau of Justice Statistics.

Bowker, L. (1977). *Prisoner Subcultures*. Lexington, MA: D.C. Health.

Calhoun, J., and Coleman, H. D. (2002). Female inmates' perspectives on sexual abuse by correctional personnel: An exploratory study. *Women and Criminal Justice, 13*(2/3), 101–24.

Charlton, L. (1971, April 25). The terrifying homosexual world of the jail system. *New York Times*, p. 40.

Chonco, N. R. (1989). Sexual assaults among male inmates: A descriptive study. *The Prison Journal, 69*, 77–82.

Clemmer, D. (1940). *The Prison Community*. New York: Holt, Rinehart and Winston.

Culbertson, R. G., and Fortune, E. P. (1986). Incarcerated women: Self-concept and argot roles. *Journal of Offender Counseling, Services and Rehabilitation, 1*(3), 25–49.

Davis, A. J. (1968). Sexual assault in the Philadelphia prison system and sheriff's vans. *Trans-Action, 6*, 8–16.

Devereux, G., and Moos, M. C. (1942). The social structure of prisons, and the organic tensions. *Journal of Criminal Psychopathology, 4*(2), 306–24.

Eigenberg, H. M. (1992). Homosexuality in male prisons: Demonstrating the need for a social constructionist approach. *Criminal Justice Review, 17*(2), 219–34.

Eigenberg, H. M. (2002). Prison staff and male rape. In C. Hensley (Ed.), *Prison sex: Practice and policy* (pp. 44–66). Colorado: Lynne Rienner Publishers.

Feray, J.-C., and Herzer, M. (1990). Homosexual studies and politics in the 19th century: Karl Maria Kertbeny. *Journal of Homosexuality, 19*(1), 23–27.

Fishman, J. (1934). *Sex in Prison: Revealing Sex Conditions in American Prisons.* New York: National Library Press.

Flanagan, T. J. (1983). Correlates of institutional misconduct among state prisoners: A research note. *Criminology, 21*, 29–39.

Fleisher, M. S. (1983). Review: Who rules the joint? The changing political culture of maximum-security prisons in America. *American Anthropologist, 85*(3), 716–17.

Fleisher, M. S. (1989). *Warehousing Violence.* Newbury Park, CA: Sage Publications.

Fleisher, M. S., and Krienert, J. L. (2006). *The Culture of Prison Sexual Violence* (Final Report). Washington, DC: National Institute of Justice.

Freedman, E. B. (1996). The prison lesbian: Race, class, and the construction of the aggressive female homosexual, 1915–1965. *Feminist Studies, 22*(2), 397–423.

Freud, S. (1962). *Three Essays on the Theory of Sexuality* (J. Strachey, Trans.). New York: Basic Books.

Gaes, G. G., and Goldberg, A. L. (2004). *Prison rape: A critical review of the literature* (Executive Summary No. NCJ 213365). Washington, DC: National Institute of Justice.

Gaes, G. G., and McGuire, W. J. (1985). Prison violence: The contribution of crowding versus other determinants of prison assault rates. *Journal of Research in Crime and Delinquency, 22*(1), 41-65

Gagnon, J. H., and Simon, W. (1968). The social meaning of prison homosexuality. *Federal Probation, 32*(March), 23–29.

Garabedian, P. G. (1963). Social roles in prison. In L. Radzinowicz and M. E. Wolfgang (Eds.), *Crime and Justice* (Vol. III: The criminal in confinement, pp. 116–130). New York: Basic Books.

Gay, P. (2002). *Schnitzler's Century: The Making of Middle-Class Culture 1815–1914.* New York: Norton.

Giallombardo, R. (1966). *Society of Women: A Study of a Women's Prison.* New York: Anchor Books.

Greer, K. (2000). The changing nature of interpersonal relationships in a women's prison. *The Prison Journal, 80*(4), 442–68.

Hensley, C., and Tewksbury, R. (2002). Inmate to inmate prison sexuality: A review of empirical studies. *Trauma, Violence, and Abuse, 3*(2), 226–43.

Hensley, C., Tewksbury, R., and Castle, T. (2003). Characteristics of prison sexual assault targets in male Oklahoma correctional facilities. *Journal of Interpersonal Violence, 18*(6), 595–606.

Hensley, C., Tewksbury, R., and Koscheski, M. (2002). The characteristics and motivations behind female prison sex. *Women and Criminal Justice, 13*(2/3), 125–39.

Hensley, C., Tewksbury, R., and Wright, J. (2001). Exploring the dynamics of masturbation and consensual same-sex activity within a male maximum security prison. *The Journal of Men's Studies, 10*(1), 59–71.

James, D. J., and Glaze, L. E. (2006). *Mental health problems of prison and jail inmates* (Special Report). Washington, DC: Bureau of Justice Statistics.

Johnson, E. (1971). The homosexual in prison. *Social Theory and Practice, 1*(4), 83–97.

Jones, R., and Schmid, T. (1989). Inmates' conception of prison sexual assault. *The Prison Journal, 69*(1), 53–61.

Karpman, B. (1948). Sex life in prison. *Journal of Criminal Law and Criminology, 38*(Jan–Feb), 475–86.

Kassebaum, G. G. (1972). Sex in prison: Violence, homosexuality, and intimidation are everyday occurrences. *Sexual Behavior, 2*(1), 39–45.

Kirkham, G. L. (1971). Homosexuality in prison. In J. M. Henslin (Ed.), *Studies in the Sociology of Sex* (pp. 325–49). New York: Appleton-Century-Crofts.

Koscheski, M., and Hensley, C. (2001). Inmate homosexual behavior in a Southern female correctional facility. *American Journal of Criminal Justice, 25*(2), 269–77.

Leger, R. G. (1973). Socialization patterns and social roles: A replication. *Journal of Criminal Law and Criminology, 69*(4), 627–34.

Lockwood, D. (1980). *Prison Sexual Violence*. New York: Elsevier.

Lockwood, D. (1994). Issues of prison sexual violence. In M. C. Braswell, H. Ried, Jr., and L. X. Lombardo (Eds.), *Prison Violence in America* (pp. 97–102). Cincinnati: Anderson.

Moss, C. S., Hosford, R. E., and Anderson, W. R. (1979). Sexual assault in a prison. *Psychological Reports, 44*, 823–28.

Nacci, P. L., and Kane, T. R. (1982). *Sex and sexual aggression in federal prisons*. Washington, DC: Federal Bureau of Prisons.

Nacci, P. L., and Kane, T. R. (1983). The incidence of sex and sexual aggression in federal prisons. *Federal Probation, 47*(4), 31–36.

Nacci, P. L., and Kane, T. R. (1984). Sex and sexual aggression in federal prisons. *Federal Probation, 48*(1), 46–53.

Otis, M. (1913). A perversion not commonly noted. *Journal of Abnormal Child Psychology, 8*, 113–16.

Owen, B. (1998). *In the mix: Struggle and survival in a women's prison*. Albany, NY: State University of New York.

Pollock, J. M. (2002a). Parenting programs in women's prisons. *Women and Criminal Justice, 14*(1), 50–68.

Pollock, J. M. (2002b). *Women, Prison, and Crime* (2 ed.). Belmont, CA: Wadsworth.

Prison Rape Elimination Act (2003).

Propper, A. M. (1981). *Prison Homosexuality: Myth and Reality*. Lexington, MA: Lexington Books.

Propper, A. M. (1982). Make-believe families and homosexuality among imprisoned girls. *Criminology, 20*(1), 127–38.

Ryan, G. W., and Bernard, R. H. (2003). Techniques to identify themes. *Field Methods, 15*(1), 85–109.

Selling, L. S. (1931). The pseudo family. *The American Journal of Sociology, 37*, 247–53.

Smith, C. E. (1956). Some problems in dealing with homosexuals in the prison situation. *The Journal of Social Therapy, 2*(1), 37–45.

Smith, N. E., and Batiuk, M. E. (1989). Sexual victimization and inmate social interaction. *The Prison Journal, 68*, 29–38.

Struckman-Johnson, C., and Struckman-Johnson, D. (2000). Sexual coercion rates in several Midwestern prison facilities for men. *The Prison Journal, 80*(4), 379–90.

Struckman-Johnson, C., and Struckman-Johnson, D. (2002). Sexual coercion reported by women in three midwestern prisons. *The Journal of Sex Research, 39*(3), 217–77.

Sykes, G. M. (1958). *The society of captives: A study of a maximum security prison.* Princeton, NJ: Princeton University Press.

Sykes, G. M., and Messinger, S. L. (1960a). The inmate social system. In R. A. Cloward (Ed.), *Theoretical Studies of the Social Organization of the Prison.* New York: Science Research Council.

Sykes, G. M., and Messinger, S. L. (1960b). Inmate social systems. In L. Radzinowicz and M. E. Wolfgang (Eds.), *Crime and Justice* (Vol. III: The criminal in confinement, pp. 77–85). New York: Basic Books.

Tewksbury, R. (1989a). Fear of sexual assault in prison inmates. *The Prison Journal, 69*(1), 62–71.

Tewksbury, R. (1989b). Measures of sexual behavior in an Ohio prison. *Sociology and Social Research, 74*(1), 34–39.

Tewksbury, R., and West, A. (2000). Research on sex in prison during the late 1980s and early 1990s. *The Prison Journal, 80*(4), 368–78.

Ward, D. A., and Kassebaum, G. G. (1964). Homosexuality: A mode of adaptation in a prison for women. *Social Problems, 12*(2), 159–77.

Ward, J. L. (1958). Homosexual behavior of the institutionalized delinquent. *Psychiatric Quarterly—Supplement, 32*(2), 301–14.

Index

About the Authors

Mark S. Fleisher is senior research associate and project director at the Institute for the Study and Prevention of Violence at Kent State University. A cultural and linguistic anthropologist, he is a former administrator in the Federal Bureau of Prisons and is the author or editor of several books. **Jessie L. Krienert** is associate professor of criminal justice at Illinois State University. Together, Fleisher and Krienert are the editors of *Crime and Employment*.